DESIRING CANADA

CBC Contests, Hockey Violence, and Other Stately Pleasures

What do Tim Hortons, *Hockey Night in Canada,* and Rick Mercer have in common? Each is a popular symbol of Canadian identity, seen across the country – and beyond – on television and in other forms of media. But *whose* definition of "Canadian" do they represent? What does it mean to be Canadian? Do we create our own impressions of Canadian identity, or are they created for us? In *Desiring Canada,* Patricia Cormack and James F. Cosgrave delve into these questions, exploring the connections between popular culture, media, and the Canadian state.

Taking as their examples the popular CBC contests, Tim Hortons advertising campaigns, NHL hockey violence, television comedy, and the business of gambling, this lively, engaging book investigates the relationship between some of our more beloved popular expressions of national identity and the extent to which the interests of the state appeal in various ways through the popular media to the pleasures of citizens, thus shaping our understanding of what it means to be Canadian.

PATRICIA CORMACK is an associate professor in the Department of Sociology at St Francis Xavier University.

JAMES F. COSGRAVE is an assistant professor in the Department of Sociology at Trent University.

PATRICIA CORMACK AND JAMES F. COSGRAVE

Desiring Canada

CBC Contests, Hockey Violence, and Other Stately Pleasures

UNIVERSITY OF TORONTO PRESS
Toronto Buffalo London

ISBN 978-1-4426-4565-3 (cloth)
ISBN 978-1-4426-1391-1 (paper)

Printed on acid-free paper

Library and Archives Canada Cataloguing in Publication

Cormack, Patricia, 1963–
Desiring Canada : CBC contests, hockey violence and other stately
pleasures / Patricia Cormack, James F. Cosgrave.

Includes bibliographical references and index.
ISBN 978-1-4426-4565-3 (bound). – ISBN 978-1-4426-1391-1 (pbk.)

1. National characteristics, Canadian.   2. Group identity—Canada.
3. Pleasure—Political aspects—Canada.   4. Pleasure–Social aspects—
Canada.   5. Canada—In popular culture.   6. Popular culture—Canada.
I. Cosgrave, James F., 1959–   II. Title.

FC95.5.C67 2013   306'.0971   C2012-908157-4

The University of Toronto Press acknowledges the financial assistance to its
publishing program of the Canada Council for the Arts and the
Ontario Arts Council.

Canada Council   Conseil des Arts
for the Arts   du Canada

University of Toronto Press acknowledges the financial support
of the Government of Canada through the Canada Book Fund
for its publishing activities.

For

Andrew Malcolm (1958–2011)

and

Christopher Kennedy (1986–2009)

A 'state' . . . ceases to exist in a sociologically relevant sense whenever there is no longer a probability that certain kinds of meaningfully oriented social action will take place.

Max Weber

What . . . is the state? Where does it begin and where does it end?

Émile Durkheim

Contents

Acknowledgments

We would like to thank all of our friends and colleagues who took an interest in this work and provided support of many kinds. Patricia would like to thank each of the members of the St Francis Xavier University Sociology Department (past and present), who have helped out in myriad ways. Thanks also to colleagues from other departments: Yvon Grenier (Political Science), Sam Kalman (History), Robert Kennedy (Religious Studies), Joseph Khoury (English), and Jeanette Lynes (English).

Thanks to Carla Haley-Baxter, St Francis Xavier University, for her help in manuscript preparation at all stages and for her enthusiastic support of the project.

James would like to thank his colleagues at Trent University–Oshawa for their support, and Amber Ashton in particular for her manuscript assistance. He would also like to acknowledge funding support awarded by The Symons Trust Fund for Canadian Studies (Trent University).

We are especially grateful to Ed Ksenych (George Brown College), Lynda Harling Stalker (St Francis Xavier), Alex Marland (Memorial University), and Judy Kennedy (St Thomas University) for their valuable comments on parts of the text. Kieran Keohane (University College Cork) offered us the opportunity to present some of our work in progress at the Theory and Philosophy Summer School, Cork, Ireland. We want to express our gratitude to Kieran and Carmen Kuhling (University of Limerick) for their hospitality during our stay.

Finally, thanks to Siobhan McMenemy and staff at University of Toronto Press, and to the anonymous reviewers who gave great attention to the earlier versions of this book and helped revise it towards its current form.

DESIRING CANADA

CBC Contests, Hockey Violence, and Other Stately Pleasures

Introduction

There's no place for the state in the bedrooms of the nation.

Pierre Trudeau

Consider that famous Canadian political assertion. It is about the relationship between personal pleasures and the state. We take it as our point of departure for this book, treating its status in popular culture and collective memory as important and instructive. In other words, Canadians have made Trudeau's comment famous, and continue to circulate it, for a reason. The relationship between the state and our pleasures is connected to our sense of being Canadian.

In this book we examine everyday pleasures, Canadian identity, and the state. On the face of it, at least, there is a huge gulf between mundane, everyday pleasures and the powerful agencies of state – laws, policies, courts, organizations, and ministries and their associated officials. In fact, this gap is critical to our sense of freedom as citizens – the state has no business in the innocuous pleasures of adult citizens, to paraphrase Trudeau. Certainly, when Trudeau, then federal Minister of Justice, made this declaration, it marked a change in the regulation of a range of sexual behaviours, including homosexual pleasures. Following on similar reform in Britain, the Canadian state's authority was to be removed from this area of pleasure because it was deemed to be imposing wrongly on legitimate and private activity. Indeed, Trudeau made his declaration in the context of his famous omnibus bill, C-150, which proposed to liberalize sexuality, contraception, abortion, divorce, and gambling (while restricting guns and drunk driving). This was a turning point in Canadian relations between the state and pleasures and identity.

Since that time, a body of academic work has chronicled the Canadian state's changing role in regulating desires, especially the desires touched on in Bill C-150. Some of these studies have traced the liberalization of a particular pleasure. Others have shown how the Canadian state has overtly or covertly continued to practise various types of regulation and surveillance of its citizens.[1]

We offer here a different discussion of state, identity, and desire. Note that Trudeau's pronouncement has typically been taken as signalling the state's retreat from many areas of private pleasure. The most obvious interpretation of his words emphasizes the removal of the state from these sites of pleasure and its implicit legitimation of them. But his utterance signals more than the removal of the state: it also signals a new relation between the state and the pleasures of its citizens – a relation, we suggest, that is rooted in the cultivation rather than the regulation of pleasures. As a consequence, Canadian identity has been rewritten along the lines of this pleasure/state relationship.

In this book we argue that the state has not really retreated from everyday life, pleasure, or national identity – it has only *appeared* to have done so. This seeming disappearance and its implications frame this book's discussion of everyday pleasures and Canadian identity. This three-way dynamic begins with the many sentiments and celebrations that accompanied the country's centennial in the late 1960s, a time when Canada was invited to begin to think of itself as a liberal, tolerant, and permissive society. This new relation to pleasure and the state was to be central to a new Canadian identity. We suggest that Trudeau's one-liner is still repeated endlessly because it has allowed Anglo-Canadians to feel modern, liberated from a colonial past. With those words, Canadians could begin to desire on their own terms – or so it appeared. (In Quebec, Charles de Gaulle's 'Vive le Quebec Libre' 1967 speech was doing its own work of identity, pleasure, and nationalism.)

In 1968, Trudeau became Prime Minister of Canada, and he and his Liberal Party turned Bill C-150 into law (more accurately, that bill repealed or reformed many laws). During that year's federal election, political foes had tried and failed to use the omnibus bill against the Liberals. Not without reason, they saw Bill C-150 as a radical shift in Canada's moral grounding. But Trudeau seemed to have understood well that our relationship to pleasure was becoming more and more our way of *understanding and constituting ourselves as citizens.* So it was politically astute of him, besides being legally important at that point in Canadian history, to acknowledge that the right to pursue pleasures, as part of our very sense of citizenship, was on the rise.

His words amounted to a signal that state institutions would now be obligated to manage the relationship between citizens and themselves more and more in terms of how pleasure was understood. From that point on, both citizenship and the state would have to be negotiated in terms of the shifting idea of legitimate pleasure. The state would now have to concern itself with a new type of citizen, one who thought more and more in terms of consumption. Indeed, the state would now have to make itself *consumable*.[2] How it addressed and invoked the citizen would have to take account of the many places now available for people to 'find themselves' and their pleasures. Today, much of the state apparatus is geared towards promoting or publicizing its services, offices, and policies. The state now has to make itself recognizable and attractive to citizens. This in turn feeds back into the framing of the citizen through state discourses and procedures.

In the classic conception, the citizen is a reasoning individual who makes civic decisions based on sound judgment and careful deliberation. What, then, are the implications of this new notion of citizenship? And what are the implications of the state itself being consumable? As we will see, this idea of identity, pleasure, and the consumable state has opened up a cultural space for private corporations to take over much of the work of national identity. It requires those who hope to gain legitimate power as elected officials within the Canadian state to present themselves in terms set out by these corporations.

The state has long been an institutional denier and regulator of pleasure, so it is perhaps difficult to view it in terms of the pleasures it *fosters*. While citizens are certainly shaped by the ways in which pleasures are restricted by law, we must not overlook that modern states also *use* pleasures in order to advance their own interests, shape their citizens, and build nationhood. Every state must manage the pleasures of its citizens to ensure its own legitimacy, and this is especially so for states that are rooted in the purported goods of democracy and individual freedoms. The management of pleasure is very much a state's business, for the state takes its shape and assumes its reality when it speaks concretely about its citizens' pleasures and their limits. Even tyrannical political systems must shape desires and foster pleasures. The willingness of citizens to support and identify with such regimes – to march in parades, conceive and denounce enemies, and fight in wars – can be analysed in terms of how this is accomplished. As Stuart Hall (1984) explains: 'though the state may be an abstract and general force, its power has to be *materialized* – i.e., it must acquire real, concrete, social organizational form, with real tasks, using and disposing of real resources' (19–20).

Certainly, the relationship between the state and our pleasures changes over time, reflecting broader societal transformations. The state must shape desire, but it must also respond to everyday practices and shifts in moral outlook. Some activities appear to become liberalized (e.g., gambling, sexuality); others become stigmatized (e.g., smoking, drinking and driving). Hence, pleasures must be thought about in terms of the social factors and interests that seek to either liberate or constrain them. It is of ongoing sociological interest to consider what gets seen as a threat to the state and/or to the 'social fabric' at various times.

To be sure, state/culture dynamics have contributed to the particular historical interplay of regulation and pleasure in Canada. An example is the weakening of the Protestant value system in English Canada. The pursuit of pleasures entails a social self that conceives of the possibilities for gaining access to and experiencing various pleasures. Society has to 'allow' these pursuits in terms of values, policies, and laws; indeed, society itself becomes structured around them. The Canadian philosopher Charles Taylor even argued that in the modern era, politics in the Western world has become organized around the ideal of serving the individual's pleasures (Taylor 2004). Academics have variously called versions of this cultural shift the 'consumer society,' 'narcissistic society,' 'postmodernity,' 'late modernity,' and the 'risk society.' More and more in popular culture we are asked to think of ourselves in individualized, 'self-actualized,' pleasure-seeking terms rather than in terms of older notions such as submission to community and service to others. One opinion tracker, Michael Adams (1998), has found this true of Canadians: 'As I see it, the new mental posture of Canadians has been shaped by three major quests: for personal autonomy, for pleasure and for spiritual fulfillment. In all three pursuits, the accent is on "personal" ... The stereotype of Canadians as respectful and reserved, and not that imaginative, is fast losing its validity' (6). As a part of this personalized pleasure seeking, individuals are expected more and more to assess their own personal risks and to make decisions based on their own calculations. (We will see this latter dynamic especially in our discussion of gambling, resource distribution, and the Canadian state.)

Hence, we view Canada as a set of analytical problems that invite discussion and analysis. How, for example, is desire shaped in particular directions and in the direction of certain projects? We thus pose the problem of desire in terms of practices and relations that seek and express pleasure but that are also managed – that is, socially controlled and exploited. This approach leaves us room to discuss pleasure and enjoyment even while we focus on the interests of authority and regulation. Indeed, we will be suggesting that the interest in order takes on special significance in a country where the motto 'Peace, Order and Good Government' continues to inform cultural habits in various ways. (In our discussion of CBC audiences, for example, we see both resistance to and acquiescence to state-mandated authorities.) In a similar vein, the deviance and crime of citizens would appear to be anathema to state interests, yet the state *uses* both in various ways. Remember here that the state defines and monitors who and what is criminal even while drawing resources and discourse into these efforts (Foucault 1977). The state's definition of criminality is even sometimes expedient; as a demonstration of this, consider gambling, which has been legalized for the utilitarian purpose of revenue generation. Here we can question the moral grounds of state actions themselves, as well as the particular impositions the state makes on citizens' conduct.

From the perspective of political stability, citizens find it legitimate that they be able to manage their own pleasures. Yet at the same time, the state's legitimacy rests largely in its capacity to regulate pleasures and control its citizens; indeed, citizens look to the state for help in formulating their own understandings of legitimate and illegitimate pleasures. We may even find pleasure and identity in the limits the state imposes. In 2010, for example, the federal government announced that the regulation of men's authority, especially with regard to wives and children, would be central to its handling of new immigrants. This shut down from the start the right of immigrants to claim cultural differences as a rationale for mistreating women and children; doing so would be exceeding the limits of Canadians' collective tolerance. Canada's immigration study guide, 'Discover Canada,' now states that 'Canada's openness and generosity do not extend to barbaric cultural practices that tolerate spousal abuse, "honour killings," female genital mutilation or other gender-based violence' (Canada, 2010a, 9). Delineating clearly what constitutes legitimate action has strengthened Canadians' view of themselves as defenders of the vulnerable, as 'civilized' rather than 'barbaric.'

It would be inaccurate to say that the new relationship between state and citizenry involves no more than promoting pleasure. But we do point out that even the *restriction* of pleasures is now being discussed in the *language* of pleasure. Since Trudeau's 1967 statement, some pleasures have receded from the state's purview, while others have become *more* regulated by the state. As already noted, some hitherto morally insidious pleasures, such as gambling, have been redefined as legitimate entertainment – indeed, they have come to be promoted by the state. At the same time, though, state policies and campaigns are warning us about the effects of indulging in legal pleasures. And even this relationship is tricky. For example, tobacco is a legal substance, yet its use is increasingly restricted. Health Canada and other state agents spend tax dollars warning about the dangers of smoking, and this is helping make it a much more deviant act than in the past. Even so, tobacco taxes are helping fill government coffers. Furthermore, the restrictions on tobacco (including high taxes) are producing new problems in managing pleasure – problems that are more readily understood as problems of citizen desire. That there is a healthy black market in cigarettes points to the resistance of citizens to the state regulation of health, as well as to the resistance of those members of Aboriginal communities involved in cigarette smuggling to state prescriptions of legality and order. The state's approach to smoking allows it to enjoy the best of two worlds – to be concerned about citizen health and to generate money from addictions.

The official status of smoking is now unclear, in part because it is now understood purely in terms of its effects. In the cultural context of the belief in the liberal body – that is, one's body is the legitimate site of pleasures as long as those pleasures do not infringe on the rights or pleasures of others – smoking has become deviant on the assumption that it harms *other* parties ('second-hand smoke'), not oneself. Smokers are warned about the health effects of tobacco but are not prohibited from using it. Hence fetuses, children, co-workers, and strangers on the sidewalk are invoked to limit this pleasure, in contrast to the older ideas of vice in which the smoker's own pleasure and dependence on tobacco would be considered sinful. Presumably, if scientists were to produce a tobacco product that could be consumed without harmful effects on the body – or, better, with *healthful* effects – the deviant status of this act would quickly recede. This notion of deviant pleasure differs from older ideas of smoking as a bad act *in itself* – that is, as a sign of weakness or self-indulgence that is connected to the pleasure that tobacco provides. The same holds true for the state's relation to alcohol promotion and restriction. This too is now framed in terms of secondary harm – car accidents and fetal alcohol syndrome. Similarly, the regulation of 'obscene' sexual materials began to be discussed during the 1980s in terms of their third-party harm to women rather than any long-standing definition as that which offends community sentiment. In 2010, Canada's prostitution laws were deemed unconstitutional on the ground that they made the conditions of sex workers more dangerous. Again, the argument has shifted from direct moral grounds (vice) to the practical consequences of these actions, leaving the moral standing of the actions themselves unclear. So even in cases where the state seems to have become more restrictive, the ground for this restriction has become framed in terms of the pleasure and safety of others. Similarly, perceptions of gambling have shifted: it was once condemned for its particular relation to material gain, but the focus now is on its ill effects. Clearly, the new effects-defined idea of deviance signals that the role of the state has changed drastically and that so has the very concept of citizenship.

We have titled this book *Desiring Canada* for a number of reasons. First, to highlight the basic sociological presupposition that what people want, long for, or enjoy is not a product of individual tastes or organic inclinations; rather, it is a highly socialized and organized practice. In other words, Canadians *learn* their desires – those desires are not innate. Indeed, we suggest that there is a particular *Canadian* style or type of desiring. But while desires are not natural, they certainly come to seem that way. Our discussion must then also answer the question of how certain pleasurable objects or practices come over time to seem natural or inevitable. This holds for national identity itself. A national identity is an accomplishment; moreover, it is one that is achieved across the range of interactional and societal locations and levels, from the personal, the everyday, and the institutional and organizational, to the level of the state.

Second, Canada, like all democratic modern nation-states, must be viewed as a desired object in the hearts and minds of its citizens. Canada, being a modern nation-state, is what Benedict Anderson famously described as an 'imagined community,' that is, an abstract community that in order to survive must continuously be invoked – collected and recollected – in the imaginations of its members. Anderson (1983) defines national self-identity as the belief in the fated socio-political collecting and ordering of a people in a territory and history: 'It is the magic of nationalism to turn chance into destiny' (19). We are trained, especially as children, to identify ourselves with our nation and to feel this identity at a visceral level. We note in this context that in 2009 an elementary school principal in New Brunswick received death threats and nationwide media attention when he exercised his right not to play the national anthem every day at his school. The school's superintendant intervened and insisted that it be played daily.

Nationalism is the most obvious state-promoted pleasure – witness the 'joyful' nationalism that developed in Canada during the 2010 Olympics. Ritualistic celebrations of national heroes, historical events, and geographic places all work to link our imaginations to the federal state and its representatives. Oddly, even old enemies of the state – take state-executed Métis rebel Louis Riel – have been recast as heroes and conscripted into official history. Indeed, the conscription of Riel – or 'inclusion,' to use softer language – can itself become a national point of pride. Michael Billig (1995), though, argues that we should look to everyday life in order to understand nationalism rather than to heroes and occasional massive state spectacles. Nationalistic symbols of state infuse ordinary life, and because of their propinquity, they are consumed in less than conscious ways. Discussing England, he points to flags, coins, foods, sports, and subtle practices that circulate through daily life to signify and reproduce the notion of a nation-state. These practices come to seem natural and almost invisible because they are so taken for granted. Lines of demarcation and categories of thought also become ritualized. As an example, he offers the apparently commonsense division of the news into 'national' and 'international' segments. Following on Billig, we ask how these daily practices become pleasurable, specifically in Canada, and in which cultural sites they occur and why.

We argue that while Canadianness is a nationalism, this identity has distinctive characteristics that are produced by particular state/pleasure dynamics. Canadianness is more than the various cultural, ethnic, and regional differences to be found within the country; it also involves a mediation of those differences, an imagined community premised on a space that the differences already assume, but that get collected into an identity – 'Canadian.'

States depend on national sentiment, but nation and state do not always coincide completely. 'Nation' implies a natural community of people, often based on a sense of common history, ethnicity, race, language, or culture. 'State' implies the institutions and agencies that administer and govern a particular population within a given geopolitical territory. Also, the state 'performs' its power through various official ceremonies and rituals – the opening of Parliament, the welcoming of foreign officials, the celebration of national holidays, state funerals, the repatriation of dead soldiers, and so on. Hence some groups think of themselves as a nation, a people, in search of a state. Other states are pulled apart by their efforts to contain more than one nation. The state then comes to depend on feelings of unified nationalism to give it support and legitimacy, but also to help it appear.

Canadians are sometimes described as a statist people – that is, as looking to and trusting state institutions, officials, and policies to manage problems of all sorts. In other words, they find pleasure and identity in being administered through the state. This is one of the more interesting features of Canadian identity. What does a nation, people, or culture look like – what characteristics does it produce and take on – when the state plays a large role in the project? What problems arise with the notion of administering a nation, people, or culture? Richard Gwyn (1995) has gone as far as to assert that 'rather than a nation-state . . . we are really a *state-nation*. Our state has formed us and has shaped our character in a way that is true for no other people in the world' (17–18, emphasis in original). Gwyn argues that Canada led the way in linking the welfare state to the experience of civil life both imaginatively and literally. He suggests that the Canadian values that should be defended are tied to the values of the state. In other words, in Canada the state seems to have preceded and induced the nation. Mary Vipond (1992) explains that 'only after the formation of the Canadian state out of several different colonies was the attempt to create a Canadian nation begun' (xi). This process may seem oddly artificial, but only because we often wrongly and romantically imagine that states spring up to house groups that already feel some allegiance – that new states naturally arise around self-identified peoples rather than by conquest and the buying and trading of territories among states. In this sense, if Canadians are statist they at least guard against essentializing nationality and make room for the multiplicity of identities that is central to the Canadian federation. However, Canadians may run the risk of essentializing the state itself. That is, if we are suspicious of ethnic nationalism, we are not historically highly suspicious of the state.

Curiously, when Mattel set out to make a 'Canadian Barbie' as part of its line of national dolls, it put her in a Mountie uniform. While other Barbies were presented in terms of social class (English Barbie dressed in equestrian attire) or ethnic notions of culture (Jamaican Barbie dressed in traditional folk costume), Canadian Barbie dressed as an agent of the state itself. Presumably, for Mattel this was the clearest and most obvious signifier of Canadianness – seemingly, we are a state-loving people. Perhaps, too, Mattel was on to something in its linking of symbols of state and play, with the male Mountie being a long-standing symbol of honest and rugged masculinity in Hollywood romances. But as we will discuss, there are parts of everyday life where the state does not seem to penetrate easily. Moreover, even if statist desires do exist, we still have to look at their particular shape and conditions of existence. In and around certain pleasures we find certain desires for the state; around other pleasures the relationship to the state is different – even ambivalent or rejecting.

In his discussion of the relationship between Canadian nation and state, historian Ramsay Cook (1971) famously argued that Canada could be more accurately characterized as 'nationalist-state' than as a nation-state (5–6). The nationalist state depends on a type of cultural homogeneity and conformity that reinscribes a simple and static world view. In this way, citizens are invited to think of their national institutions and history as fixed and inevitable, such that legal and cultural arrangements made in the past are elevated into sacred contracts that cannot be changed. This, he says, overlooks the practical, negotiated, and contingent nature of all legal and social contracts. He writes that habits of mind arise from this simplistic way of thinking that stand in the way of practical decision making and change. Nationalist sentiments are cultivated by powerful groups, including academics, to maintain or remake Canada in their own image. Interestingly, as a historian, Cook is warning about the dangers of a nationalist historical consciousness, which easily turns the state and its history into a reified and ossified thing that also freezes the nation or people as historical actors – an issue that will arise in our discussion. Cook is also highlighting the fact that nationalism is far more than a set of feelings – it is a way of knowing and acting.

Finally, the title *Desiring Canada* is meant to highlight that Canadians have learned to desire *desire* itself as a part of their identity. In other words, for decades Canadians have enthusiastically supported an industry of narratives – books, contests, debates, surveys – that are premised on the impossibility of achieving an identity. These popular narratives have characterized Canada, variously, as 'unknown' (Hutchison 1942), 'unfinished' (Hutchison 1985; Cohen 2007), 'lost' (Cohen 2003), 'vanishing' (Hurtig 2002), 'mysterious' and 'elusive' (MacGregor 2007), and 'unfounded' (Cooper 2007). While some of these narratives are alarmist, these characteristics are not always presented as a problem for Canada – indeed, often they are identified as the country's signal strength. Other popular contests and books offer to produce lists of Canadian things – inducing the endless pleasure of collecting and recollecting, as we will see in our discussion of CBC contests. Of course, there must be a certain irony in this notion of a never-ending search, for to take it completely seriously would be to invite cynicism or despair. That said, the popularity of this pursuit connects pleasure (having) and desire (wanting) in an interesting way. As Keohane (1997) puts it, 'Canada exists as symptoms of the real thing which doesn't exist, but which has real effects' (17). Indeed, the pleasure of wanting – desire – seems to be developed in this deferral. There is even something playful and seductive about never fully coming into existence. As we will discuss, this relationship between pleasure and desire gets played out in various ways that involve the state.

Clearly, then, in discussing Canadian identity, pleasure, and desire we are not directly discussing Quebec, but the Canada that is imagined as a federal whole. Since the 1960s Quebec has moved very much towards solving its problems of identity by creating a nation within Canada based at least in part in linguistic difference – as officially acknowledged by the Government of Canada. Quebec is officially now a 'nation' within Canada, but not a state. Quebec does arise in the following chapters, usually as an 'other' to Anglo-Canadian pleasures and desires – sometimes it is treated as a threat to Canada, for example. Quebec is often a background figure discussed, characterized, and vilified without the Québécois voice being invited into the conversation. In other words, the work of Canadian identity and state invokes ideas and talk about Quebec as it does about Aboriginal Canadians, immigrants, and Americans.

In chapter 1, 'Contesting Canada at the CBC,' we look at how the CBC manages its state-mandated responsibility to provide entertainment and national identity to its audience. Here we consider the state in terms of law and policy, especially cultural laws and policies that are meant to induce a sense of nation in Canadians. The CBC has the unenviable job of making the state and nation disappear into play and pleasure. We examine two CBC contests that solicited audience desire for cherished Canadian things. One of these contests asked the audience to choose Canada's seven most 'wonderful' things; the other asked the audience to compile a music playlist for the newly elected U.S. President Barack Obama. We watched these contests unfold, noting the relationship between CBC producers and the audience, and found a strong need on the part of the producers to direct the audience's desires towards particular Canadian objects, themes, and ideas. The contests ultimately offered the CBC itself, and its management of Canadian pleasure, as a necessary thing for Canadians to desire. Even so, the audience's playful and irreverent responses to this management of its desires also showed resistance and offered alternative versions of Canadian pleasure.

In chapter 2, '"Always Fresh, Always There": Tim Hortons and the Consumer-Citizen,' we consider Tim Hortons as a site of everyday, simple pleasure that is also closely linked to ideas of Canada and Canadianness. Here we find the state in its performative and ceremonial mode – one that can rely on nationalist figures such as the soldier, the veteran, and the immigrant. If the state's disappearing act into play in chapter 1 was made impossible by the need to administer Canadian identity and pleasure, the state makes a different appearance on this commercial terrain. Since it has no official mandate, Tim Hortons's employment of national sentiment can capitalize on mundane pleasure much more freely than a state-mandated agent like the CBC. A close look at decades of Tim Hortons's marketing tells us that it has developed a particular relationship to commemoration and memory, including a relationship to the state and the military. In fact, we find it to be so influential that agents of the state – the armed forces, politicians, the CBC – have made use of Tim Hortons for their own continued legitimacy – that is, in order to appear. Here we discuss the shift of national discourse to the private sector and the implications for citizenship and politics.

Perhaps chapter 3, ' "Our Game": Hockey, Civilizing Projects, and Domestic Violence,' offers the most obvious and clichéd version of a Canadian pleasure – hockey. If there is a single activity that marks the pleasures of the 'people' in Canada, it is hockey. It is 'our game.' How does the state appear/disappear here? In this chapter we discuss how hockey is situated within state- and nation-building projects, as aided by colourful allies such as CBC commentator Don Cherry. Hockey is both a commercial product and a symbol used by the state. We explore the anomalous persistence of violence on the ice and the tolerance for it and argue that the hockey fight is a form of 'domestic violence' that relates not only to the hockey 'code,' but also to projects of identity and state building. Here we consider the state as the legitimate institution of violence – it declares wars, suspends rights, and conscripts, deports, quarantines, arrests, and imprisons its citizens. The hockey ice surface is a culturally unique site in Canada, one that allows a controlled, symbolic enactment of the state's right to violence. This violence is domestic in the sense of being ours and being accepted as inherent to the game (as was, for decades, the attitude towards violence in the home). Here the state disappears and appears by way of a 'stacking' of culture sites – the state into Coach's Corner, Coach's Corner into the CBC, and the whole spectacle into the symbolic arena of the ice surface.

Chapter 4, 'Peace, Order and Good Gambling,' explores a strikingly Canadian relationship between the state and pleasure. Here the state appears in terms of the management and redistribution of wealth and resources and also in terms of how citizens are framed. Historically, gambling in Canada has gone from being illegal and sinful to being promoted and monopolized by the state. It is assumed that the state, rather than private enterprise, should own and benefit from gambling. With gambling, the state is directly involved in a commercial activity, in that it is selling a product (or experience) that is mass marketed to citizens as entertainment. The social good of gambling is measured in terms of its secondary effects, such as support of amateur athletics or community charities, rather than in terms of the nature of this particular pleasure. Moreover, the citizen is formulated as an individual risk taker and is oriented to as a consumer. We argue that the role of the state in gambling enterprises points towards a utilitarian relationship to citizens. While there is an obvious state involvement (appearance), this also allows the state to disappear by recasting the citizen along individualized and utilitarian lines. Here we see that the state's involvement in pleasure reflects a particular type of state moralism that exemplifies 'Canadianness.'

Comedy is our final topic. In chapter 5, 'The Funny State Apparatus,' we discuss the relationship between popular Canadian comedy and the state. Here we find the state presented in such a way as to reduce the imaginative space between the nation or people and state practices, authority, and apparatuses. While humour and comedy are often treated as inherently disruptive of order and authority, we find a particular style of comedy in Canada that is also supportive of authority and the state. This type of humour is more accurately characterized as parody than as satire, in that it gently challenges the powerful but does not full-out attack power's agents or organizations. Much Canadian comedy is self-referential of Canadian institutions and practices such that only the socialized Canadian audience can understand it. These self-references shore up and make natural these social arrangements. In this chapter we look specifically at comedian Rick Mercer, one of Canada's most popular comics and a CBC celebrity. We find that while he routinely attacks politicians and state bureaucrats for incompetence and corruption, he uses his humour to demonstrate a supportive and sacrificial relationship to the Canadian state itself. Mercer uses his comedic body to celebrate the armed forces and police, state technologies and scientific research, and the fit, patriotic citizen.

Clearly this discussion of desire, pleasure, identity, and state is complex. That is one reason why we offer everyday, seemingly inconsequential pleasures for consideration in this book – contests, cups of coffee, hockey fights, lotteries, and jokes. The everyday is both obvious and obscure by virtue of its very ordinariness – its familiarity and ubiquity make it seem unimportant. It is always difficult to think of the familiar in a way that makes it strange and hence open to inspection. Yet the everyday is significant, for it is just the place where habits of mind are made and remade, especially by way of our rituals of pleasure.

We hope that our analysis of everyday pleasures will be somewhat disruptive of taken-for-granted Canadian relations to the everyday so that its connection to national identity and the state will become more obvious. It is interesting in this context to note that ordinary objects are often tossed around in popular culture to represent Canada – donuts, hockey sticks, toques. Perhaps this is a Canadian claim to humility. But the place of these signifiers of Canada is not often inspected in a serious way. How do they link up with bigger things like law, policy, and institutions? We hope that by considering everyday pleasures in detail we will make a complex topic more tangible and solid so that the workings of state, identity, and pleasure in Canada can be brought to the fore. We hope, as well, that our readers find pleasure in this inspection of Canadian pleasures, now that pleasures are becoming such an important aspect of being Canadian.

1

Contesting Canada at the CBC

Canada Lives Here

CBC slogan

We're excited about the new (U.S.) President and we want him to be excited about us, so we're asking our audience to help compile the list of our most definitive Canadian songs!

Denise Donlon, Executive Director, CBC Radio

We begin our discussion of the complex relations among everyday pleasures, identity, nation, and the state by looking at Canada's iconic cultural institution, the Canadian Broadcasting Corporation (CBC). The CBC is a unique cultural site in Canada. As this country's publicly owned national broadcaster since its founding in the 1930s, it has special responsibilities within a federal cultural-nationalist policy – responsibilities that make it different from private broadcasters in terms of what it is expected to offer its audiences and how it is to operate. And while it competes in the media market with broadcasters that are far less regulated, and whose mandates do not extend far beyond simple profit making, CBC television and radio have been able to maintain a respectable share of an increasingly fragmented audience. Here we encounter an important manifestation of the state's mandate to provide entertainment – one that gives pleasure and at the same time fosters national identity.

Many Canadians love to hate the CBC, and its ardent supporters are among its harshest critics. Indeed, much of the enjoyment of being part of the CBC audience centres on the endless opportunities to debate and discuss its mandate – that is, its obligations to Canadians. Canadians are drawn to the CBC in part because the CBC is a place where Canada gets made and remade. The particular pleasure of being part of its audience arises in part from the conflicting expectations that have been placed on the organization and its people. In other words, the ongoing debate over the CBC's role is a part of a larger, ongoing crisis of national identity. Furthermore, the CBC encourages this crisis – in our view, it is key to the CBC's legitimacy as a cultural institution. For its audience, the CBC is more than a conduit and champion of Canadian culture; it is also a cultural object of vital importance, and it presents itself as such. Ambiguity and contradiction are essential to its cultural work and to its very survival.

The CBC's detractors find endless ammunition in the very terms of its official mandate, as will be clear from the audience responses to the two contests we will consider in this chapter. Those detractors often contend that the CBC is bureaucratic, paternalistic, and parochial and that the state and its agents should get out of the culture-and-entertainment business, because their presence in it only serves to render the citizen-audience a target of policy. For them, the CBC is too much about socializing Canadians to desire the state's own interests. And in truth, the CBC's executives hardly deny this is so. Richard Stursberg, at the time the Executive Vice-President of CBC English Services, put it this way in a opinion piece in 2009 titled 'A Memo to Its Detractors': 'What is CBC's "mandate"? We think it is to successfully address the central cultural challenge in English-speaking Canada: We are the only country in the industrialized world that prefers foreign TV shows to our own. Turning this problem around is – has always been – our most important cultural challenge and our most intractable one.'

Setting aside the issue of how accurately Stursberg has characterized the TV-viewing habits of the rest of the industrialized world (which, famously, have made American shows such as *The Oprah Winfrey Show* and *Desperate Housewives* international hits), his words are instructive as well as typical of how 'preference' (read 'desire') has long been understood at the CBC. While the CBC's mandate is to 'turn around this problem' of externally oriented desire, Stursberg also calls this challenge 'intractable' – that is, likely to continue. Detractors might point out that his argument in defence of sustained government financing of the CBC seems to depend on both the socialization of Canadian cultural desire and the intractibility of that desire.

A look at the 1991 Canadian Broadcasting Act (or any previous version of that act) reveals that this tension is seeded into the very legislation that mandated the CBC. According to the act, the CBC is obliged to:

- 'reflect Canada and its regions' back to itself, but also more actively to 'contribute to shared national consciousness and identity';
- generate this unifying national consciousness and identity, but also 'reflect the multicultural and multiracial' nature of Canada;
- defend high culture against the incursion of mass and/or foreign culture (i.e., 'enlighten'), but also cultivate a broad, popular audience ('entertain'); and
- produce programming in Canada that is 'predominantly Canadian,' but also produce programs that are 'distinctively' Canadian.

Clearly, the Broadcasting Act demands much of the CBC in terms of nation building. The act obligates the CBC to perform a number of social and political functions that may be difficult to implement in actual programming without generating strain and ambiguity, especially – we suggest – in terms of the corporation's relationship to its audience. For example, on the one hand the CBC is mandated to 'reflect' what is deemed to already exist – and the 'goodness' of what already exists (mainly, Canada's regional, cultural, and racial diversity) is not to be questioned. Yet on the other hand, the CBC is required actively to *generate* a unifying collective identity and consciousness. Similarly, it must somehow find ways to square the circle of educating its audience while also entertaining it. (The *Test the Nation* reality-contest programs – of which there have been three to date – address these challenges directly.) Finally, the CBC is to produce Canadian programming even while defending the uniqueness of Canada's diverse components. On top of all these obligations, the CBC must survive in a political climate that measures its success by the yardstick of the media market.

By law, the CBC's content is safe from government interference; but in reality, constant threats of budget cuts have required the corporation's executives to focus sharply on getting the most audience for the least expenditure. Cultural entities must lobby the government for support; and because of that, when the government's understandings of the purpose and value of culture shift, so must the ways in which workers in the cultural sectors (now called 'industries') appeal to the government. This is why culture is being discussed more and more in terms of the numbers of people it employs, the jobs it creates, the revenues it generates, and the audiences it attracts. (Of course, it is dangerous to defend culture as just another industry, given that Canada could survive economically by producing other things.) As the official broadcaster of the Canadian identity, the CBC also has had to respond to changes in the broader media environment in order to appeal to Canadians: by renewing TV and radio programs, by developing Internet programming, and by transforming its look and its various modes of delivery. In 2009, the CBC gave a facelift to its TV news programming: the sets became more colourful, hosts now stood up to present the news, interactive screens and graphics became more prominent, and an aesthetic of movement was introduced into program delivery. The stated goal of all this was to make the news more immediate and transparent for viewers. Critics characterized the changes as the 'CNN-ification' of the broadcaster (Dixon and Bradshaw 2009).

The questions and contradictions that surround the CBC invoke ideas that are deeply embedded in questions of collective pleasure and identity. In other words, these contradictions do not appear in the Broadcasting Act by some fluke of policy making. Nor are they a product of sloppy bureaucrats and politics. Rather, they are signifiers of how difficult it is to use culture and mass media to do the work of nation building. Our goal here is not to take a side in the endless debate that requires each Canadian to be 'for' or 'against' the CBC. This divisive way of discussing the CBC only generates constant animosity; it also allows the continuous deferral of a sustained and careful look at *how* the CBC induces desire and pleasure. In fact, we will be arguing that debating what the CBC does has itself become an important part of Canadian identity and desire. Instead of getting trapped inside that debate, our goal then is to investigate just how the socialization of cultural desire and the maintenance of the crisis of desire are sustained. The CBC is so important to the Canadian cultural landscape that it will reappear in our discussions of hockey and humour. At the end of this book we will place the CBC in a broader context of desire, citizenship, and the state.

In this chapter we look specifically at CBC contests. These contests seek to collect valued Canadian things, people, places, and culture through audience participation, opinion, and voting. This type of programming is in part a response to the surge in popularity of 'reality TV' over the past decade. Truly, reality TV has become television's dominant genre, encompassing everything from 'makeover' programming (of bodies, cars, homes, childrearing habits, budgets, love lives, driving skills), to occupational programming (unusual, risky, terrible jobs), to 'just living' programming (celebrities, unusual families, mismatched roommates), to competitions (designing clothing, baking cakes, selling things, even finding romance), to oddities (the supermorbidly obese, addiction and mental illness, disability, unusual medical conditions, very large families) . . . the list is endless.

There are a number of reasons why any broadcaster would be attracted to the reality-contest genre of entertainment. Most important, this type of programming is relatively inexpensive to make because audience members do much of the work of generating and sustaining the content (in contrast to genres like scripted drama, which depend on unionized writers, actors, set crews, etc.). With the advent of online voting and debate, this form of entertainment requires little more than keeping the lines of communication open and running. In its broadest sense almost all programming has expanded to include this aspect of entertainment; almost every show, whatever the type, now has an interactive website that feeds back into the televised or radio content, making audience opinion central to the entertainment. Another attraction of audience-centred entertainment is that it is populist – at least on its face. Thus television hits like *American Idol* (and its counterpart *Canadian Idol*) solicit expert opinion but allow the popular vote to choose the ultimate winners. In the *Idol* model, the expert panel's attempts to sway the audience to its views are key to the entertainment. Such shows actually cultivate the tension between the panel and the voting audience, with the former rendered as elitist, capricious, or market oriented, leaving the viewing audience as the morally superior authority. Also in the *Idol* model, the 'underdog' or 'every person' contestant is often recognized by the audience at the outset and is then repeatedly defended by voters from the judges' attacks. We might argue that the vindication of culture as the purview of the audience is both the message and the pleasure offered by the *Idol* shows and their ilk. This type of show challenges expert, 'official' judgment; moreover, its interactive technologies offer to return the audience to a grassroots and face-to-face form of governance found in the early American town hall. As we will see, this rhetoric of populism is not so easily managed in the CBC contests.

Contests are not new to CBC broadcasting. In the realm of high culture, CBC radio has always provided prestigious awards in classical music performance and composition through competitions adjudicated by experts. On a more popular and grassroots plane, its early talent contests set out to unearth unknown talent from all regions of the country, but again with a focus on musical performance and composition of a particular taste level. These contests relied mainly on expert judges to choose winners, presumably because the contests sought to uphold the standards of high culture and also because interactive technologies were not in place to provide quick feedback between judges and audience. For example, CBC's 'Singing Stars of Tomorrow' (1943–56) and

'Nos futures étoiles' (1947–55) featured competitors singing 'art songs and operatic or oratorio arias' (*Canadian Encyclopedia of Music* [2012]). 'Opportunity Knocks' (1947–57) also featured light classical music. In this latter case, the judges considered studio audience polls and mail-in votes. This populist gesture notwithstanding, clearly the aim of these competitions was to popularize a particular type of music rather than feature the favoured music of the period (big bands, romantic crooners, and early rock and roll).

While the CBC has retained the talent competition genre, many newer contests have borrowed features from the popular contest TV genre with the unique objective of collecting and inventorying Canadianness. The most important criterion for selecting the winning thing – be it a place, an object, a piece of music, a novel, or a historical figure – is its relationship to Canada and Canadian values. For example, in 2004 the CBC aired its 'The Greatest Canadian' contest. In her study of this contest, Rak (2008) noted that the nominated Canadians were promoted by Canadian celebrities, who framed the nominees themselves in terms of celebrity (e.g., CBC TV star George Stroumboulopoulos provided the pitch for Tommy Douglas, characterizing the Protestant minister as a rebel along the lines of American actor James Dean). Rak concluded that this type of contest encouraged a national consciousness organized around the celebration of individual heroic biographies rather than broader and more complex historical realities. Similarly, Fuller and Sedo (2006) found that the CBC radio contest 'Canada Reads' upheld and defended particular conceptions of Canada such that the winning novels were chosen less for their literary value than for the lessons they taught readers.

The two CBC contests we discuss here – the 'Seven Wonders of Canada' TV and radio contest, and the 'Obama's Playlist' radio contest – put *things* into competition – that is, symbols and signifiers of Canada. In these contests, audiences were invited to locate and choose things that represented Canada in some way. As we will discuss, these things amounted to signifiers of strongly predetermined and clichéd ideas about Canada, ideas that were then recirculated and renewed by the ritual of 'contesting' them. Not only that, but the very processes of collecting and choosing pointed to particular aspects of how Canadian self-desire is managed. We suggest that pleasure is meant to be derived not only from the circulation and celebration of important nationalist signifiers, but also from the disciplined and domesticated nature of those practices. In the following case studies we describe how the CBC audience resists experts' and producers' attempts to manage their opinions;

and how these contests try to reinscribe the pleasure of locating identity work on the CBC. In other words, while authority is questioned at the level of the particular workings or administration of opinion within the contests, on a broader level these contests sustain and even reinforce a desire for state-mediated culture and identity. Hence, programming aimed at collecting an identity through popular contests, such as the ones we consider here, are inherently very different from popular contests found on private broadcasters. The former may collect notions such as Canadian public opinion, but they are not tasked with collecting Canada *through* public opinion. As we will explore, CBC contests exist to educate, direct, and regulate the identity or self-desire of the audience for Canada and things Canadian. Audience opinion cannot be allowed to function without the active massaging of opinion in particular directions by the CBC producers.

It is our contention that the audience pleasures generated by popular CBC contests help make Canadian identity a topic of playful 'contest' (rather than a tiresome and anxiety-laden political debate) and that by making contests out of identity work, the CBC is able to deflect controversy from itself. Furthermore, CBC contests inevitably reinscribe the CBC as a location and authority of national-identity work. In other words, part of the work of 'contesting Canada,' or making Canada an object of playful contest, is to make the CBC itself beyond contest.

For the CBC this foray into interactive popular contests raises issues that are unique to it. One such issue is that any attempt to elicit or employ popular taste or opinion runs up against what has been called the 'Masseyist' position that the CBC's job is to cultivate and raise the levels of taste and opinion, rather than simply to entertain. Cuts to the CBC's 'high cultural' institutions (such as the CBC radio orchestra, founded in 1938) have encouraged some audience members to regard the popular itself as a threat to the CBC's very mandate (and, more broadly, to the shape of culture in Canada). But at the same time, resorting to opinion helps legitimize the CBC as a nation-building institution within a society that is growing more and more suspicious of the long-held authority of educated elites. The constant representation and circulation of opinion supports the idea that politics and policy should arise in this inductive, grassroots manner.

Given that the 'Seven Wonders of Canada' and 'Obama Playlist' contests attempted to collect Canadian things, we must in this chapter also consider the practice of collecting as an active way of making meaning and identity. Put another way, the things a nation collects as its own

cannot seem arbitrary; rather, they must seem to be natural manifestations of *a people*. If we could collect anything and everything under the
rubric of 'who we are,' then identity would have no meaning. What, then,
makes a people *a people*? Clearly, chance and disorder must somehow be
transformed into destiny and order. The CBC's assertive slogan 'Canada
Lives Here' nicely captures the idea that the CBC is a unique imaginative
place that collects Canadians, *as* Canadians, and enlivens them as a community. The claim underpinning this is that only the CBC can gather
and mediate Canada and Canadianness. By characterizing its abstract
and electronically mediated community as a place (a 'here'), this slogan
also invokes pre-modern face-to-face associations, with individuals taking common values and world views for granted. In other words, the
slogan both generates an imagined community and – just as important –
naturalizes this community and itself.

Hence, the implicit organizing question of these contests – 'What or
where is Canada?' – can be asked only *after* the assumption has been
made that there is already a 'we' that may constitute something like 'collective Canadianness.' Furthermore, the asking of such a question assumes an *other* or others – those *not* us – that our 'we-ness' stands over
and against but that 'we' nevertheless require in order to buttress our
sense of who we are. Our 'we-ness,' then, depends on making and reaffirming symbolic boundaries. Anthropologist Mary Douglas (1966) put
it thus: 'The idea of society is a powerful image. It is potent in its own
right to control or to stir men to action. This image has form; it has external boundaries, margins, internal structure. Its outlines contain power to
reward conformity and repulse attack' (141). Douglas's work reiterates
Émile Durkheim's classical assertion that all collectives represent and
reinscribe – indeed, they bring themselves into existence – through their
particular practices of naming, collecting, and ordering things: these
'collective representations [express] the ways in which the group thinks
of itself in its relationships with the objects which affect it' (1982, 40).
These things that affect the group have been invested with collective
meaning and are thereby honoured (Durkheim 1965). For Durkheim
and Douglas this also means that it is not just *what* collectives collect but
the *system* of classification as well that tells us how that collective thinks.
The various objects and symbols it collects must be considered within
the logic of the system of which they are a part. For members of a collective, this underlying logic of classification becomes a commonsense,
taken-for-granted way of understanding the world and is largely invisible
to them. Based on this observation, we can make the assumption that

the classification system used in an organization like the CBC will tell us about the taken-for-granted world view it promotes. For Durkheim, collective representations, which are visible in a variety of social institutions and practices, do not survive if they are not ritually reaffirmed (Durkheim 1965). He means here that ritual does not *support* identity from the outside, as an epiphenomenal add-on; rather, it is *constitutive* of identity, necessary for its appearance and support. From his point of view, the CBC's contests should be studied both as systems for organizing and constituting identity and as ritual enactments of those systems through the reaffirmation of sacred objects.

However, collecting does more than ritualistically reinscribe a collective's pre-existing epistemological and ontological assumptions. It is also a particular *political* practice in itself. It tells us about the ongoing attempt to manage inherent contradictions of order, desire, and identity. Hence, structures of classification can be understood as symptoms of these contradictions rather than as simply solving the problem of order, as Durkheim would have it. Interestingly, scholars who discuss collecting also locate control, order, and even violence in this practice. Walter Benjamin (1968), reflecting on his own obsession for collecting books, said: 'For a true collector the whole background of an item adds up to a magic encyclopedia whose quintessence is the fate of his object' (60). Naomi Schor (1994) is even more explicit on this point: 'a collection is composed of objects wrenched out of their context of origins and reconfigured into the self-contained, self-referential context of the collection itself' (256). All acts of collecting – even the most apparently innocent practices of private collecting – involve some level of superstition and violence. This observation, when applied to the work of the nation-state, echoes Max Weber's famous definition of the state as the legitimate site of the administration of violence – both physical and symbolic (1946a, 78). Pierre Bourdieu elaborates on the links among collection, state authority, and violence:

> If the state is able to exert symbolic violence, it is because it incarnates itself simultaneously in objectivity, in the form of specific organizational structures and mechanisms, and in subjectivity in the form of mental structures and categories of perception and thought. By realizing itself in social structures and in the mental structures adapted to them, the instituted institution makes us forget that it issues out of a long series of acts of *institution* (in the active sense) and hence has all the appearances of the *natural*. (1999, 56–7; emphases in original)

Bourdieu invites us to recall that one cannot separate the real governing and managing of people – collecting and organizing them in space,
law, and policies – from the more abstract or symbolic collecting and
organizing of national identity. In other words, we cannot separate the
objective historical practices of, for example, 'collecting' First Nations
peoples into reservations or residential schools (and separating them
from family, language, religion, and collective memory) from the subjec-
tive practices of collecting a notion of Canadianness. Like other groups
that have been similarly collected and ordered, they must first be understood to be lacking in internal order and in need of collection by
some external force that brings its own taken-for-granted understanding
of what order looks like. With the official adoption of multiculturalism
in the 1960s and 1970s, the interplay between the concrete and symbolic
management of Canadians became far more subtle (relative to these
earlier practices), but no less 'a long series of acts of institution.' In our
discussion of the two CBC contests, these issues of collection will arise
repeatedly. Who has the authority to impose order in these contests?
What is the source of their authority? What is, and is not, Canadian in
these contests? Why? How do these contests provide the opportunity for
the CBC and its audience to reorder Canada's history of imposing order
on its territories and the people within it?

CBC and Cultural Nationalism

Before we look at these contemporary contests, we must situate the CBC
in Canada's broader history of making a nation by attending to culture.
The CBC (or its forerunner, the 'Canadian Radio Broadcasting Commission') came into existence in 1932 as part of the federal government's
interest in using a national public radio network to generate and sustain
a national identity. The CBC was more than the national public broadcaster; it was also the regulator of Canadian broadcasting until a separate
agency, the Board of Broadcast Governors, took over this responsibility
in 1959. Right from the beginning this project met resistance, largely
because it was first designed as a bilingual system that would mix French
and English broadcasting. Pressure from Anglo-Canadians soon forced
the creation of the 'two solitudes' in CBC broadcasting; henceforth, the
CBC would be separated into two culturally and administratively distinct
units. Although by law the CBC was supposed to promote communication and identification across this linguistic divide, in effect these two
units did not do so. In fact, over time the French-language service in

Quebec (Société Radio Canada) became aligned with Quebec nationalist sentiments (as did much of the intellectual and cultural elite during the Quiet Revolution of the 1960s) – so aligned, in fact, that in 1976 the Canadian Radio-television and Telecommunication Commission (CRTC) investigated that service for violating the Broadcasting Act's directive to promote national unity (Nesbit-Larking 2007). That this investigation was ordered by Prime Minister Pierre Trudeau, a federalist, underscores the connection between federal projects and broadcasting policy.

As Paul Nesbit-Larking notes, this interest in nation building runs like a red thread through the story of Canadian broadcasting (51). In much the same way that the CPR and CNR linked Canada from coast to coast in the decades after Confederation, the CBC was literally (albeit electronically) intended to bind Canadians together into a single imaginative unit, as a defence against American imperialism. Historian Mary Vipond (1992) contends that as far back as the first magazine publishing, Canadian cultural protectionism mixed 'the puritanical, the economic and the nationalist' (26). As Harold Innis (1951) famously argued, political control over large territories requires the 'binding' of space by a communications medium that can transport messages quickly and easily. A political economist, Innis was interested in how populations were administered; more recent media theorists have expanded on his idea, asking whether 'sheer mediation' of space by state-supported transportation and media technologies has become itself the primary imaginary unifier in English Canada, whatever content those technologies carry. Maurice Charland (1986) calls this 'technological nationalism' and explains that it 'promises a liberal state in which technology would be a neutral medium for the development of a *polis*. This vision of a nation is bankrupt, however, because it provides no substance for the *polis* except communication itself . . . Canada, then, is the "absent nation."' (198).

This constant absence sustains English Canada's crisis of identity as well as the legitimacy of publicly owned and state-mandated broadcasters like the CBC. After all, these technologies do not so much unite Canadians in dialogue as bring Canadians into existence through the experience of communication technologies themselves – without irony, the CBC's 'Canada Lives Here' slogan pulls Canada into the network of transmission lines, airwaves, and fibre-optic cable.

In this sense, the experience of listening to or viewing the CBC is more important than what is actually being broadcast at that particular moment. Of course, every ritual is comprised of repeated concrete practices, so there is every reason to assume some connection between content and form such that CBC's programming echoes this theme of sheer mediation. The earnest work (or content) of the contests we examine in this chapter helps sustain the crisis of identity on which the CBC's ritual of desire rests. When we look back on the history of the CBC, we find that the content of early broadcasting often was the state itself – government speeches, royal visits, celebrations of national birthdays, and the like. This particular history of the Canadian state as content does not undermine Charland's position. The state appeared in three ways: as technology, as officialdom, and as the official regulator of all broadcasting in Canada.

In the wake of the 1951 Report of the Royal Commission on the National Development of the Arts, Letters and Sciences (the Massey Commission), the Canadian federal state greatly expanded its support and administration of culture. The Massey Report reaffirmed the CBC's essential place as a cultural institution vital to Canada's sovereignty and identity. The tropes running through that report suggested a Canada in need of a strong CBC. For example, the commission reinforced the belief that Canada's vast territory presented special challenges to the work of creating a unified national identity. And while the United States was named as the main cultural threat, this danger was formulated in terms of the general influence of mass desire rather than particular cultural content. The Massey Report began on a high note, both culturally and rhetorically, with this extract from St Augustine of Hippo:

Populus est cœtus multitudinis rationalis rerum quas diligit concordi communione sociatus; profecto ut videatur qualis quisque populus sit illasunt intuenda quœ diligit.

A nation is an association of reasonable beings united in a peaceful sharing of the things they cherish; therefore, to determine the quality of a nation, you must consider what those things are.

St Augustine, *The City of God*, xix–xxiv

The document translated Augustine's *populus* as 'nation,' the import being that a nation is something brought together by the collection and celebration of things. Nothing could align better with the CBC's mandate as it appears in contests, which ritually collect cherished things.[1]

The Massey Report, a product of the Cold War's early days, was haunted by the spectre of the apparently soulless fascist and communist masses as constituted by the mass media (Kuffert 2003, 44; Litt 1992, 86).

The report began by reminding its readers that the goal of government support of culture was to create individuals who would use education to reflect and reason (Canada 1951, 7). Like so many cultural critics of that era, the Massey commissioners worried that modern mass society was becoming dominated by the values of materialism, relativism, mechanization, and bureaucracy. Cultural policy, it followed, was to act as a prophylactic against those modern tendencies by training Canada's citizens to think in terms of eternal and universal values: 'Culture is that part of education which enriches the mind and refines the taste' (7). The task facing Canada's cultural policy was to teach Canadians to discern the differences between levels of culture and come to desire the superior forms: 'the appetite grows by eating' (5).

This humanist version of culture does not easily lend itself to the administration of a national culture or to its bureaucratization. As the commission itself stated, 'there are important things in the life of a nation which cannot be weighed or measured' (4). Hence, for the Massey commissioners it was not the unique content of Canadian cultural practices that made them 'authentic.' In their view, Shakespeare and Bach would certainly be part of the national diet. That said, the Massey Report was still the product of romantic notions about a uniquely Canadian collective personality. The first substantive chapter of the report was titled 'The Forces of Geography' and began thus:

> Canada has a small and scattered population in a vast area; this population is clustered along the rim of another country many times more populous and of far greater economic strength; a majority of Canadians share their mother tongue with that neighbour, which leads to peculiarly close and intimate relations. One or two of these conditions will be found in many modern countries. But Canada alone possesses all three. What is their effect, good or bad, on what we call Canadianism? (11)

Kaufmann (1998) argues that Canadian identity has long been organized in terms of the 'naturalization of nation,' which links climate and geography to a national personality characterized by strength, honesty, and straightforwardness. In his discussion, early to mid-century nationalists like Vincent Massey were promoting cultural works (such as the celebrated and self-promoting Group of Seven painters) that depicted a harsh but also pristine wilderness that – so they imagined – both shaped and reflected the national psyche. The Massey Report harnessed this naturalized psyche in order to ratify the linkage between cultural policy and the theme of empty space, as well as to position both high culture and folk culture as protective agents against mass culture.

By the late 1960s the Massey Report's recommendations were being used to establish a state cultural bureaucracy. But the need to administer culture in a rational and legalistic way, and nationalists' growing interest in building cultural industries to support Canadian talent and sell cultural goods (Edwardson 2008), meant that culture had to become more easily 'weighed and measured' both for the *practical* sake of making policies work and for the *political* sake of ensuring that cultural policy could be *seen* to be at work. Heady ideas about the timeless or ethereal qualities of culture came to be replaced by quantitative measures of 'Canadianness,' which in turn were tied to notions about nationality, geography, and citizenship. Most famous in this regard were the Canadian content – 'CanCon' – rules requiring broadcasters to air particular amounts of 'officially' Canadian content at particular times of day. The weakness of such approaches is that they depend on distinctions that are contingent on statist conceptions of time and space – ones that in turn often highlight the awkwardness of the cultural apparatus.

In some infamous cases, Canadian artists have been told that their work is not technically Canadian. A now legendary example involved the Canadian rock star Bryan Adams, who let his anger become known after he was told by the CRTC that his 1991 album *Waking Up the Neighbours* was not Canadian content because it had been recorded outside Canada using international artists (Edwardson 2008). Adams was a well-established recording artist whose work was likely to succeed without the protection of the CRTC. For him, the CRTC ruling amounted to an attack on his identity as a Canadian.

Another example of the CRTC apparatus being exposed involved Canadian comedians Dave Thomas and Rick Moranis. Outraged that CBC producers had told them their TV show *SCTV* was short on Canadian content, they lampooned the CanCon rules by inventing the beer-swilling, half-witted McKenzie Brothers (Pevere and Dymond 1996). The awkward role of the state has also become apparent at the level of the general Canadian audience. For example, the CRTC allowed American cable TV to encroach on large urban centres during the late 1960s and early 1970s, even while rural Canadians continued to be 'protected' from foreign media content. More recently, the CRTC has expressed its interest in controlling the Canadian Internet, though at first it had deemed this technology beyond regulation.

Clearly, the Massey Commission's version of cultural bureaucracy was encountering inescapable realities. Not only did it face the practical issues of administering culture, but it was also doomed socially. As Kuffert (2003) points out, after the Second World War the assumption that a self-selected elite would lead the masses to morally edifying culture found itself threatened by the ideal of the masses' direct participation in decision making. From now on, any group or body that wanted to influence mass taste would have to establish that it was tuned in to the popular culture. This is not to suggest that the CBC was no longer understood in terms of the old Masseyite civilization/hinterland distinction, with culture characterized as food for the culturally hungry soul. A contemporary description of the CBC's mandate was that it would 'spread[] . . . cultural nourishment to outlying areas hundreds of kilometres from the amenities of urban life' (*Encyclopedia of Music in Canada* [1992]). This anachronistic characterization notwithstanding, there set in a strange reality that put an end to the Masseyite vision: 'While Canadian culture is acknowledged as the expression of Canadian identity and experience, it is not seen as the organized, spontaneous expression of a community' (Kinahan 2006, 34). If Canadian culture is not then this 'spontaneous expression of community,' we must look at Canadian identity and experience in terms of state mediations – that is, in terms of 'organized' expressions of statist incursions into culture. How is a 'community' – here, a national culture – being formed or manufactured? And how does this manufacture become pleasurable for audiences?

We suggest that contemporary contests like 'Seven Wonders of Canada' and 'Obama Playlist' help solve some of these long-standing problems by making the cultural policy apparatus less obvious and by enlisting the audience to help reinscribe and legitimate the assumptions that underpin official cultural policy. New interactive technologies also support this goal. The online opinion poll, the survey, and the interactive contest all appeal to this view that taste and desire exist in some raw and organic way and need only be tapped or, at most, brought into dialogue with other tastes and desires. Perhaps the new techniques of opinion even mask that – as Jean Baudrillard (1983) has posited – mass audiences become the object of their own entertainment and an 'alibi' for the very techniques that bring them into existence. Certainly it is true that the circulation of audience and expert talk about all things Canadian is the content and pleasure of these contests. However, while the audience's responses to these contests showed the pleasure generated by the debate around, and circulation of, cherished Canadian things, it also provided an opportunity for the audience to ask how the CBC organizes Canadian desire.

Seven (Disenchanted) Wonders of Canada Contest

The 'Seven Wonders of Canada' project began in the summer of 2007 and was broadcast on the English-language CBC radio and television service. The project, conceived as a response to a 'New Seven Wonders of the World' project, invited Canadians (i.e., those who listen to and watch the English-language CBC) to participate in collecting and then selecting Canada's seven 'most wonderful places.' These 'places' would come to be broadly interpreted as including 'things' such as the igloo, the canoe, and the CN Tower. The project's rules and parameters were set out by CBC producers and involved a panel of expert judges as well as the participation of the CBC audience. The design, the implementation, and finally the framing of the results of the Seven Wonders project would reveal tensions in the CBC's efforts to manage collective collecting desire. While these contradictions threatened the coherence and authority of the project – and even at times made it appear absurd – we suggest that they also reinscribed the apparent need for managerial, expert, and bureaucratic – what Max Weber would call 'disenchanted' – control over 'official' Canadian identity. Weber (1946b) held that the rational-legal management of modern life through state and bureaucracy destroys all that is wondrous or mysterious because its goal is calculated administration. At the same time, and as we have noted, collecting involves creating a 'magical encyclopedia' (Benjamin 1968). Thus the sensuous and magical desires that animate collecting run counter to the bureaucratic and rationalist formulations of national identity, such as those invoked by the CBC's attempts to manage this project.

While the Seven Wonders project aimed to invoke wonder, it ultimately produced disenchantment and incoherence because the mechanisms (or form) of management came to overshadow the sensuous and magical practice (or content) of collecting. The project's stated goal was to 'encourage a national dialogue about our country'; in practice, though, it rather ritualistically reaffirmed the administrative–symbolic role of the CBC as a necessary arbiter and collector of things Canadian. Besides creating cherished things, statist-nationalist attempts at enchantment and sacralization also generated popular cultural consternation at, resistance to, and mockery of such exercises. Clearly, statist-administrative projects of enchantment (e.g., creating 'culture' or a 'people') need to be constantly invoked.

At the same time, the CBC audience, while participating in the Seven Wonders project in great numbers, both criticized and subverted it by dismantling and thereby exposing its disenchanting logic. Some audience members participated in the project by questioning the CBC's authority to organize Canadians' collective self-desire. The 'wonder' these disruptions injected into the discourse celebrated the excess, confusion, and disorder that authors like Walter Benjamin have identified as an inherent albeit repressed aspect of the practice of collecting. The same disruptions brought to the fore an aspect of Canadian popular culture that has often been prominent in comedy programs such as *This Hour Has 22 Minutes* and *Royal Canadian Air Farce* – that is, the mockery of Canadian officialdom and the refusal to take mandated Canadianness too seriously. More on this point is found in chapter 5.

In many ways the Seven Wonders project was a child of the 1991 Broadcasting Act. It was to be multicultural and multiracial and to preserve the two distinct French and English systems. It was intended to generate 'distinctively' Canadian cultural objects, present all regions to the entire country (while preserving regional differences), and encourage debate. Rather bizarrely, the CBC was to 'contribute to shared national consciousness and identity' but *without* inviting the two official-language groups to talk to each other.

The Seven Wonders project was broadcast on English-language radio through the *Sounds Like Canada* show and on English-language national TV through *The National* newscast. The use of radio *and* TV heightened the potential for audience participation; it also shored up the project's authority by linking it to the sober and official national newscast (itself anchored by a national icon, Peter Mansbridge). While the project was managed through *Sounds Like Canada,* the final deliberations and decisions of the judges were broadcast during *The National.* The project itself was the brainchild of CBC producer Ian Clayton, who explained that he came up with the idea after hearing about a 'New Seven Wonders of the World' project (N7W). He felt that Canada had so many wondrous things that it deserved its own exclusive list (CBC 2008a). The CBC's Seven Wonders project was modelled on the N7W project, with some notable differences. Both projects involved popular participation to choose natural and artificial wonders. In the N7W project, though, the natural and artificial contests were run separately, whereas in the CBC project, they were mixed. Also, in the N7W project, the criteria for selection remained broad, while in the CBC project, they were more specific. Both involved a panel of expert judges, but in the N7W project, the judges narrowed the nominations and then returned their list to the online voters. In the CBC project, the judges alone made the final decisions. It was central to the N7W project that the people of the world would choose its wonders, with the goal of dissolving regional and national boundaries. According to the N7W website, the 'citizens of the world' would participate in the 'world's first ever global election' (New 7 Wonders 2008). But unlike the CBC's Seven Wonders project, the N7W final wonders were presented without ranking; and since they depended on the popular vote, they could not be readjusted to ensure 'diversity of location.' As we will discuss, 'diversity of location' would come to dog the CBC project.

The project as first presented to the CBC audience entailed soliciting nominations and 'pitches' (justifications for each nomination from the nominator). This was to be followed by debate, then by audience voting. The list of the fifty-two most popular nominations was then to be handed over to three judges, who would make the final choice of Canada's seven wonders. The criteria for nominating and pitching each of the wonders, the voting procedures, and the panel of three judges were all set out at the beginning, with little explanation about how this structure had been established. Once under way, the project became mired in its own procedures, and it was quietly modified as it approached its conclusion (as we will see, the word 'conclusion' must be treated broadly here). These ongoing modifications were presented to the audience as consequences of peripheral technical issues rather than as necessitated by the administrative assumptions of the project itself.

The project launched itself by announcing the names of the three judges and the criteria for selecting the wonders. The criteria to be used by both the audience and the judges were announced to the CBC audience and posted on the CBC website:

1. Essential 'Canadian-ness' – historically significant, character filled, valued;
2. Originality/uniqueness of the pitch and place;
3. Spectacular physical site or amazing human creation;
4. Ability to inspire;
5. Range within the final seven – diversity of location, type of wonder.
   (CBC, 2007a)

The three judges were announced as Ra McGuire, Roy MacGregor, and Roberta L. Jamieson. The criteria for choosing them were not revealed, which implicitly invited the CBC audience to consult their CBC biographies, which were to serve as an after-the-fact justification for the panel's composition. The presumed expertise of the judges was supported by the social and cultural capital they had generated through their production of Canadian symbolic goods (Bourdieu 1993). But in addition to that, their achievements and identities in Canadian culture were made official within the contest itself as a consequence of their having been chosen as judges. The CBC had sanctioned them as arbiters and representatives of Canadianness.

McGuire is a musician and member of the rock band Trooper. His short CBC biography implied that his experience touring the country for three decades, writing songs on the road, had made him a good choice for a Wonders judge. McGuire was framed by his participation in the production and dissemination of Canadian popular culture. His expertise rested at least partly in the idea that his music is inherently Canadian – confirmed perhaps by his having penned the song 'Real Canadians.' Presumably, his position on the panel was justified by the CBC's mandate to protect and encourage Canadian culture. But this circular mandate served 'Canadianness' without having to define what was Canadian about cultural practices other than their geographic origin, the citizenship of their producers and consumers, and self-referential titles. McGuire also served, somewhat ironically, to justify the expert administration of the popular. But again, problems of legitimacy arose. If the popular is by definition that which does not require expert mediation and sanction – the popular being simply what the 'people' like – McGuire's authority was here oddly arbitrary.

The second judge, Roy MacGregor, is a newspaper journalist, author, and novelist who writes about Canada and Canadian identity. His status as an expert was justified partly by the long list of national newspapers he had written for, and also by his books about Canada. The CBC website explained: 'His new book *Canadians*, sets out to explain Canada to Canadians' (CBC 2007b). The idea that Canada needs explaining to Canadians is a persistent theme on the Canadian cultural landscape – a theme that serves to perpetuate the 'crisis' of identity. MacGregor's best-selling book is a romantic narrative structured around the mythic figure of federalist Pierre Trudeau in conjunction with 'ordinary' Canadians, nature, geography, and the like. It is one of a large canon of popular texts that focus on identity as a 'problem' for Canadians. This industry rests on a commonplace idea that 'national identity is the quintessential Canadian issue' (Lipset 1990, 42), a perennial topic for Canadian journalists, academics, and artists. Persistent concerns about Quebec's

possible separation and debates about multiculturalism also suggest
that, whatever Canadian identity is, it is in crisis. Since Canadian identity
is often posited or framed in the language of 'crisis,' concerns about
identity become naturalized and, we suggest, themselves culturally productive (especially of careers, recognition, and profit). Entire industries
are committed to the endless Canadian search for identity, which helps
place the CBC – and authors like MacGregor – in a position to 'solve' our
identity issues where others cannot.

Roberta L. Jamieson had the longest and most formal list of qualifications. Unlike the two white men who preceded her on the website, she
was identified first by her ethnicity (Mohawk), and only then by her impressive list of political and intellectual accomplishments: Chief of the
Six Nations, CEO of the National Aboriginal Achievement Foundation,
Ombudsman for the Province of Ontario, lawyer, Harvard graduate, and
holder of honorary degrees. It is peculiar that while Jamieson would
have been placed first in an alphabetical list of judges, she was at the
end of this one. From the reader's point of view, then, we moved from
McGuire, the 'lightest' judge (representing the popular and folksy),
to MacGregor, the 'middleweight' (the journalist-expert on Canadianness), to the 'heavyweight,' Jamieson. We see in this listing a discursive
framing of social positions, from the popular to the official. This build-
up to the weighty Jamieson also helped deflect any interpretation of her
as a double-token – an Aboriginal woman – and as some sort of hollow
gesture towards inclusiveness. She was, after all, not 'just' a woman or
Aboriginal. She was, so it seemed, a person of 'firsts': 'the first woman
ever to head Canada's most populous reserve,' 'the first woman to hold'
the position of Ontario Ombudsman, 'the first non-parliamentarian to
be appointed ex-officio member of a Special House of Commons Committee on Indian Self-Government,' and 'the first Canadian aboriginal
woman to earn a law degree.' Indeed, Jamieson was presented on the list
as a heroic figure who had overcome institutional barriers of discrimination to acquire administrative power. It followed, by the tone of this discussion, that these various institutions had been improved by her power
as an official within them. In other words, her gender and her ethnicity
served ritualistically to purify the practices and administrative authority
of these institutions (and also to radically sever them from their discrimi-
natory past). By extension, the weighty Jamieson served to justify the administration of popular opinion in the Seven Wonders project. To resist
her authority as judge would have been to question the very goodness
and rightness of women and Aboriginals as authorities, and to silence

two social groups that had long been voiceless. Any audience member who suspected tokenism would have been thrown back by the question of who could possibly have deserved this position more. In short, Jamieson was being presented by way of a rhetorical hat-trick: a list of official qualifications, historical oppression, and deep institutional affiliation. To read this woman's biography cynically would have been to risk questioning the good faith of the CBC.

Once under way, the CBC audience members enthusiastically took up the Seven Wonders project. But they were far from passive participants. During the period of nominations, pitches, and debates, some questioned the criteria they had been given – for example, by asking why these criteria were not open to debate. As the project unfolded, and audience participation was closed down so that the judges could begin their deliberations, anger over the management of their choices became manifest. Many complaints were posted on the CBC website, most of them critical of the project's design and handling. These bloggers often perceived the agenda as paternalistic. They repeatedly raised the issue of the judges overriding the popular vote. Feelings of futility were expressed. As one blogger put it: 'Pure CBC. Canadian opinions, thoughts, concerns, and votes only count when they coincide with the corporation's social agendas.' Another said: 'This is a travesty. A joke without humour' (CBC 2008b). Other participants used unofficial sites to inject some sought-after humour into the project. One blogger raised the possibility of famously busty Canadian-born actress, Pamela Anderson, as a 'natural wonder.' Another asked whether Anderson should be counted as one wonder or two and whether she should be classified as a natural or artificial wonder. The blogs offered a democratic forum for citizens not just to participate but to sidestep the official voice of the CBC and its judges. As frivolous as such examples might appear to the earnest project of determining Canada's seven wonders, they point to the dynamic cultural responses of the 'people' to power and authority, in a mocking and carnivalesque rejoinder to officialdom's seriousness (Bakhtin 1985).

During the period of open discussion, nomination, and on-air debate, the term 'geographic correctness' emerged. This acknowledged the evolving consensus among the producers and judges that criterion #5 ('Range within the final seven – diversity of location, type of wonder') would require that the Seven Wonders be evenly distributed across the Canadian map. The spectre of imposed diversity was treated with embarrassment by the CBC hosts but was formulated as a necessary evil if a sense of Canada and Canadianness was to be reproduced. Thus the televised map of Canada – which formed the backdrop and working surface for the final decisions of the judges – came to represent a literal and symbolic version of the CBC's mandate of national identity achieved through ethnic, regional, and cultural diversity.

So, which fifty-two places/things were shortlisted by popular audience vote? Twenty-eight were natural phenomena rather than strictly 'places' (from very general things like caribou herds, the prairie sky, and the Northern Lights, to specific natural objects like the Bay of Fundy and Niagara Falls). Twenty were technologies (the CN Tower, the igloo, the canoe, highways, rail tunnels, bridges, buildings, settlements, whole cities, the *inuksuk*). Finally, there were two monuments (the Vimy Ridge memorial on Canadian ground in France, and the world's largest Easter egg in Vegreville, Alberta), one food item (the Montreal bagel), and one trophy (the Stanley Cup). Interestingly, while the definition of 'places' had been expanded to include skies, settlements, and animal herds, it was not expanded to include the various 'peoples' and their histories. (The sole exception to this was the nomination of Nonosobasut Rock by a grade two class in Newfoundland. They provocatively contended that this rock should be treated as a symbol of the Beothuk peoples, who had vanished as a result of colonial contact.) Indeed, instead of treating places as historical and political symbols, the list contained mostly natural and technological wonders. And while the inclusion of so many technological wonders may seem to point towards a more historical and political discourse, they fit nicely into Maurice Charland's discussion of 'technological nationalism' in which communication and transportation technologies become symbols of community. Mary Vipond (1992) similarly argues that Canadian identity is built not on communications but rather on the 'myth' or story of communications (xiii). As we have noted, the CBC is itself a prime example of a technology that symbolically binds its audience into a national whole by instantaneously overcoming space. As Charland (1986) puts it, 'the CBC exists by virtue of a discourse of technological national-building, and reproduces the rhetoric which legitimates it and the Canadian state' (197). Within all these transportation/communication signifiers found on the short list of wonders, this tradition of technological nationalism positioned the CBC to make itself the ultimate referent of the Seven Wonders project.

As the CBC Seven Wonders project drew to its conclusion – a conclusion that, as we shall see, became infinitely deferred – tensions and contradictions within the project became evident. The project was in one sense very successful. Online voting was reported at over one million, with more than 25,000 nominations cast. However, the project was also hampered by audience complaints and questions. One common grievance concerned the relay of decision-making power to the judges. Their role and authority had been set out clearly at the beginning of the project, but complaints still arose. One blogger's poem nicely captured this frustration:

> I wonder how they picked the Judges.
> I wonder why our votes didn't count.
> I wonder if Canadians will accept the Judge's decision instead of the popular vote.
>
> (CBC, 2008a)

In response, the CBC insisted repeatedly that the project was only an 'exercise' in generating debate, recognition, and celebration of Canada's wonders. In other words, the final list was to be treated as secondary to the process; that is, debate and discussion were ways of generating a collective self-awareness and appreciation and were to be seen and enjoyed as such. The presumption here was that audience members had begun to miss the point of the project and had mistakenly fetishized and naturalized the contingent wonders as essential and necessary. As Benjamin suggests of individual collectors, they had begun to treat these wonders as sensuous real objects that could be meaningfully collected and cherished. But instead of deflecting criticism, this rhetoric of 'exercise' focused attention back on the process itself and on the issue of the legitimacy of the expert judges. If it was only an 'exercise,' why were the judges retained? What were they ensuring or guarding? After the project 'concluded,' the CBC's response to the problem of the judges was to issue two lists of wonders: the judges' and the voters' lists. Ultimately, the CBC generated many more lists, including – curiously, given the stated mandate of national identity – *regional* lists. This gesture of producing endless lists risked throwing the whole contest into jeopardy, for it thereby lost coherence. That is, doing so undermined the indulgent pleasures inherent to collecting things – arbitrary choice, imposed order, exclusivity. Only the CBC's authority to administer the making of lists remained, even if the lists were becoming absurd.

These tensions became obvious as the project approached its climax. During the televised broadcast of the final list, the three judges were clearly anxious and defensive (CBC 2007b). They expressed their relief that they would soon be finished with what had become a frustrating and

futile 'exercise' in the course of which their authority had been roundly
questioned. After they had agreed on the official seven wonders, one
judge unenthusiastically said, 'Well, that's it. I can live with it.' Another
judge responded, 'I'm sure there'll be many who can't. This is no fun.
Reaching a conclusion is not a happy moment. It's a ridiculous notion
to try to encapsulate this country in seven notions.' He quickly recanted,
saying 'I've enjoyed every second of it' and adding that he had learned
lots of 'information' and that the project was 'fun' and that it had succeeded in 'capturing the imagination of the country.' All three judges
suggested that they had been overwhelmed with wonders ('Starting with
every individual who has chosen to make Canada their home,' added the
Aboriginal judge without apparent irony); that they had been impressed
with the level of participation (asserting, with gross inaccuracy, that it
was higher than for many federal elections[2]); and that it 'usually takes
a crisis' to generate so much enthusiasm (unmistakably a reference to
francophone Quebeckers, who had not been invited to participate but
who represented an ongoing threat to national unity). Ultimately, the
judges and the hosts fell back on the cliché of the humble Canadian, asserting that the project generated 'bragging rights' for a population that
was hesitant to brag about itself (except, of course, for bragging about its
humility) and that the list represented a 'classic Canadian compromise'
(in other words, it represented its process).

The actual televised exercise served as a visual lesson for its audience.
Viewers were initially confronted with a blank map of Canada, with the
various wonders named and identified by visual icons. On that map, the
even placement of the wonders – over which the judges agonized, vacil-
lated, and traded choices – served to instruct Canadians about the administered spatial uniformity of the choices that had been made. It also
visually reaffirmed the idea of Canada as a bounded place ('this is where
"we" are'). In this way, the wonders became anointed as collective representations of orderly Canadianness. Bourdieu (1999) explains the ritualistic importance of such official 'mapping': 'Taking the vantage point
of the Whole, of society in its totality, the state claims responsibility for
all operations of *totalization* . . . and of *objectivation,* through cartography
(the unitary representation of space from above)' (61).

Through its implicit teaching of geography, as well as its sanitized history, the project made visible an accumulation, dissemination, and recirculation of informational capital. Put another way, the exercise was a
didactic lesson in constituting a 'legitimate national culture' (ibid., 62).
Richard Day (1998) makes a similar point in his discussion of how

cartography and geography are used in the Canadian administration of multiculturalism, arguing that this ongoing administration requires a concrete and visual 'spatialization of the concept of diversity' (58) that 'must be arranged according to a conspicuously planned pattern' (60). From within this pedagogic and administrative context, the judges' seven wonders were announced: the canoe (classified as representative of Canada as a whole, but pinned onto the map in Ontario), the igloo (the 'North'), Niagara Falls (Ontario), Old Quebec City (Quebec), Pier 21 (Atlantic region), the prairie skies (the prairies or 'the West'), and the Rockies (the west coast). After the project had officially ended, CBC radio collected its collecting project thus:

> When we launched our quest for the Seven Wonders of Canada, we knew it would be difficult to narrow the list to seven. It was even more difficult than we'd anticipated. The number and passion of your nominations was overwhelming. As exciting and challenging as it's been to name Seven Wonders, more than anything we're buoyed by the dialogue this campaign has begun. On Sounds Like Canada and The National we plan to continue this conversation about our country over the coming months. In the meantime, we've compiled several alternative Canadian lists, inspired by submissions. (CBC 2007c)

Yet nowhere did this statement question the design and administration of the project. It presented the 'difficulties' it faced as technical (the number and passion of nominations), as if fewer nominations and less passion would have solved its inherent problems. The website statement also said 'we're buoyed by the dialogue this campaign has begun.' The 'we' in this statement could be read to mean 'we' as Canadians or 'we' as CBC producers; but it seemed to refer to the latter, because in the rhetorical move of returning this dialogue back to Canadians to pursue, the statement went on to say that the CBC would continue to mediate this conversation. Unwittingly, this statement was pointing out that the point of the project had been to reinscribe the CBC as a necessary institution. Finally, this statement closed by offering more lists – wonders organized by provincial and territorial boundaries, as well as animals, food and drink, people, roadside attractions, and views – that is, an endless articulation of things, but as managed and mediated by the CBC.

The blog on *The National*'s website signed by the executive producers for the radio and TV shows was even clearer in its effort to set the audience straight: 'If you were disappointed with the Seven Wonders of

Canada outcome, please read on: We truly regret you are disappointed. In fact, that is the last thing we wanted.' Referring to the technical problems inherent in managing the huge numbers of participants and voters, it continued: 'What started as a modest project . . . took on a life of its own.' Quickly, however, the statement began to chide the audience for complaining about a process that it had implicitly condoned by its willing participation:

> We had . . . always made it clear the Seven Wonders . . . would be decided by our judges . . . We think they did an excellent job at meeting key criteria of this project, including creating a list that represents as many Canadians and regions as possible. It's why we felt we needed judges in the first place, to try and level the playing field in a country with an uneven population base, uneven internet access, and areas where a majority of Canadians don't listen or watch English radio or television and therefore wouldn't be as likely to participate . . . We showed the judges grappling with their decisions. Anyone who watched knows how difficult it was and how seriously they took their responsibilities. (CBC 2008c)

The producers were arguing that they, the CBC generally, and the judges needed the authority to vouchsafe representation, to ensure that regional differences would not overshadow the capacity of 'conversation' and 'dialogue' to generate extra-regional alliances. Yet if 'conversation' and the like cannot be trusted as methods to generate identity and celebration of Canadianness, why were Canadians invited to participate in the first place? Finally, the CBC was characterizing the audience as childish, chauvinistic, and unappreciative of the hard work and goodwill of others. The executives' statement concluded with the same passive-aggressive tone with which it had begun: 'Having said all that, we obviously feel terrible that such a project would lead, in some quarters, to anger.'

On this note, let us return to the issue of humour and its subversive capacity. Consider the bloggers' jokes about nominating Pamela Anderson as a wonder. Was she one wonder or two? Was she a natural or artificial wonder? Clearly these jokes referenced both her famously large breasts and her further technologically aided enhancement of them. So, what made these jokes funny? Certainly there was nothing inherently funny about nominating an eye-catching actress as a wonder. This joke was funny partly because it was absurd, considered within the confines of the project's stated criteria. Anderson was not a 'place' or 'thing' except in the highly sexualized idea of her as a site or object of corporeal pleasure. There was a level of aggression in this treatment of Anderson. Her body had become a 'democratic' site of visual, onanistic pleasure, especially of a heterosexual male world, via the global popularity of her television show, *Baywatch*. As a site of pleasure, Anderson's body indiscriminately and unpatriotically exceeded the boundaries of the nation-state, and this Canadian joke jealously repatriated and reordered her as our exclusive object. At a misogynistic level, the joke sexually disciplined Anderson. It was what Freud (1938) identified as a 'smutty joke' – that is, one that acts as a 'denudation of a person of the opposite sex' (694) and that also allows the listener to be 'bribed by the easy gratification of his own libido' (695–6).

But as Freud also argued, jokes are rooted in an infantile aggression towards social order in general. That is, jokes are often aimed *indirectly* at institutions and organizations that cannot be *directly* attacked because of their status as sacred (702). Of course there is something childish about promoting Pamela Anderson as a Canadian wonder. Anderson has become a famous icon for challenging the accepted boundaries of clothing, modesty, and good taste, as well as those of nature and technology. We can imagine, with juvenile delight, our hapless panel of judges trying to figure out where to pin her disproportionate, pornographic, and cybernetic image on the map of Canada in a lesson of 'geographic correctness.' Freud would have suggested that the cathartic release induced by the Anderson joke was a product of its juxtaposition with the earnest, pedantic project of the CBC – the joke's ultimate target. In this sense, the joke was not on Anderson, but on us.

Nothing could better demonstrate the thesis of our discussion than an examination of these official and unofficial blog entries. Taken together they explain why it was necessary ritualistically to exclude the raw, popular, unmediated objects of collective self-desire, while ritualistically reasserting the rational-legal, expert administration of desire and identity. The CBC blog entry also helps explain why the CBC ended the project by offering endless lists. It was a kind of symbolic gesture that threatened to drown the audience in a meaningless and bottomless exercise and that inverted Benjamin's formulation of collecting as a sensuous, magical appreciation of things in our world. The audience was being told implicitly that 'if-you-want-populism-you-can-have-populism-until-you-choke-on-it.'

We began this discussion by proposing that the rational-legal administration of desire and identity in the Seven Wonders project risked killing off wonder and enchantment by subjecting both to administration.

We found that it did so, and more. At least in the case we have discussed here, such administration requires Canadians to desire administration in *itself* as a disciplinary good. Presumably, Canadians were supposed to learn from the CBC's Seven Wonders project that proper Canadian desire desires the mediation of the CBC, including the periodic ritual reinscription of the good of the CBC on the hearts of its audience. Between the 'poles of disorder and order,' the CBC must perpetually institute the Canadian 'people'; in so doing it must naturalize its own symbolic violence in its effort to be Canada's most 'cherished thing.' But given that collecting also involves the lusty 'thrill of acquisition' (Benjamin 1968, 60), Canadians – as demonstrated by the Anderson joke – have loudly asserted that they want to guard their objects and their collecting desires from such statist and bureaucratic mediation.

Obama Playlist Contest, or 'Obamarama'

A few weeks before the 2009 inauguration of U.S. President Barack Obama, the CBC announced that it would be hosting a contest titled '49 Songs from North of the 49th Parallel.' The CBC audience would be encouraged to compile a list of 'definitive' Canadian musical pieces for an 'Obama playlist,' which would be broadcast on Obama's inauguration day. The contest followed on the president-elect's widely reported pre-election interview with *Rolling Stone* magazine, during which he revealed his own tastes in music – which it seems are sophisticated, popular, multi-ethnic, and eclectic. His own playlist, though, was not filled with Canadian signifiers.

In comparing the Seven Wonders contest to the Obama Playlist contest, one is immediately struck by the streamlining of the latter. In fact, many of the elements of the Seven Wonders contest that became controversial – complicated criteria for choosing wonders, an appointed expert panel of judges, the didactic overtones of the final moments of the contest, the chastising of the audience – were seemingly absent from this one. Most audience members who did question it – at least in its early stages – were concerned less about its rules and procedures than about the meaning of contest itself. For them, the gesture of compiling forty-nine songs that were to 'represent our country to the world' (as the CBC put it) constituted a more primary and problematic issue of representation. Why was the CBC inviting Canadians to 'celebrate' the inauguration of a U.S. president? As many bloggers noted, the CBC was revealing itself as supporting a democratic, left-leaning (in the American context), multi-ethnic president. As they pointed out, the CBC would never have called for a 'McCain Playlist,' had Republican candidate John McCain won the election (CBC 2009a).

Certainly the on-air atmosphere during the 49 Songs/Obama Playlist contest was celebratory, even hagiographic. Some of the radio hosts referred to the contest as 'Obamarama.' The graphic accompanying the contest's announcement on the CBC website showed a '49' sharing a single pair of audio headphones (the '4' filled in with the pattern of the American flag and the '9' filled in with the Canadian flag), the implication being that Obama's election signified at least some cultural and musical if not greater political unity. The audioclips of Obama's speeches that preceded the on-air nominations for songs placed him in the company of Abraham Lincoln, John F. Kennedy, and Martin Luther King, Jr. One Radio 2 guest, Afro-Canadian poet and academic George Elliott Clarke, called Obama the 'first Canadian President,' explaining that Obama's multi-ethnic parentage and international education embodied Canadian values of multiculturalism and multiracialism. And while many audience members shared Clarke's pleasure as they compiled a personalized playlist for the incoming president, others interpreted the gesture as 'sycophantic,' 'embarrassing,' 'corny,' and indicative of Canada's perpetual 'inferiority complex' (CBC 2009b). Some audience members likened it to an unattractive teenager hoping against hope to catch the eye of the popular kid. Others found the corniness endearing. One American listener was clearly just puzzled. After challenging his friends to name one Canadian prime minister and getting one response, he stated, 'I am just thinking, if American(s) don't care about politics of Canada, why do Canadians (as represented by CBC) care so much about U.S. (?) I found it strange' (Ibid.). As we will discuss later, this issue of American recognition of Canada is complex and contradictory. In fact, the enthusiasm and embarrassment were two sides of the same coin: here, they just happened to be embodied in the musical desires of Barack Obama.

The audience members who entered the contest most eagerly generated some of the most salient questions for this discussion. On the CBC website, some debated the very meaning of the contest (Ibid.), which was asking them variously to locate 'definitive,' 'favourite,' and 'representative' Canadian songs. Was definitive the same as favourite? Was the list meant to reflect Canadian tastes or to generate Canadian themes? Was it to showcase Canada's exceptional talents, or was it to serve as an overview of Canadian music? Should it topicalize Canada itself in the music in an explicit way, such as in the lyrics? Should it be international and multicultural and thereby overcome versions of national identity tied to culture? It is noteworthy here that only a tiny number of bloggers complained about the contest's MAPL rule. MAPL, which stands for **M**usic, **A**rtist, **P**roduction, and **L**yrics, is a measurement system that the CRTC has set out to determine what counts as Canadian content for the purposes of broadcasting. All radio stations in Canada must play a minimum amount of 'CanCon' during their broadcasting day (and keep a log of this music and when it was aired). It is not surprising that the CBC would turn immediately to the CRTC to define what Canadian music *is*, dodging the potential problem of too much 'non-official' music making the list by broadcasting it over a number of days. By letting the CRTC in effect set the rules, the CBC would be able to avoid being seen as imposing its own (as had been so problematic in the Seven Wonders contest). From an administrative perspective, this solved the audience's problem of what is Canadian and representative of Canada. Thus, Nickelback – a generic-sounding, popular hard rock band without any recognizable Canadian themes in their music – was legitimately voted into the contest.

As the Obama Playlist contest unfolded, some of the same problems arose as had plagued the Seven Wonders contest. This time, though, the contest's rules and procedures – which had been overtly stated at the outset of the Seven Wonders contest – were only hinted at. When the contest was announced, there was no discussion of vetting the shortlist of one hundred songs, or of creating separate categories for different types of music, or of 'pitches' being considered. Under the 'rules' link on the CBC website (CBC 2009c), only the MAPL rules were mentioned as a reason why a musical piece might not appear on the list of nominated songs. Radio 2 hosts repeatedly stated that the votes would be 'tallied' by the CBC staff. The host of the classical music show *Tempo* apparently thought that music genres would go head-to-head, since she called out for her listeners to make sure that classical music made it to the list (CBC 2009d).

When the hundred-song shortlist was presented, the audience was told that the hosts and producers had considered not only the number of votes cast but also the quality of pitches (many of the participants listed their favourite piece without defending their choice, presumably because there was no clear indication that pitches would be considered), and issues of diversity of music genres. Hence, without prior notification they presented the audience with four categories ('A,' English language pop/rock/folk; 'B,' French language pop/rock/folk; 'C,' classical; and 'D,' spiritual, soul, blues), explaining that each listener would be allowed to vote once each day within each of the four categories. This announcement was posted in both French and English, although all other postings had been up to this point in English only (available in French at a separate link) (CBC 2009e).

Here is the response offered to audience members who questioned the contest's internal coherence and the forthrightness of the producers:

> Howdy folks. Glad to see such enthusiasm about the music. As for the process, well, nothing is perfect, is it. But here is some explanatory info., which may not satisfy, but hopefully will help clarify, re: the presentation in categories, decided by producers working on the project at Radio 2 – sure, it's presented so as to ensure a final list hopefully including regional, linguistic cultural balance etc. It's meant to be something of a reflection of Canada's musical DNA, if you will. And at this point it is totally down to you – the 49 pieces of music with the greatest number of votes, from each category, will be included in the final play list. (Also, all of the music on the shortlist adheres to MAPL standards as set out on the Obama's Playlist website.) So no, the shortlist was not tabulated 'a long time ago.' Listeners had a huge amount of input. And now it's entirely in your hands. So go on, vote! (CBC 2009b)

Ultimately, the Obama Playlist contest came to resemble the Seven Wonders contest in terms of its assumptions about how to administer the popular vote and how to preserve diversity. But there was also a stark difference: in the Seven Wonders contest, the rules had been set out explicitly and become a focus of lively debate for audience, guests, and hosts; whereas in the second, the rules were not explicit and did not become a focus. Though there were complaints, this lack of transparency did not generate mass audience resistance. The history of Canadian cultural policy helps explain the Radio 2 audience in terms of both its deference to regulation and its musical choices. In fact, as we will discuss, these forms of audience (self-)desire are intertwined. If we consider the final forty-nine pieces of music selected in the Radio 2 contest as a manifestation of a particular social-political desire, one that is both the product of regulation and a reassertion of it, the types of music selected show themselves as more than the sum of individual tastes or even notions of Canada. These choices also reflected the history of Canadian cultural policy, not only in that their popularity was partly a product of their having been aired under MAPL rules for decades, but also because they thematically expressed and reinforced myths of state cultural policy. Put another way, we suggest that the content of Canadian content regulation included the artistic thematization of these myths.

Not surprisingly, many of the artists who made their way onto the final list were well-established stars, now sexagenarians and septuagenarians (thirteen were already in the Canadian Academy of Recording Arts and Sciences' Hall of Fame). In fact, many were institutional 'products' themselves. For example, Gordon Lightfoot's 'Canadian Railroad Trilogy,' which was barely squeezed out of first place in category A, had been commissioned by the CBC for a broadcast celebrating Canada's Centennial in 1967 (CBC 2009g). Similarly, Gilles Vigneault's 'Mon pays' had been commissioned by the National Film Board of Canada in the mid-1960s. In this tight circle of institutional self-referentiality, it is not surprising that one song, Stompin' Tom Connors's 'The Hockey Game,' celebrated the CBC's decades-long weekly mediation of Canada (called, of course, 'Hockey Night in Canada') – 'Hello out there, we're on the air. It's hockey night tonight.' These songs made space and the technological mediation of space their central themes. The relationship between the myth of space and the imagining of America (cum Obama's taste) will be explored below. We have inspected the 'final forty-nine' musical pieces in terms of cultural policy history and mythology and have reorganized the CBC's genre distinctions ('A,' 'B,' 'C,' 'D') into three thematic categories of our own: (1) 'A Message to Americans,' (2) 'Nothing Is Up Here / Here Is Nothing,' and (3) 'Requiem Massey.' These categories offer a way of understanding the cultural dialogics that led to the existence of the contest, the interplay between the symbolic import/administrative form of the contest and the desires and tastes of the audience, and the substantive contents of the selections.

A Message to Americans

And the men who hold high places
Must be the ones to start
To mould a new reality
Closer to the heart
Closer to the heart.

Rush, 'Closer to the Heart'

American woman stay away from me.

Guess Who, 'American Woman'

Democracy is coming to the U.S.A.

Leonard Cohen, 'Democracy'

Those participants who saw the Obama Playlist contest as rhetorically aimed at Obama (or who incorrectly believed he would be sent the playlist) discussed their nominations in terms of sending some kind of message. Some of the forty-nine songs that were thus defended were clearly celebratory and supportive of Obama's hopeful 'Yes, we can' presidential campaign. Many songs were about peace, democracy, and social change ('Universal Soldier,' 'Quand les hommes vivront d'amor,' 'Closer to the Heart,' 'Rockin' in the Free World,' 'Hymn to Freedom,' 'Rise Up,' 'Democracy,' 'Wondering Where the Lions Are'). In their pitches, the audience framed these songs in terms of hope ('Mr. Obama I hope that you can turn it around, because the US could use a smart superhero just about now'), but also in moralizing or ambivalent tones ('the usa has never known us or our music') (CBC 2009b). Here we consider a few of the most popular songs.

Leonard Cohen's 'Democracy' was an obvious choice for the CBC audience (it placed fourth in the English Pop and Folk category). Most of the audience members who explained why they nominated this song thought of it as carrying an explicit message. Cohen's song-poem begins by rhetorically removing any claims on democracy from the United States and then predicting/pleading for it to be delivered from the rest of the world: 'Democracy is coming . . . from the ashes of the gay' and Tiananmen Square. As the song progresses, the agent of change presses into the country (metaphorically rendered as a ship – 'sail on, sail on') and is relocated to include disenfranchised Americans – 'from the sorrow of the street' – along with the promise of sensual celebration – 'we'll be makin' love again.' Cohen's song is prophetic of Obama's campaign and election victory ('It's coming to America first; the cradle of the best and the worst'); at the same time, it is spoken from an estranged point of view ('I like the country, but I can't stand the scene'). It preserves an exteriorized position while locating the United States as the ultimate site of real change and renewal. As a message to Americans, it retains the difference between the United States and Canada such that the Canadian singer can direct his words at U.S. domestic policy. Canadians often point to domestic policy as an essential difference between the two countries, with Canada the more socially caring of the two. 'Democracy' is rendered in Cohen's lyrics as protection and love of the weak, of minorities, of the poor and oppressed, rather than as something more technically political, such as voting rights. As one blogger put it, 'it basically advocates for peace and freedom' (CBC 2009b).

Rush's 'Closer to the Heart' (recorded in England in 1977) won the first spot in category A and was discussed both in terms of the hope that Obama represented and as message from Canada in terms of its high expectations of him. The lyrics certainly lend themselves to such a message, but placed in the context of music history, this choice raises interesting questions about how music can be employed to speak about oneself and hail others. In their discussion of Canadian 1970s rock, Testa and Shedden (2002) explain that rock magazine readers still nominate Rush as one of their favourite groups, flattering the group as a 'thinking man's' band and at the same time flattering themselves (201). Testa and Shedden describe this British-influenced art rock as 'unapologetically white,' 'pretentiously operatic,' and 'immensely wordy' (201). They also note that Rush dedicated one of their albums to Ayn Rand, the radically right-wing and individualist philosopher who is popular especially with young men. Rush's interest in this philosophy is well documented, which raised interesting ironies in the context of this contest. Following on Nietzsche's critique of modern culture's 'slave mentality' that makes gentleness a virtue over power (Nietzsche [1887]1989), Rand popularized the romantic notion of the heroic, misunderstood artist fighting against mediocrity and compromise. The famous complexity of Rush's music apparently proves their political commitment to art and radical creativity over the mainstream and the ordinary. In their discussion, Testa and Shedden come close to characterizing Rush's typical fan as a middle-class, white, male teenager safely ensconced in his parents' suburban Canadian home, imagining his own radical detachment from it all. In other words, the construction of alienation and detachment easily swings back into the slave mentality it is meant to reject and becomes an opportunity for what Nietzsche called 'ressentiment,' the obsessive concern and apparent condemnation of the powerful other who is in reality envied. Ressentiment disguises envy as a morally superior position in that it refrains from violence and power and gleefully awaits the day when the powerful collapse under the weight of their own excesses. For the powerful, on the other hand, the existence – much less the hostility – of the slave hardly appears within their experience. As the blogger quoted above noted, 'they' don't know us. This helps us understand why the playlist contest would aim to generate a collection of valued cultural objects *not* to be shared with Obama.

The act of demurring to offer this gift is central to its meaning. It is important to collect this music under the assumption that it is *impossible* for Americans to recognize it. The appreciation of the music must remain beyond Americans' reach in order to ensure the moral and intellectual difference between Canadians and Americans. As we will discuss, much of the music collected in the final forty-nine Obama songs can be understood in a Nietzschian context. In his discussion of the history of Canadian literature, Glenn Willmott (2001) argues that Canadian literature embodies – sometimes consciously and ironically and sometimes with little self-awareness – this relationship of ressentiment towards the United States. In other words, a whole collective Anglo-Canadian self-understanding has been built in and through this emotion and circulates between authors and their readers, making the Canadian imagination a 'photographic negative, a mirror at the margin of empire' (135). Michael Dorland (1988) argues that ressentiment is at the heart of the Canadian imagination in general and allows the state to take on the role of protector of the weak citizen without having to show its own power.

Willmott's observations help explain the popularity of The Guess Who's 'American Woman,' nominated as a reprimand of the United States (and in one case as a reprimand of the CBC's apparent 'anti-Americanism'). This Canadian and American hit, recorded during the Vietnam War, feminizes the United States as a dangerous *cultural* seducer ('Coloured lights can hypnotize / Sparkle someone else's eyes') and international and domestic oppressor ('I don't need your war machines / I don't need your ghetto scenes'). In his discussion of this song, Edwardson (2003) explains that it became a hit during the height of Canadian cultural nationalism (topping the charts in 1970, the same year the CRTC instituted radio CanCon rules) and that The Guess Who's singer Burton Cummings 'often went into very anti-American rants, characterizing American women as "hookers" and "sluts"' (342). It is interesting that Cummings himself confuses his own metaphor – America is a bad woman; American women are bad – nicely demonstrating the danger of using minority groups as images for the apparently oppressive society in which they live. Willmott (2001) finds this extension of ressentiment onto women (and even children) in the earliest Canadian poetry. He quotes Charles Mair's nineteenth-century poem 'Tecumseh' in which a British-Canadian speaker promises that the exploited will eventually rise up and punish America by throwing their 'unhealthy' infants and 'lawless' women from their beds and into the streets (136). In the broader political context of the contest, 'American Woman' was nominated while Canada was militarily engaged in Afghanistan, undercutting its long-standing self-image as a post-conflict peacekeeper (as UN 'Blue Helmets') and as a refuge for American draft dodgers. So, while it is in many ways topically outdated,

'American Woman' does the work of reinscribing the apparent gulf between the two countries, with Canada maintaining the morally superior and culturally protective position: 'American woman stay away from me.'

Nothing Is Up Here / Here Is Nothing

Mon pays, c'est né pas un pays, c'est hiver.
(My country, it's not a country, it's winter.)

Gilles Vigneault, 'Mon Pays'

Frozen land and frozen miles and frozen land and frozen time.

Stan Rogers, 'The Canadian Dream'

A land so wide and savage.

Stan Rogers, 'Northwest Passage'

Long before the white man and long before the wheel,
when the green dark forest was too silent to be real.

Gordon Lightfoot, 'Canadian Railroad Trilogy'

It seems as if this country has lost its will to live . . .
But we can still step proudly because Canada is really big.

Arrogant Worms, 'Canada's Really Big'

I hate Winnipeg.

The Weakerthans, 'One Great City'

As the above lyrics show, The Arrogant Worms and The Weakerthans were not the only artists on the final Obama Playlist to make geography their theme. The Arrogant Worms' ironic anthem, 'Canada's Really Big,' stands out on this list because it pokes fun at the Canadian pursuit of identity through the sheer occupation of empty space. In fact, they echo Dowler's (1996) argument that this preoccupation covers over more concrete issues of sovereignty. As they sing, 'the economy is lousy, we barely have an army.' In the context of the contest debate, their song also poked fun at what one blogger called 'stoic anthems of the wilderness' (CBC 2009b). The forty-nine songs list was filled with such pieces: 'The Canadian Dream,' 'Canadian Railroad Trilogy,' 'Four Strong Winds,' 'Mon Pays,' and 'The Wreck of the Edmund Fitzgerald' were all written around themes of vast and unforgiving natural forces and spaces.

In company with The Arrogant Worms, The Weakerthans' 'One Great City' parodies the romanticization of place with its hateful ode to the city of Winnipeg. Yet 'Departure Bay,' 'Home,' 'Bobcaygeon,' 'A Case of You,' 'Montreal -40c,' 'Wheat Kings,' and 'Evangeline' all celebrate a particular place or lament leaving some idealized place.

According to Bennett (2000), in contrast to musicological research that seeks to understand popular and other forms of music by analysing the musical text, many contemporary academics of popular music seek rather to examine the relationship of music to 'institutions and collective cultural sensibilities.' Theorists of popular music seek to grasp 'how music is used in everyday contexts to create cultural spaces and articulate collective forms of cultural identity' (183). The local contexts and physical environments where music is created and received must then be taken seriously. While many of the forty-nine songs represented the sensibilities of particular locales, the articulation of collective forms of cultural identity is understood here as shaped by the cultural policies that have sought to create a national cultural identity that can synecdochically play on themes of the local. Even those songs that thematically and historically have been aligned with Quebec nationalism were not nominated under the guise of a strong separatist agenda (raising the interesting question of the appropriation of Quebec's signifiers by federalists following on the Canadian government granting 'nationhood' but not 'statehood' to Quebec). This is not surprising, for Quebec nationalists would typically tune in to the francophone CBC service, Radio Canada, which not only is broadcast in French but also is famously more pro-separatist in its content.

The juxtaposition of the light-hearted with the many more earnest nominations raised tensions about the intended tone of the contest. Many bloggers defended their nominations against both parody and serious criticism by arguing that it was 'just' a bit of light fun (CBC 2009b). In other words, for these listeners neither the contest nor the content were to be questioned, apparently because doing so would have threatened the enjoyment of listening, debating, and voting. With the myth of empty space thus defended, listeners also made sure they posited *themselves* as empty space. One listener was featured on Radio 2 stating (without apparent irony) that Canadians are the most humble people in the world and hence best suited to generate the playlist. This theme of humility, found in much of the CBC's content, renders Canadians moral agents when set against the mythically overbearing, ever-present Americans.

  The themes of empty space also work anachronistically to empty Canadian territory of its colonial history, especially with reference to Aboriginal peoples. The Canadian cultural policy of full assimilation and
'civilization' of these groups into European culture meant aggressive
control over every aspect of their lives. (The Indian Act of 1867 prohibited religious practices such as the potlatch and the Sun Dance and
required 'Status Indians' to renounce that status if they wished to vote in
elections.) This highly administered emptying of territory and collective
memory then became naturalized by themes of emptiness (put another
way, Aboriginal people became naturalized as pre-cultural savages). 'Canadian Railroad Trilogy' aligns the 'white man' with the 'wheel,' both
of which came onto the scene and found a 'forest too silent to be real.'
This song certainly draws into question the frenzy of industrialization
and nation building that underpinned the drive to expand the railway,
in that it commemorates the toil and deaths of railway workers. Yet the
Aboriginal people are not mentioned in this song except in terms of
their metaphoric existence within nature. Even today the state continues
to evoke the 'empty' North in order to extend sovereignty over it. Note,
for example, how the 2008 announcement of a new ice-breaker by Prime
Minister Stephen Harper was framed in terms of the spirits of European
explorers and Stan Rogers's 'Northwest Passage':

> The ghosts of Hudson, Franklin, Amundsen, Larson, Bernier and all the
> rest will watch as the Diefenbaker crashes through the pack ice, and they
> will hear the echo of the words of the late, great Canadian folk singer Stan
> Rogers: 'Ah, for just one time, I would take the Northwest Passage to find
> the hand of Franklin reaching for the Beaufort Sea, tracing one warm line
> through a land so wild and savage, and make a Northwest Passage to the
> sea.' (Canada 2008)

This myth of empty space continues to divert attention away from Canadian administration of peoples and territory and towards the idea that
that territory must be defended against the designs of outside aggressors –
and kept imaginatively empty.
  The work being done by these popular songs also explains why so many
lyrics are highly ironic. They point to the effort expended on insisting on
nothingness – that such effort is both absurd and highly political. As The
Arrogant Worms so cleverly point out, there seems to be no content to
Canada in terms of wealth or power – the only assertion is that we exist
by virtue of taking up space. By this logic, if Canada were to take up even
more space, there would be even more reason to 'step proudly,' even if

the reason for taking up the space (and guarding it from being filled up with people or history) is unclear.

In the context of this contest, it was stranger still to offer the theme of empty space to President-elect Obama. This hardly counted as a clear message: How would the new president interpret this as a way to get to know Canada? Yet it did resonate with the aim of the project itself, which was to generate a playlist for him that was *not* to be sent to him. That is, it was a collection of songs *not* to be shared, which served to reinforce the idea that the president-elect would not be able to see, hear, or understand the message. Rhetorically, this helped shore up the differences between the two countries. Presumably, Americans practise a cultural and political life of export, conquest, and domination, whereas Canadians practise a cultural and political life of self-consumption, border vigilance, and administration. As we discussed earlier in this chapter, the myth of the technological mediation of space both overcomes and maintains that space. In other words, while our technologies of communication and transportation have made the problem of space physically less and less real, the myth (of overcoming) requires that in our minds, this space remain vast. Space is overcome not in the sense of being killed off, but rather in the sense of having been traversed or travelled, crossed again and again, in the collective imaginary. It is imaginatively traversed also to guard against it being filled up with political history. As The Arrogant Worms put it:

We can still step proudly because Canada is really big[.]
It's the second largest nation on this planet earth
And if Russia keeps on shrinking
Then we will be first!
We gotta lot of land.

Requiem Massey

If anybody asks me, I'm goin' up yonder.
                              Measha Brueggergosman, 'Goin' Up Yonder'

We'll gather lilacs . . . until our hearts have learned to sing again.
                              Ben Heppner, 'We'll Gather Lilacs'

During the Obama Playlist contest, debates among listeners were often animated by broader concerns about Radio 2's shift away from exclusively classical, opera, and jazz to include popular styles such as rock, folk, and country. Many audience members expressed their hope that Radio 2 would return to its earlier, more 'highbrow' content, as supported by their music choices. Other Radio 2 bloggers accused these people of supporting music that was not distinctly Canadian (although it met MAPL regulations). Unlike the relatively contemporary pop and rock selections, many of the pieces in this category were exceptionally international in nature. This was the case with Glenn Gould's recording of Bach's *Goldberg Variations*. For some listeners, that Gould was the performer did not make this piece sufficiently Canadian. Early on, *Tempo*'s on-air host encouraged voters to ensure that classical music would appear on the final list, since such music would 'compete against Joni Mitchell, Leonard Cohen, and other Canadian greats' (Nesrallah 2009). It turns out that classical music would not have to worry about being washed out by middlebrow (or lower) Canadian tastes, for it had been given its own category. Canadians would not after all appear (to themselves via the imaginary American listener) to be a bunch of folk music lovers or hard rockin' 'hosers.'[3]

Generally, the category C listeners displayed a version of Canadian cultural content that echoed the assumptions found in the Massey Report. On the face of it, these listeners were not interested in sending a concrete political message: this music was directed at the cultivation of discriminating tastes. Yet the category C bloggers aligned high culture with Obama's promise to lift America out of its social and political habits. After the inauguration, one such listener was vindicated:

> You will notice that Barack Obama's personal playlist for the inauguration featured Itzhak Perlman and Yo-Yo Ma . . . This music . . . has eternal qualities, unlike the ephemeral tunes we enjoy today and forget tomorrow. The beauty, seriousness, and quality of this music are in tune with the values Barack Obama urges the American people to espouse. This is the kind of music we crave, we long-time devotees of Radio II. (CBC 2009f)

Another listener was more explicit about the politics of cultural policy:

> Perhaps, instead of sending President elect Obama a sample of our protectionist Can Con philosophy, we should try . . . a sample of the open minded, wide ranging musical tastes that we as Canadians share . . . Cue Beethoven's 5th . . . Let's open our borders, our minds and ears to it. That would be how CBC would have handled this 'contest/promotion' prior to 9/1/08. Still holding a candle-light vigil for classic CBC stereo. (Ibid.)

From the point of view of Radio 2's category C listeners, culture is art and hence speaks to themes that transcend time and space (and certainly the contingencies of the nation-state). Attempts to appropriate art to further nationalist ideas certainly exist – for example, Bach can be said to belong to Germany or to Gould, who has always been a favourite of the CBC – but they continually escape these bounds. The songs found in the other categories can be said to speak to these same universal themes (especially as nature is unlimited and absolute); that said, they are more effective at shoring up ideologies of state. On the other hand, Gould's famous obsession with the Canadian North is not as easy to connect with his interpretation of the *Goldberg Variations*.

Indeed, the jazz and classical categories allowed the audience to play with references across borders and time and to celebrate American culture and Canadian talent. 'Go'n Up Yonder' is a famous American spiritual performed by a Canadian artist who discovered her own African-American slave ancestry; similarly, Oscar Peterson's jazz (which included 'Hymn to Freedom' and 'Place St Henri') acknowledged Afro-Canadian-American history at both a biographical and a musical level; and Moe Koffman's 'Swinging Shepherd Blues' embodied the coolest of mid-1950s American-style jazz. Composers Marjan Mozetich ('Affairs of the Heart') and Jesse Cook ('Mario Takes a Walk') were born outside Canada, while James Ehnes's violin piece was written by an American, Samuel Barber. At both a musical and a demographic level, this music category most effectively plays across history, genre, and lineage, creating a complex, multilayered effect. Certainly, listeners expressed pride in the talents of these Canadian artists, but this music does not talk *to* Americans or *about* Canada in the same ways as the music in the other categories. This music is very much a celebration of music itself – it is 'go'n,' praying, 'walking,' 'gathering,' 'singing,' and 'swinging' – and recommends primarily itself. So while the blogger quoted above characterized classical music as 'serious,' such music is least serious about its cultural nationalist work. Of all the music, it was perhaps most a 'gift' to Obama in its sheer utterance of joy.

This group of listeners made it clear that they saw a connection between the promotion of 'popular' music and the administration of Canadian desire by the CBC. As holdover Masseyites, their understanding of the role of such contests took issue with the assumption of simply collecting opinion and reaffirming the equality of all types of expression. For them the administration of Canadian desire into categories that could not be challenged suppressed the issue of taste as a measure of quality, value, and reflection. They would have agreed with political philosopher Hannah Arendt that the musical pieces they had chosen were 'durable': having been established as works of art, they were beyond the particular historical and political concerns of Canadian cultural policy (Arendt 1961). However, it is also on this point that we can view the ways in which conflicts over 'culture' were suppressed by the contest itself. The listeners' choices were expressions of taste preferences (in terms of performer and genre of music), but they also represented a struggle to represent 'Canadianness' on the basis of these preferences. Perhaps in microcosm, the choices could be taken to signify the various versions of Canada that had been struggled over through historical efforts at Canadianization: Masseyist 'high culture' Canada; cultural-nationalist Canada (exemplified by The Guess Who's 'American Woman'); and cultural-industrial Canada, where the quantitative orientation to Canadian products for sale on the market (millions of Rush albums sold!) becomes a state-cultural objective (Edwardson 2008). In any case, we note the administration of taste itself through the contest in the service of state-nation interests in the representation of identity.

Conclusion: Can the CBC be Contested?

The CBC is not a direct arm of the state, but it is the manifestation of and perpetuator of state policy as it pertains to national culture and identity. That is its task and responsibility. It also seeks to hold off government criticisms of irrelevance or wasteful use of tax dollars by appealing to large, popular audiences. Caught between these two somewhat contradictory aims, CBC's popular contests work hard to keep their audiences concerned about national identity and culture. The cultural nationalist assumptions that mandate and politically sustain the CBC as an institution are buttressed by the audience during such playful pursuits. The CBC's mandate is visible not only in the themes of these contests (collecting Canadian things), but also in how they are administered. In other words, the administration and direction of the audience's self-desire is of central concern for those running these contests. As the public broadcaster in Canada, the CBC has a stake in generating a particular version of the public sphere and in making itself part of that sphere. We found that CBC audience members took up these contests with enthusiasm. Their comments ranged from defence of these contests (and their administration) to outright attacks. In fact, audience members often turned on one another in their efforts to defend particular notions of the role of the audience, the purpose of the contest, and the job of the CBC in general. Regardless of their differences, however, most audience members made it clear that they perceived the CBC as an important site of collective nation building. Even those who suggested that these contests should be seen as light-hearted fun defended the importance of the CBC as a place for such fun. In other words, there is something unique and important about having one's fun at the CBC.

Comparing the two contests, we found more audience-generated criticism and debate during the Seven Wonders of Canada contest than during the Obama Playlist contest. This could be because the former contest ran much longer and its mechanisms of administration were made clear from the start. The difference could also be related to the types of things that were being collected in the two contests. While the former vaguely collected things, the latter collected music. As we have discussed, what constitutes Canadian music was widely debated by the CBC audience, yet the highly socialized nature of these choices (going back to their almost half-century-long protection and exposure through CanCon regulations) was largely taken for granted. Indeed, the themes these songs elicited – misrecognition, empty space, ressentiment – repeated long-standing ideas of how Canadians have been encouraged to think of themselves and their culture. These very themes in turn fed back into the need for statist regulation and administration. The intimate relationship between the institutional administration of culture and the audiences' musical tastes (both in terms of recurrent lyrical themes and their willingness to have their tastes massaged and managed by CBC producers and the CRTC) suggests a deeply socialized consumptive desire aimed at reproducing the cultural apparatus itself. The valued myths of vast, empty territory, misrecognition, and ressentiment have allowed for cultural and administrative policies that organize Canadian identity and desire towards the state's discipline. Aboriginal peoples, immigrants, and regional ethnic enclaves (and even the general masses' lust for American popular culture) all serve to justify the administration of culture and to summon this administration to the centre of Canadian identity. Michael Dorland (1996–7) has made just this argument, asserting that the history of protecting the cultural distinctiveness of Canada has led directly to the state becoming the central agent of cultural life. In fact, Dorland contends that the state has become entirely coequal with the public sphere. In this vein, Paul Rutherford (1993) has found ample evidence that in consuming American popular culture, Canadians do not lose their identity – they in fact *make* that identity by consuming this material as evidence that American culture is radically different. This raises an important question: What, then, is being protected?

In the days of Massey and his cohort, assimilation of culturally suspect groups was the goal of cultural policy. This value has been replaced by what appears to be its opposite – diversity. But in our examination of the two CBC contests, we have found that diversity can itself become a disciplinary good. In both contests the CBC enforced its value of diversity and showed that lessons about diversity must be provided when these contests are being administered. In the Seven Wonders contest, this lesson was organized spatially, with the map coming to represent preassumed regional identities and differences. Regarding the mythic 'North,' this space also came to represent the past – that is, the early Aboriginal cultures before Western contact. In the Obama Playlist contest, the theme of space – this time empty – also arose. As discussed, the myth of empty space allows the highly administered history of Canadian space to be suppressed even while the myth of technological nationalism is sustained. It also allows the Aboriginal groups who lived (and continue to live) in these spaces to be conflated with nature. In the second contest, the administration of diversity took the shape of administrating types or styles of music, reinvigorating the old 'mass' versus 'Massey' debates about the role of culture in national identity and desire. The styles of music defended by the CBC producers under the value of diversity came to stand for ethnic, linguistic, and racial differences; but at the same time, interestingly, those styles helped ensure a diversity of taste cultures in a multicultural society, and this included protecting the 'high culture' position of the classical music category. Perhaps we see some residual Masseyism here, with the continued valuation of high culture, albeit through its administrative protection. In this context, the resort to a popular contest showed that the Massey ideal of the education of Canadians towards cultural discernment had faded. While this interest could be protected (within a song category), it could not be allowed to assert its most basic value judgment – that *not* all cultural expressions are of equal value. The valuing of cultural expression is now located in policy apparatuses that must reproduce diversity above all. In both contests, diversity (as understood by the CBC's producers and directors) was not to be sacrificed to the popular vote. Clearly in this view, diversity was essential to Canadianness. Canadians were a community *because of* their differences. Yet there was also an underlying suspicion that the popular desire did not naturally reproduce diversity, which had constantly to be both taught and administered. Perhaps popular opinion has become a stand-in for a disciplinary collective self-desire.

It is widely accepted in English Canada that Canadian things – especially cultural things – need to be collected and preserved because they are endangered by American cultural imperialism. Hence, contests that propose to collect Canada also propose to *defend* Canada. But as Dorland argues, because the object of defence is not so much territory as cultural practices themselves, a far more abstract ideology arises that lends itself to the mixing of policy and identity in Canada. If the primary thing to be collected and defended is 'unique Canadianness,' then this work is complex and subtle. Dorland (1996) follows on Ramsay Cook (1971), both of whom suggest that because the state has come to take on the serious work of defending Canadian culture, the state itself has become the primary signifier of Canadianness. In other words, that the state mediates culture for Canadians is the primary difference between Canadians and Americans, which raises the question of whether Canadian cultural desire is primarily desiring of the state (with cultural content as a secondary product).

If Canada exists only by way of emptiness, mediation, and misrecognition, then only the pleasure of discipline can bring it into existence. If Canada exists by way of diversity, difference, and tolerance, then no value judgment can outweigh another (other than the value of the administration of cultural taste towards diversity itself). This is the emptiness of nihilism mixed with masochism. As we discuss in subsequent chapters, such wholly negative formulations of identity chase Canadian desire into some unlikely places in its effort to build a sense of self – including a national coffee chain.

2

'Always Fresh, Always There': Tim Hortons and the Consumer-Citizen

You're Home.

Slogan found on entrances to Tim Hortons restaurants

Outside of Hockey Night in Canada and – with reverence – Don Cherry, there are few institutions or companies that have blended into the character of the nation so completely as Tim Hortons.

Rex Murphy (2009)

The 'way of life' of an ethnic group, a community, or a nation takes the form of an articulated constellation of bits of enjoyment.

Kieran Keohane (1997)

In the previous chapter we saw that the CBC struggles within a heavy official mandate that makes the production of nation, citizen, and pleasure a difficult – perhaps impossible – task. In this chapter we consider a wholly different cultural location that makes a similar offering of Canadianness – Tim Hortons coffee shops. As we will discuss, Tim Hortons is a commercial enterprise operating outside of official state mandates and has positioned itself within a consumer landscape as a kind of public sphere. As Tim Hortons has increasingly marketed itself as the cultural site for the articulation of Canadian values, agents of government and state have come to use it as a legitimate place for their own public appearance. Put another way, the dynamic of the appearance/disappearance of the state and its agents into ordinary pleasures discussed in this book now occurs, at least in part, in the context of a commercial enterprise. It arises through the figure of the consumer-citizen.

Tim Hortons was established in 1964, with one shop in Hamilton, Ontario, selling only coffee and donuts, and has since become Canada's most successful and omnipresent purveyor of coffee, snacks, and meals, with more than 3,000 outlets nationwide. Its national competitor Starbucks has approximately 1,000 outlets; McDonald's has about 1,400. For three consecutive years, readers of *Canadian Business* magazine judged it Canada's 'best managed brand' (Gray 2004, 2005, 2006). In 2010 *Advertising Age* named it one of its 'World's Hottest Brands' (*Advertising Age* 2010). The company was sold to American Wendy's International Inc. in 1995 and was repatriated to Oakville, Ontario, in 2010. While owned by Wendy's, Tim Hortons made its most aggressive move on its representation of Canada and Canadianness to Canadian consumers. It is now a publicly traded company, with the vast majority of its restaurants run as franchises. Since the 1990s it has expanded into the United States and parts of Europe. It plans to open more than 100 outlets in the Persian Gulf.

Other companies have used nationalism as a branding strategy in Canada – the Hudson's Bay Company, Canadian Tire, Molson, Roots. The Bay (now wholly American-owned) and Canadian Tire both emphasize their Canadian stories: in the former case as tied to British colonial expansion and as represented by the famous eighteenth-century 'point' blanket; and in the case of Canadian Tire, as the story of two entrepreneurial brothers starting from a single shop and expanding into the rest of Canada. Both play on classic Canadian themes of ruggedness and endurance – themes that we will also see in our discussion of Tim Hortons. Roots began as a small shoe company established by Americans, albeit who had been inspired by their experiences at summer camp in Ontario. In the late 1980s and early 1990s, however, it started a craze for its sweatshirts emblazoned with Canadian symbols – canoes, beavers, leaves. Catherine Carstairs (2006b) suggests that the branding of Canada through Roots signalled a cultural shift away from economic, political, and cultural protectionism (discussed in chapter 1) towards 'a more consumer-oriented and branded' nationalism (235). This 'Roots nationalism' is

a consequence of Canadians' inability to create other meaningful forms of nationalism. Canada's multicultural heritage makes ethnic nationalism impossible, while the ongoing struggle with Quebec separatism and other forms of regionalism has made it difficult to create what some scholars have described as voluntary or 'civic' nationalism – a common understanding of what it means to be a citizen. (237)

During this same period, Molson used its 'Canadian'-named beer to brand itself as the essence of Canada. In Molson ads, 'Joe' the 'average' Canadian ranted about misrecognition and stereotype. As Erin Manning points out, while those ads were very popular, there was nothing critical or new in this formulation of Canadian identity. The speaker was white, male, and young; he railed against being confused with Americans ('I have a prime minister, not a president'); and he was anti-American ('I believe in peace-keeping, not police-keeping; diversity, not assimilation') (Manning 2000). Manning contends that this commercial's popularity was 'insidious' because it defined nationalism as 'benign, entertaining, innocent, and seamless' (3). This Joe character is also now ironic, given that Molson is owned by MolsonCoors, a Canadian–U.S. company, which has effectively blurred the lines of national difference between the two countries in the context of globalized commerce.

This 'I am Canadian' ad was so popular that politicians came to parrot its lines (2). Sheila Copps, the Heritage Minister at the time, screened it at a meeting of the International Press Institute in 2002. The particular conference session was on American cultural imperialism, during which Copps stated: 'For Canadians, culture is just not another good. It's not just entertainment. It's the expression of the soul and identity of who we are' (International Press Institute 2002 Congress Report). Apparently for Copps this ad campaign spoke about Canadian difference more than it did about the commodification of national identity and insidious nationalism. For the purposes of our discussion, it is instructive on just that point. As a representative of the state and heritage, Copps seemed to be arguing that Canadian culture and identity were located in the commodity and its branding.

In this chapter we argue that Tim Hortons has been the most successful and long-standing private commercial enterprise to brand itself by way of overt national identity and pride. As we will show, politicians and agents of the state make their way to Tim Hortons in order to present themselves to the public. No other commercial enterprise binds together the social and political roles of consumer and citizen more closely than Tim Hortons, which simultaneously offers, in Carstairs's terms, a 'civic' and 'commercial' nationalism. It has made a claim on what Jürgen Habermas (1989) would call the 'public sphere' – that is, the site of collective debate and discussion about the common good. Of course, Tim Hortons has the advantage over other companies in that it is a coffee shop, with all the associations of community, conversation, and public co-mingling. As we will show, Tim Hortons has carved out this political space by aligning itself with Canada's apparent collective values.

During and after the Second World War there was an explosion of academic writing on commercial culture and democracy. At the same time that the Massey Commission in Canada was warning about the dangers of American mass culture, European and American cultural critics were turning their attention to the same phenomenon. Generally, they held that by definition, mass and consumer culture undermines democratic sensibilities rooted in reason and deliberation. The exiled Frankfurt School intellectuals Theodor Adorno and Max Horkheimer found their new American home to be a cultural wasteland in which mass-produced cultural products (such as Hollywood movies and popular music) remade audiences in their own image so that the masses came to crave the formulaic and undifferentiated products they were fed (Horkheimer and Adorno 1969). This highly influential version of the consumer-citizen dominated academic ideas of mass and consumer culture until recently. Contemporary thinkers place more agency in the hands of audiences and consumers to interpret and fashion messages and products. Feminist scholars (e.g., Joyrich 2005) have argued that a fear of 'feminization' or weakening of rational, masculine culture was at work in much of the early criticism of the mass and commercial consumer. Moreover, historians such as Lizabeth Cohen (2003) have pointed to commercial activism – boycotts, strikes, and the like – as the first avenue of enfranchisement for women and Blacks in America. By these accounts, commercial culture runs the gamut from threat *to* democracy to tool *of* democracy. For our purposes, however, the issue at hand is the citizen's relationship to public and collective debate around the pubic good. In other words, how do topics of public concern arise and become objects of common discussion by way of commercial advertising and marketing? For our purposes, the best way to frame the question of consumerism and citizenship is offered by Don Slater (2000), who discusses the topic in terms of the public sphere: 'Ideas of modern consumption arise firstly in the ideal (or dystopia) of a liberal and commercial society comprising free individuals pursuing their interests through a free association in the public sphere' (183). Tim Hortons makes use of this consumer-citizen who is individualized in his or her desires, but it also capitalizes on the fact that this social actor is left with little community, identity, or history. In other words, Tim Hortons offers back what private industry, and the ideology of the free enterprise, have removed from the public sphere.

Tim Hortons's status as a Canadian icon and institution has become a truism repeated endlessly by academics and journalists.[1] Many journalistic stories feature Tim Hortons as a purveyor of national identity; others discuss Tim Hortons in terms of rituals of welcome and hospitality.

As Tim Hortons represents 'home,' journalists can discuss strangers as initiated into Canadian life by way of their first ritualistic tasting of the food (Delaney 2005).

In a similar use of Tim Hortons to measure social space, the proximity of people to Tim Hortons has been employed at a professional health conference to define the Canadian rural: 'You know that you are rural if there is no Starbucks or Second Cup . . . You know that you are remote if there is no Tim Hortons' (Health and Health Services 2002). As a gauge of social distance, Tim Hortons is also used to draw a line between friend and foe. When a famous Canadian convict was released from prison in 2005, newspaper accounts picked up on her comment about wanting to visit Tim Hortons. According to the *Globe and Mail*, 'convicted sex killer Karla Homolka giggled on national television and said the first thing she wanted to do with her newfound freedom was quaff an iced cappuccino. From Tim Hortons' (Mahoney 2005). The company responded by insisting that there was no connection between Tim Hortons and Homolka. At the same time, even the perfectly legal banning of a problematic customer or the dismissal of an employee grabs headlines – 'Patron Makes a Double-Double Take Over Ban' (Fletcher 2010); 'Tim Hortons Fires Single Mom Over Free Timbit' (TheStar.com 2008) – raising the question of whether this coffee chain has become a kind of space to which all citizens may claim access, save only our murderers. Ironically, as Tim Hortons receives so much supportive attention from the media, it is vulnerable to bad publicity. Notice how the *Globe and Mail* both reports on and helps create this media phenomenon: 'In a terse press release, the company blamed an overzealous manager for the firing, which threatened to become a public relations nightmare as the story gained traction in the media Thursday' (*Globe and Mail* 2009a).

In advertising, Tim Hortons is even obliquely referenced by unrelated companies piggybacking on the sentiments associated with the brand. For example, a TV ad that encourages new Canadian immigrants to set up their banking needs before they arrive shows these prospective Canadians practising being 'Canadian' while still in their country of origin. One scene shows a man in an obviously hot climate being pulled behind a car on skis. Another shows a man trying out Canadian vernacular speech by attempting to pronounce the phrase 'double-double,' a way of ordering coffee associated with Tim Hortons (CBC 2004a) and found in the *Canadian Oxford Dictionary*. But perhaps the strongest acknowledgment of Tim Hortons's place in Canadian life has been the recurring skit on the comedy show *Royal Canadian Air Farce* (an example of the mediation of Canadianness that we find in comedy programming, which we take up in chapter 5). Here two rude and disaffected teenage girls (the 'T-Hoes') take sips from customers' coffees, chew gum loudly, berate customers, and complain incessantly. This skit nicely takes up the tension between the general marketing of the coffee chain and its vulnerability to complete subversion by the low-paid and often part-time counter staff.

Tim Hortons has so much momentum in popular culture that ideas and rumours about it surface independently of advertising. The most enduring myth is that the chain's coffee is loaded with caffeine, nicotine, and/or monosodium glutamate (MSG) – that is, that there must be 'something' in the coffee to account for its popularity. The popular media keep this myth alive simply by discussing it. To explain what they called Canadians' 'addiction' to the coffee, CBC's *Disclosure* TV program investigated these claims and found them unsupportable (CBC 2004b). This talk of hidden substances serves only to add to the mystique of Tim Hortons coffee. The suggestion is that Canada is a country of caffeine addicts – it is only the source of that addiction that must be found. The company's website, under 'Frequently Asked Questions,' states that 'there is absolutely NO nicotine or MSG in our coffee. Tim Hortons coffee has NO ADDITIVES whatsoever' (Tim Hortons 2011a). Of course, for those committed to conspiracy theories, the fact that the company has had to make such a claim 'proves' both addiction and manipulation. This lore frames the relationship to Tim Hortons coffee in terms of citizenship, addiction, and even conspiracy. It also plays on a long-standing narrative of suspicion surrounding advertising that says that our pleasures and desires must be the result of hidden manipulation.

Paul Rutherford (1993) points out that this theory of consumer desire became popular in the late 1950s, when TV ads became a new social force behind consumerism (34). It was suggested that advertising executives were inserting hidden images and messages to excite the base, Freudian unconscious mind. In 1973, Wilson Bryan Key published a best-seller on this theme, titled *Subliminal Seduction*. In the case of Tim Hortons, the notion of hidden ingredients resonated with the level of sentiment on which the marketing works – national feeling lies 'under the skin' and circulates without apparent origin.

So, the status of Tim Hortons as Canadian icon and institution is widely accepted. Still lacking, however, is an analysis of the means by which it has achieved this status and the broader implications of this commercialized nationalism. While many advertisers attempt to align themselves and their products with vaguely nationalist feelings, Tim Hortons has waged a decades-long marketing campaign that touches on the most celebrated of Canadian values and that has aligned those values with celebrations of warriors, foreign diplomacy, troop life, and other rituals of state. In other words, Tim Hortons has worked to organize a particular relationship between consumer-citizen, state, politics, and pleasure.

The Rise of the Café Canuck

As Canada's dense urban streets make evident, coffee shops and cafés have exploded into everyday life since the 1990s. The top coffee chains are often located literally beside one another and in turn are surrounded by non-chain shops that appeal to particular clienteles of their own. As marketing experts point out, what appears to be competition between companies for the same customers is also mutual support and expansion of a product, for the 'need' for coffee (and the organization of work and social life around coffee) has no natural limit. The competition among coffee purveyors is perhaps, then, more ersatz than real; and meanwhile, the proliferation of coffee shops has allowed customers to stake *themselves* against one another in battles of identity.

This personal consumptive positioning cannot be fully explained by the taste of the coffee alone. That positioning also depends on the *meaning* of the coffee in one's cup. As Pierre Bourdieu (1984) has pointed out, *taste* is an effective marker for discrediting and excluding others and for enhancing one's own social standing. The old saying that 'you can't argue with taste' would seem to defend people's right to like whatever they want; in fact, though, taste is a means for maintaining class barriers. Complex cultural objects and practices are considered beyond the comprehension of those without a certain level of education and training. Those others can be dismissed as 'disgusting' (literally, from the Latin 'against taste') because they consume objects that are 'simple' and 'easy' (486). Bourdieu would argue that this notion of taste even extends to the coffee in our (branded) cups, in that what we find pleasant to the palate is a product of cultivation or learning. As Howard Becker (1953) discussed in his classic study of marijuana users, most adult pleasures require training before they become recognized as pleasurable. Hence, there is no natural or biological attachment to our various coffee preferences.

In *The Meaning of Puck*, sports writer Bruce Dowbiggin (2008) explains 'how hockey explains modern Canada.' He does so in part by organizing taste distinctions in terms of an 'emerging urban/suburban-rural split,' with Starbucks signifying the urban and Tim Hortons the suburban-rural. Class and cultural linkages also arise when we examine Tim Hortons sports sponsorships (Timbits programs, Tim Hortons Hockey Day, the Tim Hortons Brier). In other words, Tim Hortons not only capitalizes on class and cultural demographics in Canada but also builds 'taste cultures.' Those cultures in turn contribute to Tim Hortons's bottom line as well as to Canadian collective identity. As we will see, themes of rural life, nature, and strong community are not just demographic realities (as if Tim Horton markets only to these types of people). They are also general ideas that help work up a particular nationalism linked to purported values of populism, collectivism, and inclusion.

William Roseberry (1996) contends that coffee may be the contemporary commodity *par excellence* because it allows people to articulate their identities (and even their politics) through their consumptive differences. So while differences among individuals have traditionally been rooted in religion, ethnicity, locale, politics, and the like (social positions often inherited rather than chosen), difference and identity are increasingly being constructed through individual choices around consumption. The subtle and endless meanings that coffee allows make it the ideal commodity for the work of identity. As we will discuss, this type of consumer identity seems to reject highly divisive and value-laden identities tied to older forms of social differentiation by offering a celebration of personal diversity and difference. But as Bourdieu suggests, this type of consumptive identity holds its own forms of judgment and distinction and should be taken seriously as a social practice. The passions and animosities that have maintained distinctions among people (kinship, ethnicity, race, religion) are being echoed in the visceral ones that coffee drinkers make among one another – distinctions that in turn are rooted in those of both morality and taste.

For some coffee drinkers the long-standing association of coffee houses with urban sophistication is important to their consumptive pleasure. Modern political and economic freedoms that challenged traditional power and authority were articulated and defended in the new social space of the seventeenth- and eighteenth-century British coffee house (Laurier and Philo 2004). Habermas (1989) posits that the early coffee houses in London allowed for a mixing of people hitherto segregated by feudal social-class barriers; as a consequence, innovations associated with modern liberal freedoms, such as the free press, were able to arise. This linkage between democracy and the coffee klatch is echoed in Canada by Democracy Watch's 'Coffee Party,' a non-partisan populist organization that works for corporate and government accountability (and that is set in opposition to the right-wing 'Tea Party' movement in the United States).

Socially, the coffee house or café is also linked to the rise of the *flâneur*, Baudelaire's term for the modern urbanite who treats the city as something to consume. As Arendt (1968) puts it, the *flâneur* 'inhabits a city by strolling through it without aim or purpose, with one's stay secured by the countless cafés which line the streets' (21). In other words, cities that include cafés generate spaces in which people linger, pose, and visually consume one another in terms of their sophistication of gaze, dress, posture, and gait. Because coffee shops – and their products – clearly announce their brand names on signs and on takeout cups, one's coffee choice becomes part of an overall 'presentation of self' (Goffman 1959) within urban space. Charlene Elliott's (2002) study of Starbucks demonstrates this. She notes that Starbucks requires the acquisition of a pseudo-Italian lingo (servers are 'baristas,' a medium coffee is a 'grande,' etc.), which customers are encouraged to learn and employ as part of the pleasure of demonstrating their cultural competence. More important, Starbucks outlets and their customers 'play with the map' to generate a sense of worldly sophistication and taste by associating coffee with exotic places and names (countries of origin are grouped together not by geographic proximity but rather by the exotic images and ideas they invoke). The descriptions of these coffees are often sensual and provocative, which links them to white stereotypes of the sexual characteristics of exotic others – 'wild,' 'spicy,' 'full-bodied,' 'smooth and satisfying' (116).

Because coffee consumption is so socially and politically charged, it is almost impossible to consume coffee in a public space without making a statement about oneself. That is, it is a 'conspicuous act' (Veblen 1953) to embrace or reject expensive coffee drinks, fair trade practices, organic beans, or franchised national stores, for such acts speak to other consumers as moral positions. In this regard, Thompson and Zeynep (2004) interviewed Americans who identified themselves as anti-Starbucks consumers. Some of them rejected Starbucks on the grounds of taste distinctions – for them, Starbucks offered fake sophistication and was aimed at consumers who had not developed taste discrimination. Small, owner-run coffee shops were deemed authentic by these consumers. Others rejected Starbucks for more political and economic reasons, such as the threat it posed to local businesses. These authors point out, though, that both groups used their coffee-drinking choices to give themselves an identity and personal autobiography. In this chapter we will see how Tim Hortons has linked the most personal of stories and feelings with broad national sentiment and values and that this has taken coffee consumption beyond displays of either taste or personal politics.

As a relatively inexpensive, accessible, and nevertheless exotic pleasure, coffee consumption is now an important personal, social, and political practice in everyday life. Nevertheless, the meaning of this consumption tends towards two extremes: it is tied either to personal taste performances or to the politics of local and international trade and social justice. As we have seen, these aspects of coffee consumption are highly complementary, but they also tend to exclude narratives of nation and national identity. Canada, unlike many countries, lacks a national history associated with the production, trade, or gastronomy of coffee. It is all the more interesting, then, that Tim Hortons has managed to tie national sentiment, values, and memory to its product.

War and Peace in a Coffee Cup

In 2008 the Dominion Institute conducted a nation-wide survey asking ordinary Canadians about the First World War and the history of Remembrance Day. The results indicated a gap between the respondents' knowledge of war history and their desire to commemorate it:

> The study reveals that less than half (46%) of Canadians knew that Remembrance Day marks the end of the First World War. Only 42% of Canadians aged 18–34 could correctly identify what this date commemorates. Just 16% of respondents could identify both Germany and Austria from a list of five countries against which we fought. Nearly one quarter of Canadians (22%) were unable to identify Germany as one of Canada's opponents.

Yet, the study continued,

> the survey also found that nine in ten (92%) 'agreed' (59% strongly / 33% somewhat) that 'it is important to commemorate Canada's military history.' And a similar proportion (90%) agreed (53% strongly / 37% somewhat) that we should 'be doing more to educate our young people about our military history.'

Similarly, the institute's 'Canadian Icons' survey (2009a) reported that 'only four in ten (41%) Canadians can identify Sir John A. Macdonald and only one half (49%) can identify the Governor General based on their picture.' Terry Fox (89%) and Celine Dion (88%) were the most recognizable.

The Dominion Institute, founded in 1997, promotes and measures Canadian historical knowledge. It conducts surveys to evaluate what Canadians know (and, importantly, what they *don't* know) as measured by its 'Canadian History Report Card.' It also makes the case for more resources for historical education. In 2009 it merged with Historica, a similar organization dedicated to fostering Canadian identity through historical knowledge. Historica is best known for its 'Heritage Minutes' TV ads, which promote heroic and romantic notions of Canada's history. Katarzyna Rukszto (2008) has written that these short ads aim mainly at generating a dramatic emotional response from viewers and that they 'send a uniform message: that Canadians are marked by creativity, strength, unity, and above all, tolerance' (179). Rukszto also notes that the Heritage Minute ads were developed expressly to counter the effects of Quebec nationalism. Certainly, an examination of the Heritage Minute archive shows that most of these ads present a pre–Quiet Revolution Quebec.

In spite of all the organizations working to generate a historical self-awareness in Canadians, this project seems largely to have failed. Yet the *desire* to commemorate those who served in war seems strong. Perhaps the Dominion Institute has discovered that national identity or patriotism requires little historical content – that it may even *thrive* on a lack on content. After all, if war commemoration is about pride and emotion, the details of when and how Canada participated in the First World War are irrelevant. As the Heritage Minute ads show, it takes only a minute to generate emotion. But that emotion does not necessarily cultivate an interest in exploring the details and ambiguities of Canadian history. In fact, while Rukszto generally supports the Historica–Dominion Institute's dedication to 'citizenship and identity in Canada' (Dominion Institute 2009b), she also suggests that surveys and TV ads may be *undermining* the goals of deeper historical education.

French academic Pierre Nora (1996) has famously formulated the connection between historical knowledge and memory. Memory has traditionally been grounded in local authorities and in stories passed down through generations such that active memory and historical knowledge are one and the same thing. Nora argues that the difficulty in making people historically knowledgeable in modern society rests in part in the loss of traditions of collective memory in contemporary life, so that legitimate sources of memory come to be questioned. The wisdom of the older generation is assumed in traditional societies as much as it is obliterated in modern ones.

Nora argues that this cultural void generates a general *nostalgia* for the past without the collective and sacred rituals of memory. Modern societies, he maintains, attempt to simulate the past without the mechanisms to do so. Such sentiments of nostalgia depend on the coupling of idealized periods in the past with dissatisfaction in the present. In other words, the past is not a link to the present, but an escape from the dissatisfactions of the present. It is a play of difference rather than continuity, and it posits a fictional time when 'there is no gap between desire and its fulfillment . . . The world is always fully and unambiguously present' (Hodgins 2004, 100). Often, as is the case with Tim Hortons advertising, this dissatisfaction is rooted in a vague notion that in the 'past' there was more communal unity and identification, as well as commonly understood standards and values. Hence, much of Tim Hortons's advertising – even when it involves stories set in the present – generates a longing for a lost past. This helps explain why rural communities feature prominently in their stories, the present-day rural itself being a spatial trope for the past. Similarly, while the *functioning* of Tim Hortons is altogether modern (technologies of rapid, mass production of products and services), the *presentation* of Tim Hortons (from packaging, interior design, uniforms, signage, etc.) is deeply nostalgic. But as we will show, Tim Hortons does far more than generate vague nostalgia; it has placed itself *in* this past, where it offers a solution to the problem of nostalgic longing.

One way to begin this investigation into Tim Hortons as site of collective memory is to examine its 'commercial personality' on the coffee landscape. In stark contrast to Starbucks and other popular coffee chains in Canada, Tim Hortons is the down-to-earth character on the coffee scene. When it added espressos and cappuccinos to its menu in 2011, Canadian media commentary (including a screed by the CBC's Rex Murphy on *The National*) generated mock hysteria that no-nonsense Canadians would soon be undermined by the indulgent urban values associated with these drinks. It is interesting that when Tim Hortons announced these earnestly sophisticated drinks, the photograph accompanying the press release showed them decorated with innocent happy faces. These menu additions notwithstanding, Tim Hortons's emblematic cup of coffee, meant to represent the company as a whole, remains the unadorned brew in the plain brown takeout or beige ceramic mug.

More recent additions to the Tim Hortons menu emphasize unpretentious fare – steeped tea, oatmeal, soup, sandwiches, and chili. These products are highly 'fetishized,' as Karl Marx would put it – they seem to appear out of nowhere, lacking any connection to their own history as commodities that have been produced in a particular place at a particular time by particular people and under particular conditions (Marx [1867]1967, 71). Certainly, there is no Juan Valdez character picking coffee beans that links Tim Hortons coffee to a particular region or country. On its website's 'Frequently Asked Questions' page, under 'Where does Tim Hortons get its coffee beans from?', the company answers simply: 'Tim Hortons uses a premium blend of 100% Arabica beans from several of the world's renowned coffee-producing regions' (Tim Hortons 2011a). Only recently has Tim Hortons made some concessions to the public demand that coffee – in particular – be traded and grown fairly. These campaigns are not, however, central to its advertising.

As noted, even the language used by Tim Hortons customers is derived from Anglo-Canadian slang. Penfold (2008) suggests that the donut is a working-class signifier of Canadian down-to-earth common sense and sincerity. In short, there is little to intimidate the customer: Tim Hortons, even in its downtown outlets in large Canadian cities, lacks 'the specifically metropolitan extravagances of mannerism, caprice, and preciousness' (Simmel 1950, 421). This type of branding takes on a stark anti-fashion stance, if fashion is understood as the frenzied recycling of styles and trends. As we will show, the respite from movement and whim, from this empty present, and from the endless multiplicity of modern Canadian life (including the multiplicity of multiculturalism), is a central theme in Tim Hortons ads. It also aligns with the company's theme of populism, which in turn allows politicians (especially) to use Tim Hortons to counter notions that they are part of the distant and uncaring Canadian elite.

The company's pervasive use of browns and sepias – which have never been changed – conveniently reference the era of early photographic reproduction around the turn of the twentieth century. This small semiotic coincidence has allowed Tim Hortons ads to create a sense of collective memory. Sepia toning, used mainly in portrait photography, references a specific, brief era in photographic technology, just before the explosion of endless commercial images into everyday life. As Susan Sontag (1977) wrote in her famous discussion of photography: 'From the start, photographers . . . set themselves the task of recording a disappearing world' (76). That Tim Hortons has succeeded in aligning itself with a romantic past – a time when even the *reproduction* of images was innocent – speaks volumes about how it has insinuated itself into a Canadian history in which it did not yet exist. As a conduit to the Canadian past,

Tim Hortons is suggesting that it was *present* in that past (or at least, like elders in traditional societies, that it is interchangeable with ancestors who *were* present back then). This adds strong resonance to its slogan, 'Always Fresh. Always There.' Moreover, in a culture where memory is personalized, nostalgic, and suspicious of traditional authorities, this commercial agent is offering itself as both the site and the source of collective memory work. Canadians are being offered a version of history and memory at Tim Hortons; not only that, but Tim Hortons is positing *itself* as the new authority for the collective practice of memory over and against other sources. In this way, Tim Hortons is working both to create nostalgia and to solve the problem that nostalgia creates. These other authorities – including the Canadian federal state and its agencies – must then turn to Tim Hortons for their own legitimacy.

The most notable break from this language of browns and beiges comes once a year with the popular 'Roll Up the Rim to Win' contest. These takeout cups are bright red and festooned with images of consumer objects (such as cars and TVs) that can be won. In anticipation of our discussion of gambling in chapter 4, we note that such promotions are taking place in a culture in which gambling has become legitimated and expanded by the state, with citizens being encouraged to take their chances on various types of gambling. There is every indication that this contest is being treated as gambling. The company posts the odds of winning, but as the winners are distributed across the provinces, those in high-population provinces such as Ontario have a smaller chance of winning. Are the customers playing the odds? One server has reported that 'you'll get six, eight, 10 . . . cups of large coffees from people who will come in the run of a day, compared to when the contest is not running' (R. Jones 2009). The odds of winning the car are about one in eight million (varying somewhat by province). While in Afghanistan Tim Hortons issued its 'Roll Up the Rim to Win' takeout cups in camouflage colours. One can only imagine the media frenzy that would have ensued if a Canadian soldier had been shot by a sniper while rolling up a bright red roll-up-the-rim cup.

Tim Hortons's marketers realize that if the company is going to become a prominent place for doing collective memory work, it must first take itself seriously as a core Canadian institution. In other words, besides commemorating important people and events in Canadian history, it must commemorate itself. One example of this self-commemoration was the 2004 collectors' coffee mug celebrating the fortieth anniversary of the company. It read 'Thank you for 40 years of friendship.' It was promoted as a Christmas gift to be given to friends and family. Clearly, this mug was meant to suit the intimacy of such a season and of such gift exchange.[2]

Over the past half-century, Tim Hortons has grown in importance as a place to remember the past and to enact the nation's present. In 2004 it became the sole distributor of the Royal Canadian Mint's Remembrance Day poppy coin. The Royal Canadian Mint's website explained that it (along with the Royal Canadian Legion) had authorized Tim Hortons as 'exclusive distribution partner' because it was seen as 'a distinctive Canadian enterprise.' Clearly, the mint and Canadian veterans both agreed that Tim Hortons had a corporate image that matched the tone of war commemoration. Later that year, when U.S. Secretary of State Condoleezza Rice visited Canada, she was taken by Foreign Affairs Minister Peter MacKay to a Tim Hortons, where the international press eagerly documented the two drinking Tim's coffee and played up the romantic intimacy of the pair sharing this ritual.

But the merging of the state with the cultural practice of going to Tim Hortons is not always so successful. In 2009, Finance Minister Jim Flaherty flew to London, Ontario, for a speech and a photo-op at a Tim's. The minister wanted to talk about his 'belt-tightening budget' but was criticized shortly afterwards for using taxpayer money to pay for the government aircraft he had used to fly to the location (Whittington 2010). While the juxtaposition of Flaherty's spending with his speech about cutting the budget was the obvious problem, the addition of Tim Hortons (apparently to show his sympathy for the common person) made it worse in terms of publicity. Opposition critics invoked the hypothetical pensioner who (apparently) might not even be able to afford to go to Tim Hortons yet who had to pay for Flaherty's flight.

Another example: in a move deemed 'Donuts over Diplomacy' by the *Toronto Star* (2009), Prime Minister Stephen Harper chose to celebrate the 2009 announcement by Tim Hortons of its plan to repatriate to Canada rather than speak at the United Nations in New York City. Harper defended his decision, arguing that the return of Tim's was of central importance to Canada and that a delegate could address world leaders. Harper called the Tim Hortons headquarters an 'important forum' for his promotion of tax breaks for companies willing to relocate their operations to Canada. By attending this event, Harper was able to align himself with the premier branded commodity around national identity and to link this with his economic policies. This choice allowed Harper to articulate his own party's avowed commitment to the economy as its first policy priority. Moreover, in a culture of political branding, it allowed the Conservative brand to stand out in a way that conventional political meetings do not. Harper had made a choice between what can appear as 'just talk' at a flaccid and ineffectual UN, on the one hand, and action – repatriation of a symbol, company, and jobs to Canada – on the other.

During the 2011 federal election, all major party leaders spent significant amounts of time in Tim Hortons restaurants, even working as servers. Major news services, for example, reproduced a photo of NDP leader Jack Layton handing out coffee at a Tim Hortons drive-through window. Playing on the company's slogan, the *Vancouver Sun* declared of the candidates, 'They've always got time for Tim Hortons' (*Vancouver Sun* 2011).

In 2006, Tim Hortons opened an outlet in Afghanistan to serve Canadian troops. Members of the armed forces had lobbied for this extension of Canada into foreign military posts, but the company was cautious in its approach. With the opening of the Afghanistan outlet, the Chief of the Defence Staff, General Rick Hillier, was quoted on the Tim Hortons website: 'I know I speak for all the men and women of the Canadian forces when I say that I'm delighted to hear this news . . . Opening a Tim Hortons to serve our troops in Afghanistan strengthens an already superb relationship between two great Canadian institutions. I would like to thank Tim Hortons for their endless support of the Canadian Forces over the years' (Tim Hortons 2006). Hillier's comments aligned Tim Hortons with the Canadian military in a way that suggests that they are national institutions of equal weight and value and that their histories run parallel. Because his words were conveniently imprecise, this pronouncement allowed Tim Hortons to embed itself into Canadian war history, as if it were, as its slogan says, 'always there.' In this way, it has become a site of war commemoration. In 2010 the company CEO visited the Kandahar base. The company press release read: 'Brave and selfless Canadians fighting the war in Afghanistan, received a personal thank you from the President and CEO of Tim Hortons Don Schroeder this Christmas, when he travelled to the Kandahar army base over the Holidays. Schroeder was part of the Team Canada Christmas Day Tour of Canadian military bases in Kandahar, Afghanistan led by Defence Minister Peter MacKay' (Tim Hortons, 2010).

While in Afghanistan, the Tim Hortons outlet became the central referent of Canada for journalists and armed forces personnel. Tim Hortons was careful in its handling of its relationship to this ongoing military conflict that was no longer simply the UN 'Blue Helmet' peacekeeping action that generations of Canadians have been taught to admire. In 2009, Tim Hortons responded to a lively petition drive asking the company to develop a campaign that would invite its customers to buy a cup of coffee for a soldier. The company's response was to direct interested customers to send gift cards to troops (and to remind customers of its active support of troops, which has included sending coffee to troops who were are stationed in Kuwait). The company did not take up the invitation to generate an active or overt 'support the troops' campaign during the ongoing conflict. Interestingly, however, forces personnel have taken up Tim Hortons as a signifier of their own identity (with all the heroic and patriotic resonances that decades of Tim Hortons advertising have provided). As we will see, much of the armed forces storytelling on websites has mimicked the style and themes found in Tim Hortons advertising (especially their 'True Stories' campaign). This is not in itself surprising, for it was the troops who pushed for a Tim Hortons in Afghanistan. An outlet there, after all, would be a natural extension of their experience training at and living on armed forces bases – usually with a Tim Hortons nearby.

Tim Hortons's general support of troops comes to a peak annually with its celebration of Remembrance Day. Like many organizations, the company allows for poppy sales at its counters, but Tim Hortons speaks directly to the customers and interprets the day for them:

> On November 11, the past and the present are one across our land. It's a unity expressed in the poppies we wear to honour the brave Canadians who served their country, both then and now. This Remembrance Day, Tim Hortons encourages you to reflect on all they've given and to wear a poppy. Together, we can show our veterans we remember them. Then, now, and forever. (Tim Hortons 2011b)

As a part of their twenty-five-cent poppy coin distribution, Tim Hortons issued paper tray liners that reproduced the typical commemorations made by many families with the help of framing stories (in which war medals, photos, and other mementos of a particular soldier are arranged within a frame). Here the frame contained a military hat, a medal, and two casual photos of soldiers (including one in which a soldier held a baby). The overall effect was sober, with the frame and mat in black, photos in black and white, and the tray liner itself dark brown. The lettering under the frame read '25-Cent Poppy Coin. Keeping the Memory Alive.' Nothing on this tray liner told whether or not these particular soldiers had returned alive from the war, but the slogan reminded the coffee drinker that many had not. As a campaign, this war memorial was atypical, rejecting the hopeful and light themes found in most advertising. This heavy message depended on the company's success at establishing itself as a respectful and trustworthy cultural site for collective commemoration.

Tim Hortons advertising also commemorates Canada's peacetime past. Certainly, many companies market themselves through this sort of nostalgia, with vague references to pre-modern production, 'homemade' products, and traditional, rural families. Others – or the same company at different moments – link themselves to nationalism by way of simple claims that they reflect national tastes or that they support national industries and workers. But Tim Hortons has been much more specific in directing nostalgia towards particular values, themes, and institutions, including even the state. Private enterprises usually try to operate as far as possible outside state regulation and supervision, so this imaginative linking of Tim Hortons to the state is unusual. At the same time, however, it shows an understanding that the Canadian imaginary is linked at least in part to manifestations of the state.

Advertising of Values

The association of Tim Hortons with Canadian themes can be traced back to its origins in the romantic life and death of its namesake. Miles Gilbert (Tim) Horton began the company with Jim Charade in 1964, opening a single donut shop in Hamilton, Ontario. In *The Donut: A Canadian History*, Steve Penfold (2008) writes that this timing could not have been better: Canada was becoming an automobile culture and was moving away from tea towards coffee drinking. But changes in transportation and taste were not the only advantages accruing to this new enterprise. As a National Hockey League defenceman, Tim Horton possessed 'all the trappings of the classic myth of white Canadian manhood' (48). Penfold suggests that Tim Horton's image as a rugged yet honest hockey player supported the image of his restaurants. He even argues that that image was so important to the enterprise that popular Toronto Maple Leafs hockey player Eddie Shack's similar foray into the donut business was stifled by his own less than trustworthy public persona (51). In the first years, the company made much of its founder's name and popularity.

In 1974, however, Tim Horton died when he lost control of his car while driving late at night between Toronto and Buffalo. While a number

of things were working against Horton that night, former marketing director Ron Buist (2003) emphasizes that his work ethic also played a part
in the accident – he had just finished playing a game against Toronto
and checked on the donut shop before taking to the highway (67). His
widow, who wanted images of her husband removed from the restaurants, inherited part of the company (which was soon bought out by
Horton's then partner Ron Joyce). With the removal of these references,
the company's connection to the hockey player began to fade. Buist
maintains that within ten years the company's link with Tim Horton the
man had weakened dramatically (58). Still, the chain has consistently
emphasized ruggedness, sport, and endurance as general themes. After
his widow's death, the company revised the Tim Horton biography on its
website to emphasize his hockey career, and his image has reappeared in
shops, along with 'Timfact' quizzes.

Tim Hortons is famous for sponsoring sports at the grassroots and amateur levels, as well as for associating itself with professional sports such
as hockey and curling through its ads. The company rents arenas to offer
free skating, sponsors local 'Timbits' children's sports, and operates six
summer camps for economically disadvantaged children. (A Timbit is a
small piece of fried donut batter, but also refers to the children who participate in Tim Hortons sports.) But the company's involvement in children's sports does not stop at financial support. Many of the company's
TV ads make it clear that Tim Hortons understands kids' hockey as a
site where the next generation of Canadians is being socialized. Hockey
has a reputation as a violent game, yet Tim Hortons ads make the arena
a place of fair play, inclusion, and cooperation. One Timbits ad shows
young Canadian NHL star Sidney Crosby ('Sid the Kid') in his Timbits
uniform as a child. Another shows the now-grown star playing gently
with young Timbits children, thereby linking Tim Hortons to the gener-
ational reproduction of hockey and hockey stars. When there was a rash
of head injuries to NHL players in 2010–11, Tim Hortons responded
(along with other sponsors, including Air Canada and ScotiaBank) by
making it clear that their corporate image could not be associated with
such violence. Tim Hortons 'encourages the NHL, the teams and general managers and the NHL Players' Association to continue to work
towards addressing concerns with head injuries' (CBC 2011). Indeed,
Sid the Kid was one of the most seriously injured players during this rash
of headshots: a concussion left him unable to play for months.

Again, Tim Hortons has been able to link itself with the past (and the
future) by forging a connection to hockey and by taking responsibility

for the sport's development. As its slogan asserts: 'We are all players. We are all fans.' The long-standing ambivalence around hockey as a violent sport – and symbol of Canada – is even taken on in its ads about children's hockey as the arena of fair play. Nationalist spectacles like CBC's *Hockey Day in Canada* are also natural sites for Tim Hortons to promote itself. As the CBC's chief marketing and sales officer commented, this partnership has allowed for mutual promotion by way of hockey: 'We are extremely proud to have our key partner Tim Hortons be a sponsor of CBC's 4th Annual Hockey Day in Canada . . . The strategy is to leverage the power of these two exciting brands through a unique programming initiative that celebrates Our Game at the grass roots level' (Tim Hortons 2003). As this statement suggests, the celebration of 'our game' is also the celebration of its roots and of the CBC and Tim Hortons themselves as brands connected to the collective imagination. Cooperative and dedicated small-town individuals – players, parents, coaches, and so forth – are recurring icons connected to hockey. One of the many ads that links commitment, community, rural areas, and hockey shows a man arriving at an isolated hockey rink before dawn during the middle of winter and toiling to prepare the arena for early-morning children's hockey. This ad is beautifully filmed and simple, with steam rising off the ice and the sun breaking the darkness of the sky as the man enacts his morning ritual in solitary silence. This understated style runs parallel with the apparent humility of the man whose labour is unseen and apparently taken for granted by the eager children who will hit the ice hours later. The viewer becomes a privileged witness to a labour of love aimed at fostering the next generation of hockey players. This ad connects values (commitment, loyalty, humility) to sacred space (the arena), ritual practices, and the maintenance of community over time. It avoids cliché by *showing* these values and practices rather than by asserting them. And, as with so many Tim Hortons ads, the product is embedded in the story as a small but essential comfort to this man's morning. In other words, the coffee takes on a character of its own as his humble companion. The man represents the traditional notion of passing on skills and sacred practices from one generation to the next by way of their ritualized enactment.

One value repeated over decades of Tim Hortons ads is mutual community support or collectivism. Historically, grassroots collectivist sentiment became associated with state policies such as socialized medicine and social welfare. The icon of this institutionalized collectivism in state policy and apparatus is CCF/NDP politician Tommy Douglas. Although Douglas was never able to lead his party to federal victory, as the 'conscience of Canada' he had a strong influence on the actions of the two federal parties that did form the government. More important to this discussion, however, is his first-place standing as 'The Greatest Canadian' in CBC's audience-driven contest aired in 2004. This popular victory does not mean that Douglas would be any more likely today to win a federal election than in his own day. Opinion polls and general sentiment show a strong belief in the integrity and honesty of NDP (previously CCF) leaders relative to their more successful counterparts in other parties. This gap between respect and actual voter support seems to indicate that Canadians have high admiration for socialist politicians and their values but do not have the same confidence in their policies. This in turn strongly suggests that collectivism lives in the Canadian imagination more than in the actual realities of policy, law, and administration. Tim Hortons ads have picked up this form of collectivist longing and run with it. In Nora's (1996) terminology, while these ads may appear deeply nostalgic, they in fact offer a way to embody the connection between past and present rather than just an empty longing. As we will see, in this way they populate or fill Canadian identity and history by providing the ritual and sacred space in which to tell stories.

Another Tim Hortons TV ad links immigration, family, and hockey. The press dubbed this one 'Anti-Hockey Grandpa' (Keller 2006). The narrative involves the tension between a young boy and his father, who appear to be new immigrants from Asia. The boy wants to spend all his time playing hockey (in the street and on the ice); his father struggles to get him to study. The second part of the ad shows the father and the now-grown son watching the son's own boy play Timbits hockey in an arena. The son asks his father why he comes to watch his grandchild play when he never attended his own games. (Here the ad introduces the real pain of children's longing for attention and approval from parents.) It turns out that his father *had* attended games (takeout Tim's coffee cup in hand) but had remained hidden. Apparently, his concern to get his son to study made him feel that he could not show his pride in his son's athletic achievements. He proves his hidden support of his son by producing a faded and creased photo of his son as a boy in his hockey uniform. Clearly this story is steeped in long-standing misunderstanding and resentment, in a secret pride that cannot be revealed for decades, and in a stubborn insistence on the part of the father than his child assimilate with Canadian culture and society by studying hard. This ad is also highly romantic in that it supports the vision of immigrants as ultimately happy and successful, and the father as wise and strict. Remarkably, it also adds a complexity to the simple, official version of multiculturalism and immigration. This ad is about pain – about language, culture, and tradition being sacrificed to the need to assimilate. That the grandfather can now enjoy watching the grandson play hockey speaks to the fact that he succeeded in integrating his family into the broader culture, even at the cost of alienation from his own son. Here, caution, humility, and pride are all mixed with an immigrant's pain of watching his children inevitably become separated from their own deep cultural knowledge and traditions. Sharing their Tim Hortons coffee becomes a sad yet important connection between these two men. It is a small, intimate comfort as they watch the grandson (inevitably) play (Timbits) hockey.

The Ministry of Citizenship and Immigration's definition of multiculturalism suggests that maintaining one's ethnic, religious, and cultural values is not at odds with 'integration' with the larger, pre-existing Canadian society, as long as those values are understood as existing in the past: 'Multiculturalism ensures that all citizens can keep their identities, can take pride in their ancestry . . . Through multiculturalism, Canada recognizes the potential of all Canadians, encouraging them to integrate into their society and take an active part in its social, cultural, economic and political affairs' (Canada 2010b). This statement does not explain how integration can be achieved while meaningful differences in values are maintained; it does, though, assert that racism, violence, hatred, and ghettos will be the result of any resistance to the multicultural ideal. It is significant here that some Tim Hortons ads (including 'Anti-Hockey Grandpa') raise themes that are rarely acknowledged in official notions of Canada. We are thinking specifically here about the theme of tension between multiculturalism and identity. The immigrant father in 'Anti-Hockey Grandpa' faces the real problem of getting by in a country that is not – all sentimental protests to the contrary – organized around his background and traditions. His mantra, 'study, study,' signifies that for him, submission to Canada's culture, school system, and economic and linguistic practices will be essential to his son's success. That father views the pleasures of hockey as undermining the hard and painful work of making his child radically different from himself – that is, Canadian. Ultimately, though, playing hockey has allowed him and his son and grandson to assimilate into Canadian society, disrupting the official notion of Canada as a mosaic of simple differences.

Author Neil Bissoondath – himself an immigrant to Canada – has reflected on this position, which he and other new Canadians are implicitly asked to take within the rhetoric of the mosaic. The mosaic metaphor

plays on the notion of distinct parts (or tiles) set side by side to create
an overall pattern (a metaphor of cold difference in contrast to hot assimilation into a new whole – the 'melting pot'). Multiculturalism asks
immigrants – especially those who are visible in their difference from
the Anglo-European norm – to do the work of signifying ethnic diversity.
They introduce a difference from this norm – viz., colour and texture to
the mosaic – and thereby allow white and English Canadians to feel good
about their 'tolerance' and to ignore the deep assimilative practices that
confront immigrants. Bissoondath (1994) also argues that immigrants
of colour like him are being asked to represent a harmless and frozen
cultural past that can neither move forward nor challenge Canadian values – especially the value of multiculturalism. For him, 'it is impossible
to avoid a whiff of formaldehyde, a hint of the sterility of museum display
cases. Impossible to ignore the image of colourful butterflies pinned to
black velvet by careful and loving hands' (42). The mosaic and multicultural rhetorics of state, then, have a number of interrelated effects:
they deny the real assimilative realities of Canadian life; they require
immigrants and visible ethnic, racial, and religious minorities to live as
temporally frozen and harmless representations of difference; they suggest that any questioning of the multicultural ideal will result in violence
and chaos; and they paper over the administrative interests at the heart
of the mosaic.

In this context of official discourse, collective narrative threatens to
tip over into cultural relativism: no longer will difference be brought
into conversation about Canadian values; it will merely be placed (like
tiles or butterflies) in juxtaposition, for all values will be officially equal
to all other values, traditions, and beliefs. As the many critics of multiculturalism suggest, this relativism cannot provide the basis for a collective
identity or narrative. The Tim Hortons story of the Chinese hockey dad
at least admits that his difference will be largely overcome and erased by
the assimilation of his children and grandchildren. In his grudging and
measured acknowledgment of the pleasure they find in hockey and its
associated comradeship, he acknowledges the pleasure of assimilation
and that he has learned to live with the loss it means to him. Unlike
Bissoondath's butterflies, he is living in real and dynamic time, which introduces a profound distance between him and his offspring. Again, the
Tim Hortons coffee shared by father and son does not signify a weepy
celebration of the Canadian mosaic, or a general appreciation of the
beauty of the mosaic as viewed from the outside, but rather a small and
intimate comfort in the face of real and irreversible change – a change

that the father encouraged through his assimilationist attitude towards his son.

Ironically, while Tim Hortons marketing and advertising is nostalgic, its nostalgia takes advantage of the gaps, contradictions, and dissatisfactions left by official Canadian versions of the past and the present. As noted earlier, the company also makes itself a witness to these realities – war, assimilation, difference – as if it were a core institution for preserving collective history and memory. By taking this stance, it is implying that other institutions and stories may be less than satisfactory or authentic. Moreover, Tim Hortons appropriates the grounds of collective storytelling and gets its customers to become the voices of these stories. Unlike the mosaic pieces found in the official images of the citizen, the Tim Hortons stories are 'hot' narratives filled with visceral joys, pains, and losses.

In the mid-1990s, under Buist's stewardship, Tim Hortons and Enterprise Advertising of Toronto began making their 'True Stories' TV ads, which were the precursors to the similar 'Every Cup Tells a Story' campaign. In both these campaigns, Tim Hortons customers and store owners generate stories featuring the everyday lives of the storytellers. Storytelling is one of the oldest and most commonplace forms of human communication, and its significance for Canada in the mid-1990s is important (even politically disruptive). Narrative as a practice is simultaneously universal and particular – that is, narrative's forms are repeatable and often clichéd even while the content of narratives is specific (if not unique). As Tim Hortons implies, everyone can *tell* a story and everyone *has* a story. Thus, as we have seen, while Tim Hortons has made itself the site and source of much collective storytelling, these campaigns seem to shift the actual telling to the customer. Rhetorically, Tim Hortons acknowledges the voices of ordinary speakers, the implication being that they do not necessarily get the opportunity to tell their stories in their everyday experience and that the voices of ordinary people are ignored and pressed out by other voices. As we will show, Tim Hortons cleverly gets its customers to do its talking, with profound implications for storytelling's place in Canadian identity.

The very first 'True Story' TV ad was remarkably quaint and banal. It told the story of an elderly woman, Lillian, who made a daily pilgrimage to her local Tim Hortons in a small Nova Scotia town. Other than the tough and determined character of Lillian herself, there wasn't much of a story here. This introductory figure did, however, set the tone for other 'True Stories' to follow. Like Lillian, the subjects were rugged, self-sacrificing, and unwavering in their goals. Most of these stories featured adventure, risk, severe weather, and personal sacrifice, running from the most heroic and extreme (in the case of soldiers in war zones) to the most ordinary (lonely students studying abroad and asking their parents to send them Tim's coffee). Keohane (1997) helps make sense of this theme of endurance within the broad Canadian narrative: 'Throughout Canadian popular culture there are discourses that celebrate an enjoyment of endurance . . . skating, cross-country skiing, canoeing, camping, trekking . . . The heroic endurance/enjoyment of the voyageurs is recreated in the contemporary practice of endurance driving' (35). Keohane seems to have a point when he links Canadians' heroism with their capacity to endure the harshness of their environment. Take for example, this passage from Roy MacGregor's *Canadians: A Portrait of a Country and Its People* (2007), which establishes the character of two young Aboriginal leaders: 'One winter in the late 1960s the group ran into a blizzard driving home from the University of Brandon . . . Cars and trucks were in ditches. The others wanted to quit, but Mercredi and Harper refused and took turns running out in front of the headlights so that the driver could stay on the pavement' (212). In this narrative, the 'stubbornness' that these men showed by running down a highway in a blizzard for 30 kilometres (against the efforts of the police and other drivers to stop them) sets them up to become political leaders in the future.

While lacking the same drama, the 'True Story' of Jean and Doug Thornton (from *Tim's Times*, 17 May 2004) worked from similar themes. This story involved the elderly couple's drive across the country from Alberta to Newfoundland. In the story, they planned their journey around stops at Tim Hortons, explaining that they warmed up and studied their maps at Tim's outlets. This trip took seven weeks and covered almost 18,000 kilometres. As Keohane discusses, driving as 'endurance' or sheer distance seems to be integral to this type of pleasure. In the photo that accompanied this story, the Thorntons held up a sign announcing the number of kilometres covered rather than any souvenirs. Tim Hortons shops offered them support on their travels, providing warmth, comfort, and even the opportunity to reorient themselves spatially on their maps. Space itself was measured and navigated in terms of proximity to the next Tim's. When the couple returned home they contacted the coffee chain to tell their story. It was a Tim Hortons story through and through. Their story, in turn, allowed the company to show itself as connecting the geographically and culturally diverse parts of the country into a whole.

A similar ad featured two pairs of travellers – an older couple in an RV and two young men in an older-model car. Both couples planned to drive across Canada from coast to coast, stopping 'only at Tim Hortons.' As they drove in opposite directions they eventually crossed paths, with the young man politely waving the older woman ahead of him as they drove into a Tim Hortons. The irony built into this story was that both pairs had declared they were probably the first ever to make this Tim Hortons journey. And both couples marked off that journey by locating Tim Hortons outlets on the map of Canada and by counting the number of Tim Hortons they visited. This ad was explicit in its promise to provide comfort and geographic orientation from coast to coast. In another ad, a man saw a takeout 'Roll Up the Rim to Win' takeout cup on the ground and bent over to pick it up. The wind took the cup and the man chased it. When he picked it up, he realized that he had traversed the width of the country from east coast to west coast.

In all these travel ads, Tim Hortons both celebrates and mitigates the huge distance between coasts. Even the Tim Hortons website has captured the sense of endless wilderness one experiences while driving across the country. Sitting in front of a computer screen, the website visitor takes on the point of view of a driver negotiating a highway winding through a dense forest. Suddenly this virtual journey stops at the doors of a Tim Hortons outlet – apparently in the middle of nowhere. After all the twisting and turning through this disorienting and apparently endless hinterland, the virtual Tim Hortons outlet offers psychological relief. It 'saves' the visitor from this uncharted, boundless, and threatening expanse of nature. With a click on the virtual doors, the viewer is back in the safety of Tim's. All of this effort to traverse and fill up Canada's space makes sense in the context of what we discussed in chapter 1 – that Canada is nothing more than the empty mediation of technologies. Here we have a version of filling in this space with social actors who take pleasure and gain meaning in the movement across space.

All narratives tell about some kind of adventure – small or large. The 'True Stories' take individuals, friends, co-workers, and families and make them sites of adventure. As we have seen, they also establish connections between friend and stranger that are at least long enough to ritually initiate the stranger to the local. Also important in these ads is the characters' capacity to make value judgments about people and places, as stories are not equal-opportunity sites of inclusion. Suspicion, fear, and disorientation have been thematic to adventure narratives since

Homer. In chapter 1, we discussed how opinion in Canada has been 'administered' as a means to integrate Canada's parts – regional, linguistic, ethnic, and so forth – into a whole. By contrast, narratives stand beside one another and elicit one another and cannot easily be reorganized to construct general ideas. The 'truth' of narratives, then, is found not so much in their veracity as in how they understand and speak about the world. They are truthful in their orientation to distinction, discrimination, and judgment.

During the 2010 Winter Olympics (hosted by Canada), Tim Hortons repeatedly ran a TV ad that depicted the reunion of a husband (evidenced by his wedding band) with his wife and children. According to a *Globe and Mail* reporter, that ad 'played like a modern Canadian heritage vignette' (Houpt 2010). From their appearance, the family seemed to be immigrating to Canada from an African country (during the winter, of course). Just before the wife arrived, the husband bought a Tim Hortons coffee at the airport. At the moment they were tearfully reunited (with the husband biting the back of his hand in an effort to retain his composure), he gave her the coffee, saying, 'Welcome to Canada.' The wife took the cup but seemed to miss its significance (i.e., she had not yet been socialized into Canadian culture); instead, she fixed her attention on the winter garb her husband had brought for her. The implications of moving to Canada became apparent to her as she examined the bulky parkas.

Two things are noteworthy about this ad. First, Tim Hortons was taking the risk of positing itself as *the* iconic and ritualistic signifier of Canada. Second, media coverage of this ad (as so often happens, this Tim's ad was the subject of intense media scrutiny) focused on the claim that it was based on a true story. This media coverage, however, missed almost everything that was significant about the ad. Claiming that this African family did not exist completely overlooked the fact that the general narrative of separation and reunion is a universal Canadian story (including the Aboriginal story). The ad was communicating that universal reality when a young woman (of a different ethnic appearance) looked over at the scene and smiled. She was a passing stranger, yet she immediately recognized what was going on, and she appreciated its profound emotional significance. Moreover, the media's focus on veracity overlooked the real social and political statement this ad was making, which was, Tim Hortons's claim to be the primary and essential signifier of Canada. This family's reunion was bittersweet because they had left Africa behind and were entering Canada as strangers. This idea was emphasized as the family walked out of the airport and was assaulted by snow and wind. The significance of the coffee as comfort could now begin to take hold for them.

In November 2008, Tim Hortons launched an interactive website, 'Every Cup Tells a Story.' In less than two years the website received more than 5,000 stories (as well as comments on and rankings of the postings). The company stated that it had launched the website in part to funnel the letters and photos being sent to them (Tim Hortons 2008). In keeping with the 'True Stories' campaign, 'Every Cup Tells a Story' encouraged customers to locate meaning in every activity associated with Tim Hortons. More important, it encouraged them to link Tim Hortons to everyday activities, from the most mundane to the most vital. The campaign took advantage of communication technologies that allowed customers to send photos and narratives directly to Tim Hortons. Many photos included babies and animals with Tim Hortons cups, brides and grooms drinking Tim Hortons in their wedding attire, marriage proposals, soldiers and tourists in foreign countries, new mothers in hospital beds, and people engaging in a host of community, sports, and family activities. Almost all the photographers were careful to capture the Tim Hortons cup in their frame (which itself says interesting things about the rituals of photography, memory, and commercialism). This product placement in the everyday experiences of Canadians was a testament to the place that Tim Hortons occupies in the Canadian consciousness. The accompanying stories also featured the cup of coffee (sometimes other beverages) as central to the activity discussed. One such story was told by a husband, who explained that being present for his wife's Caesarian section was traumatic until he saw a nurse with a cup of Tim Hortons coffee. According to his account, the sight of the cup calmed him immediately: 'That cup of coffee was a touch-point,' he wrote, 'a known, good thing in a room of the unknown' (Tim Hortons 2009).

Many of the stories that invoked fear and risk – including those of sending loved ones into military action or serious medical procedures – suggested that consuming Tim Hortons products in the final moments of separation served as a kind of good luck charm. Other stories directly embraced death and mourning. For example, one customer told about the death of her husband and featured a photo of her young daughter at Tim Hortons. The writer explained that she now had little time to spend with her daughter because she had to work long hours, but that their Saturday morning trips to Tim Hortons were a comfort. It would be hard to imagine this story being turned into a 'True Stories' commercial, for such commercials require careful scripting, direction, and design. When stories come 'directly' from customers, the risk to Tim Hortons is minimized. Every Cup stories seem more neutral than True Stories. Why run these personal stories through the Tim Hortons website? Apparently, the company's products and institutional status provide meaning to customers' lives, not just the opportunity to communicate with others.

Tim Hortons narratives have also become popular for the promotion and celebration of military life. Here is a short excerpt from the story told by a woman working at the Kandahar Tim Hortons and posted on a website in support of the 'buy a cup for a soldier' campaign:

> My alarm goes off just before 5 a.m. I pull on my bathrobe, pad down the hallway and open the plywood door to a gravel road and a line of large rounded tents surrounded by concrete highway dividers. The sun is already up, and hundreds of birds have congregated in the few trees to bid the morning welcome with their cheerful chatter. It is almost cool, but the promise of 50-degree heat hangs in the air. (J. Jones 2009)

The long, detailed narrative goes on to describe the Kandahar Tim Hortons and its customers (whose nationalities are revealed in their food tastes and ways of placing their orders). This is followed by an account of the storyteller's first air raid. The story ends with the description of a 'ramp ceremony,' the ritual of returning the dead home by plane, which includes Tim Hortons personnel in the ranks of mourners. At the end of this story, the author describes the sombre mood back at the Tim Hortons as the surviving comrades come in for coffee. Here we have come full circle from the troops requesting a Tim Hortons in Kandahar to the Kandahar Tim Hortons becoming the centre of troop narratives and rites of passage.

The True Stories / Every Cup campaigns are clichéd and mundane; their appeal lies in their familiarity. In a sense, all childbirth and wedding stories share the same range of emotions. They are rites of passage that deserve telling by virtue of the teller's having survived to tell the story. Like all narratives, these are stories of endurance and survival. Hence, old Lillian from the first 'True Story' is the archetype of the *storyteller*, not of the hill climber. It is, however, interesting that so many Canadians would turn to Tim Hortons to satisfy their need to tell their stories. What has happened to other outlets for personal and collective narrative? As we have discussed, Tim Hortons has taken decades to situate itself as the place to tell stories. Tim Hortons has been able to occupy a cultural space left open by Canada's *official* storytellers (i.e., agents of statist nation-building policies). It has then played up the social and emotional importance of storytelling at its grassroots and intergenerational levels. It has worked pain, fear, and ambivalence into these stories, but also collective national pride.

Conclusion

Returning to this book's theme, 'desiring Canada,' one might argue that the ability of Tim Hortons to become a site of national narrative and political enactment speaks to this country's ongoing crisis of identity. After all, what kind of community turns to a coffee shop for meaning? While this 'crisis' talk has become an industry and a site of pleasure in itself, there must be more at work here than the futile effort to fill up the bottomless hole of national identity. Keohane hints at an answer in the passage that we used to open this chapter: 'The "way of life" of an ethnic group, a community, or a nation takes the form of an articulated constellation of bits of enjoyment.'

Folklorists and anthropologists have long observed that a group's seemingly ordinary and mundane practices are filled with collective meaning. In *Baking as Biography*, an ethnographic discussion of the history of women's baking as service to community, Tye (2010) describes the ritual and daily work of churchwomen in rural Atlantic Canada, who built and sustained their communities by baking for family, neighbours, visitors, church teas, fundraisers, funerals, and so forth. In this chronicle of largely unrecognized work, Tye demonstrates how tea, coffee, sweets, and their consumption and production have contributed to making community. These activities affirm relationships, welcome strangers, and help mourn the dead. Tim Hortons has extended these localized rituals and their meaning to the national community, maintaining the same resonances. Tye also describes how beginning in the 1950s and 1960s these women included new, processed products in their baking, to the extent that some recipes involved little more than mixing these products. Most of the recipes that Tye found in these women's repertoires had not been handed down from their mothers; rather, they were new, modern, and convenient. Nevertheless, the mystique of home cooking, motherly love, and community care was still associated with these treats. Similarly, Tim Hortons initially employed a baker in every shop but now par-bakes its products and ships them to outlets for baking, with little apparent loss of mystique. Here, again, we find a counterpoint to the more official management of Canadian desire that was discussed in chapter 1: bureaucratic administration thwarting pleasure and identity by way of top-down management. The notions of the local and the particular and of manifest labour are important to a community's pleasure and identity.

But Tim Hortons is not so much about methods of baking as it is about methods of marketing. We have seen that their marketing strategies boldly offer up collective values that resonate with and against more official notions Canada. They offer a complexity and texture to the national experience that customers are able to recognize and enjoy. This, however, raises the question of why so many agents of state and government have aligned themselves with the company if their message is ambiguous and painful, pro- and anti-official. One answer is simply that of populism. Regardless of the ambiguities surrounding national identity, Tim Hortons has succeeded in representing the Canadian every-person. Politicians in countries like Canada struggle to show themselves as non-elitist and in touch with the concerns of ordinary citizens. This certainly seems true when one observes their eagerness to align themselves with the coffee chain during election campaigns. But there is another, more important answer – agents of state and government may recognize a cultural merging of citizen and consumer.

At the same time as the consumer has become the citizen at Tim Hortons, the citizen has become the consumer in the hands of political marketing strategists. This involves more than selling a party and its policies to the electorate. Analysts of political marketing make the case that marketing should be distinguished from the older strategy of selling: 'In politics, as in business, marketing is what happens when the product shapes itself around the consumers' demands – often before it even hits the sales floor or the ad campaign. It's the attempt to give the people what they want, sometimes before they know they want it' (Delacourt and Marland 2009, 47). Political parties and their candidates now approach the citizen by way of the most sophisticated of marketing strategies, even locating their constituents through their consumer practices (Ibid.). In some cases, this marketing orientation lasts beyond the election to become the foundation of governance itself. Richard Nimijean (2006) contends that Canada has become a 'brand state' in that political parties offer packaged images of Canada for both international and domestic consumption. In terms of the latter, national pride and apparent national values are played up towards particular political ends. The editors of *Political Marketing in Canada* ask whether the frequent indications by opinion polls that Canadians distrust the political elite and suffer from a political 'malaise' may be tied to this conflation of politics with marketing (Giasson et al. 2012). Political scientist Reg Whitaker (2001) contends that this marketing orientation towards the 'needs and wants' of citizens undermines politics as the deliberative and careful consideration of party policy. For Whitaker, what once involved party loyalty and membership within a broad ideological commitment has now become simply the attempt to satisfy, and cultivate, the immediate and capricious desires and sentiments of the electorate.

This conflation of consumer and citizen helps explain why Tim Hortons could become a type of public sphere for the enactment of political life. Tim Hortons is not just a site for the enactment of Canadian politics; it is also the *model* for it. Hannah Arendt's (1958) and Jurgen Habermas's (1989) comments on public life and the public sphere are relevant here. For Arendt, this seepage of personal desires into the public world threatens to allow private need to become confused with its opposite – the public good. This line between private and public, for Arendt, must be guarded in any democratic society because private life and public life serve diverse ends. Public life becomes degraded, semi-human, when it is deprived of the conflict and challenge of public debate, during which one must stake a position and defend it openly and coherently. Habermas's version of the public sphere is less antagonistic than Arendt's, but he similarly argues that issues of common good must arise within an ideal speech environment in which citizens can debate and decide issues of common good, outside both state and commercial interests.

Clearly, the rise of the consumer-citizen has implications beyond the effects it has on politicians and their party machines. As we have seen, consumption can become the focus of governance and state authority. In the following chapters of this book, the state itself is considered in terms of its relationship to consumptive pleasures – hockey violence, monopolized gambling, and CBC comedy. In each case we find a particular version of citizenship being offered to Canadians by way of their consumptive pleasures.

3

'Our Game': Hockey, Civilizing Projects, and Domestic Violence

True play knows no propaganda; its aim is in itself, and its familiar spirit is happy inspiration.

Johan Huizinga (1955)

At what point does the state have a place in the rinks of the nation?

Stephen Brunt (2009)

I'm trying to keep this country together. I'm the fucking glue that holds it together.

– Don Cherry, quoted in Pevere and Dymond (1996)

In this chapter, we discuss hockey in terms of its place in nationalist-statist projects and its relation to ongoing processes and negotiations of Canadian identity that involve issues of power, social conflict, and the role of the mass media. For hockey to have become the symbol it is purported to be has required a shift from the community arena to the national one – a development in which the mass media, especially the CBC, itself a national symbol, has played a central role (Gruneau and Whitson 1993, 252). If modern Canada is less unified than it once was – if it lacks a collective narrative – we can nevertheless consider the symbolic significance of hockey in the Canadian imaginary and how it continues to feature in conceptions of identity.

Hockey in Canada has much to do with national identity and pleasure. But what does hockey have to do with the state? After all, isn't hockey a natural expression of Canadian culture? Hockey is a popular pleasure, played by many Canadians for the sensual experiences of skating and shooting, checking and hitting, passing and scoring, winning and losing, and, for some, fighting. And many find pleasure in *watching* hockey for its displays of speed, skill, and aggression, as well as for the opportunity to share in the glories and defeats of a particular team. For generations, cultural commentators have treated hockey 'as if it represents an organic connection with the Canadian landscape or national psyche' (Ibid., 25). This assertion points to a desire on the part of many who speak about Canada to link hockey, naturally and inevitably, to place and 'people.' It is part of tradition, made famous by writers like Northrop Frye (1982), who assert that a 'Canadian mind' exists that is rooted in the land and its climes.

The naturalization of hockey and its links to national sentiment have allowed the state to represent itself within the cultural arena of hockey and thereby make use of its violence. In this unique arena, the citizen is domesticated (or civilized) yet at the same time taught that violence, both symbolic and real, is inevitably part of the sport.

If hockey is not the triumph of culture over nature, it nevertheless seems to fill a need for play and entertainment in the face of unfriendly winters, aided over time by the building of indoor arenas. Michael McKinley (2000) suggests that the move from frozen ponds to covered arenas created the conditions for hockey to become a spectacle, which, as this chapter discusses, has had great significance for the ongoing development of Canadian cultural and national identity. Spectacles are ways of organizing people around an event or image (Debord 1983, 2). As Robidoux (2001, 73) comments, professional hockey games are 'sentimental spectacles' that speak more about the audience than about what is happening on the ice.

This chapter examines hockey – particularly the mediated spectacle of professional hockey – as a social relation between the 'people' and the state. However much modern collectivities are characterized by difference and conflict – ethnic, religious, cultural, gendered, political, ideological, moral – hockey, as much as anything else in Canada, has a totemic status. In his analysis of totemism, Émile Durkheim ([1895]1965) considered the ways in which objects in the natural environment came to take on transcendent and supernatural power for early social groupings. Such groups were surrounded by hostile natural forces, and their need to survive them came to have not just collective significance but power over the group itself. A look at the names of hockey teams at any level reveals classic totemic references from nature – animals, plants, weather. For Durkheim, totemism was the simplest form of religion, and the totem expressed and symbolized the group's identity. In this context, a Citizenship and Immigration Canada / Dominion Institute survey of the things, people, events, places, and symbols that were most definitive of Canada found that 'hockey' was the second most common response, sandwiched between two symbols of state – the Maple Leaf (#1) and the Canadian flag (#3) (Ipsos Reid 2009).

Durkheim also wrote that all societies create 'bonds of sympathy' that make social life possible. This idea applies not only to smaller groups such as sports teams but also to larger groups such as nations. This social altruism helps us understand the sacrifices made for the team, as well as for national pride. It also helps us understand how cultural activities are defended as expressions of collective identity. For example, it is often claimed that hockey belongs to Canada or that there is an Anglo-Canadian style of play. This idea of symbolic sacrifice will loom large when we consider hockey as a site of violence.

Contemporary academic writers on the cultural significance of sport have expressed views that reveal affinities to Durkheim's insights. Michael Novak (1976), for example, considers sport to be a form of secular religion. Historically, sporting events like the Olympic Games have expressed both religious impulses and statist interests, such as the pursuit of glory and honour. Sports events themselves are organized and dramatized in a religious way. For Novak, they are 'natural religions': 'sports flow outward into action from a deep natural impulse that is radically religious' (251). They are thus capable of engendering a civil religion, including emotional and violent responses on the part of believers. In Canada, the most famous example of this type of response was the 1955 riot in Montreal that followed the suspension of Montreal Canadiens star Maurice Richard. That riot was a demonstration of the Canadiens' fervent French Canadian following and of Richard's god-like status and has been interpreted as signifying the cultural conflicts between Quebec and English Canada.

It can rightly be said that Quebec has its own national identity, and that province's love for the Canadiens is part of Canadian hockey lore. It seems evident here that 'civil religions' exist in Canada and that they continue to confront each other across an English – French abyss. Don Cherry, who unreflectively equates hockey with English Canada, manages to conflate Quebecois players with European players, who, for various questionable reasons, are suspect in their approach to how hockey should be played, and are thus, covertly, suspect in their enactment of masculinity.

Among English Canadians, an enduring Quebec hockey narrative is Roch Carrier's 'The Hockey Sweater' (1979), which tells the story of a pre-politicized rural Quebec, isolated by language (his mother's English is so rudimentary that she somehow orders a Toronto Maple Leaf sweater, to the horror of her son), religion (the priest is the hockey coach), and wealth (the offending sweater cannot be returned because the mother does not want to face writing another letter in English to 'Monsieur Eaton,' and the sweater cannot be wasted). While on one level this story speaks to the universal fear of being ostracized – all the other boys on the team have Maurice Richard's number on a Canadiens sweater – it also speaks to a non-threatening and impotent population.

In an essay that looks at the Montreal Forum's closing ceremonies, Robert Dennis (2009) discusses the political climate in Quebec at the time. In 1996, Molson, the owner of the Canadiens, was moving the team from the Forum to the new Molson Centre. This was after the second sovereignty referendum, which had been held the previous year and which was still fresh in the minds of Quebeckers. Dennis's account demonstrates the cultural significance of the Montreal Forum to Quebeckers: it was more than a hockey arena; it was also a cultural forum for transforming Quebec society from a Roman Catholic–dominated culture into a secular and commercialized society (the latter values embodied in the new Molson Centre). In changing the team's venue, Molson had to transfer the Forum's cultural significance to the new location. (Some of the seats from the Forum would be incorporated into the multi-use entertainment complex later built where the Forum had stood.) In accomplishing this transfer, Molson had to celebrate the great tradition of the Canadiens and also had to frame the Forum's cultural significance in ways that would not offend the province's voters. It seems that Molson succeeded in shifting the team to the new venue without stimulating negative post-referendum sentiments. Even so, the persistence of political conflict was demonstrated in *Le fantôme du Forum,* a TV docudrama that aired on Radio-Canada, whose subject was historical events that had taken place in the Montreal Forum. In one segment of this miniseries – a fictional one – a francophone industrial worker longs to see Maurice Richard score his 500th NHL goal at the Forum. He begs for time off from his anglophone boss but is refused. Finally, the employee is able to leave, but while descending from the bus he has taken to the Forum, he is struck by a car. He stumbles into the arena's lobby in time to hear the announcement that the Rocket has scored his 500th goal. And then he dies. The employee becomes a Forum ghost.

Dennis connects the Montreal Forum directly to religion, noting that the Forum held many Catholic events up until the 1960s. But he also shows the Forum's importance for Quebeckers' cultural and political identity. The Forum was a central public space where Quebec's transformation into a secular–democratic society was played out. It 'provided a forum for identity and solidarity suggestive of the will to make foundational changes to the nation-state' (166). We suggest that while the Forum was an important cultural site for Quebeckers to negotiate their identity, the transformation of hockey into a spectacle and symbol for Canada as a whole was a consequence of mass mediation, particularly at the hands of the CBC.

Roy MacGregor, who has written extensively on the place of hockey in Canadian culture (as both a novelist and a journalist), has suggested that 'so dominant is hockey in the national conscience' that to consider it as the 'national religion is to underestimate its reach' (2011a). The emotional response to Canada's Olympic hockey victory over the United States in 2010 testifies to this secular–religious expression. Furthermore, particular individuals may gain iconic status as a result of their deeds on the ice (e.g., Paul Henderson in 1972, Sidney Crosby in 2010), and even objects related to important games can become fetishes. Most obviously, the Stanley Cup is a sacred object, the ritual pursuit of which begins with each new NHL season. Another example: the puck that slid into the Americans' net in the 2010 victory was quickly sacralized by being placed in the Hockey Hall of Fame.

Modern democracies have been built on the separation of Church and State. Yet these states' relationships to secular religions – including, in Canada, hockey – cannot be viewed as separate, for states are using sports explicitly for nation building and to foster solidarity and national pride. These objectives have been made explicit in the 'mandate and mission' of the state-run Hockey Canada program, which oversees amateur and international hockey. Hockey Canada believes

- in the promotion of teamwork, and the belief that what groups and society can achieve as a whole is greater than that which can be achieved by individuals.
- in the country of Canada, its tradition in the game of hockey, and the proud and successful representation of this tradition around the world. (Hockey Canada 2009)

Sports sociologists Gruneau and Whitson (1993, 25) have warned against essentializing hockey in the Canadian imaginary without due consideration of the influences of social structure and history. It is thus necessary to examine the social processes and institutional interests that have contributed to and are maintaining the game's totemic status, as well as the game's definitional framing and the uses to which it is put.

'The Game' as Ken Dryden (1983) referred to hockey in the title of his iconic book, as a *game*, is enjoyed for the pleasure it gives in itself, like other forms of play. While the object of the game is to defeat an opponent, utilitarian objectives are external to the playing – that is, the pleasure is in the *playing*. Stakes and a desire to win are features of all contests, but this does not equate with utilitarianism. Utilitarianism is added when the game becomes an organized sport, a professional sport, a commercialized sport, and an object of state interest. In short, as with other forms of play, the commercialization and bureaucratization of the game are at odds with its spirit. While this may sound idealistic, we are merely contrasting the phenomenological features of play with the kinds of interests that are not intrinsic to it (Gadamer 1986). This is not to attribute 'purity' to hockey in its amateur and communal expressions, for hockey has been put to many uses by both community and commercial interests throughout its history (Gruneau and Whitson 1993).

Nevertheless, the joy of play and the experiences that accompany it allow us to understand the relationship of play to culture. On one level, we can observe the particular forms of play (and of games) that are valued and ritually celebrated by a particular culture. We can begin to grasp the pleasure offered by this play and the reasons why a culture might take its forms of play seriously. We can look at the collective organization of play (culture) and understand how it could come to express deep collective feelings: the play shapes and expresses an identity, which is dramatized and reinforced by victory over an opponent. The 'religious' aspect of sport noted by Novak is buttressed by its agonistic structure. Sports institutionalize division, an us-versus-them relationship that ritually celebrates the dramas of struggle and character, individual and collective. To the victor go the spoils of honour and esteem.

Play has been taken to represent a broad civilizing value, no less important than apparently more serious matters. Religions and wars are themselves rooted in the spirit of play, and so is civilization itself. As Huizinga (1955) expresses it, play is a condition of being *homo ludens* – 'man the player.' Sporting contests between groups, though agonistic and capable of generating strong collective emotions, are vivid demonstrations of the principle of play. Nation-states orient themselves towards sporting contests such as the Olympics, hoping to reap international honours thereby, and as a consequence, the quest for athletic supremacy becomes an instrumental project, one that subjects the spirit of play and competition to quantitative measures such as medal counts. Hockey in Canada is taken seriously as an expression of culture and is a source of identification and pride: 'our game.' For that reason, we must examine how hockey enables the state to dress itself in the robes of pleasure and identity. In this chapter, we look at hockey through the two lenses of cultural practices and state interests and analyse state–culture dynamics.

Hockey books are among the stronger sellers for Canadian publishers. Some books celebrate the game's appeal in fictional form,[1] while others analyse its place in Canadian culture. The former include Roch Carrier's 'The Hockey Sweater'; the latter, David Adams Richards's memoir *Hockey Dreams*, Ken Dryden's *The Game*, Andrew Podnieks's *A Canadian Saturday Night*, Alan Brunt's *Searching for Bobby Orr*, and Bruce Dowbiggin's *The Meaning of Puck*. Academic analyses include Richard Gruneau and David Whitson's *Hockey Night in Canada* and their edited collection *Artificial Ice: Hockey, Culture, and Commerce*, and Andrew C. Holman's edited collection, *Canada's Game: Hockey and Identity*. Add to this list the countless hockey biographies, hockey history books, and statistics-oriented compendiums that show up on bookstore shelves before Christmas every year.

The importance of hockey in Canada, like that of soccer and other sports in other nations, points to how sport can generate strong collective emotions and nationalistic fervour in ways that only the most charismatic politicians and intense political movements can match. Dowbiggin (2008) has even argued that modern Canada (outside Quebec) 'has largely had no compelling backdrop since Paul Henderson's goal against which to frame its identity or art' (71). Brian Kennedy (2009), in his discussion of the 1972 Summit Series between Canada and the Soviet Union, remarks that 'the events of September 1972 helped to create the Canada of today through giving a generation of people a touchstone moment with which to mark their participation in a shared culture.' But he goes on to question the value of the series 'in an era of increasingly multicultural Canada – that is, a Canada that is not what it was in 1972 but, rather, is increasingly populated by people for whom neither the series nor hockey has any cultural resonance' (45). This claim that Canada lacks an identity has become institutionalized, which in turn has produced various responses, such as discussions of a national-cultural crisis and calls for a post-nationalist state (Saul 1998). As we discussed in chapter 2, Tim Hortons has successfully branded itself by exploiting this gap in collective identity through its symbolic and narrative uses of Canadianness.

Multiculturalism is one possible identifier of modern Canada, except that it poses the problem of how diversity can be construed as a unity. If we are a multicultural country, who, then, are *we*? Canada's official multiculturalism suggests one way in which a contemporary state in a globalizing world can manage cultural and ethnic diversity. Put differently, official multiculturalism is a way for the state to govern such diversity, though it doesn't tell us how the state can still somehow encourage national unity or identification. In Canada, hockey is treated as a national symbol, and Citizenship and Immigration Canada encourages immigrants to recognize and become familiar with this symbol of Canadianness (Canada 2010a). Recent surveys indicate that some immigrant groups, such as Lebanese and Italians, are big fans of professional hockey. In a newspaper article discussing this phenomenon, one woman who came to this country as a child commented that in Montreal 'you are either a fan, or you are an outcast' (Friesen and Perreaux 2010).

How does hockey figure in the ongoing life of Canada in terms of state and nationhood, cultural identity, and everyday life? And how are these issues being shaped by the pressures of consumerism, multiculturalism, and globalization? These issues, too, can be discussed in terms of hockey's importance in Canadian life. Gruneau and Whitson (1993) discuss the changes that took place in Canadian society after the postwar boom, which lasted until the early 1970s; these changes included shifts in gender relations, the rise of identity politics, and the increasing importance of cities at the expense of the hinterland. Dowbiggin (2008) reiterates this argument, suggesting that the 1972 Canada–Russia series marked the end of a certain conception of Canada. He sees in hockey – Canada's 'sacred trust' – an acting out of larger societal dramas. While the idea of hockey as a microcosm of Canadian society is not new, and there are risks to overstating its explanatory power, some aspects of the sport nevertheless have a strong bearing on broader social issues.

Canada has changed a great deal since the early 1970s, as has the game itself. Canadians, especially in the big cities, have opened themselves to multiculturalism. With changing gender relations and the rise of identity politics and consumer culture, traditional conceptions of authority (patriarchal, white, male, religious) are being challenged. These developments have had effects on hockey and indeed on Canadian society in general. In their sociological analysis of Canadian hockey, Gruneau and Whitson (1993) pointed to the significance of changing gender relations for traditionalist orientations to hockey, which viewed the game as an arena for an aggressive masculinity.

One of the more visible public issues related to hockey is the persistence of violence in the game, including dangerous forms of body checking and headshots. Another such issue is the place of fighting – hockey is the only professional sport where it is tolerated. The theme of violence thus lends itself to our discussion, especially given that the violence that is allowed in hockey seems to run directly counter to other conceptions of Canadian cultural and national identity. As will be discussed, violence is pertinent for a consideration of the positioning of the state within the dynamics of identity and pleasure.

It is important to mention here the significance of the CBC-produced TV series *Hockey: A People's History*, and the book (McKinley 2006) that accompanied it (and whose back cover blurb declares it to be '*the* book on the game'). For the series, the CBC gathered together various figures, events, and other historically significant aspects of hockey to produce 'a people's history' – in effect, it used hockey for nation-building purposes. There was little mention of the CBC in the book itself, though the corporation's logo appeared on the front cover and its pages sometimes referred to important episodes of *Hockey Night In Canada* (*HNIC*). The series' significance for our purposes is that the cultural importance of hockey for the 'people' was being developed and promoted by the state through the CBC and its nation-building mandate. Thus the state was naturalizing its role in making the 'people,' even while obscuring its presence in that project.

The state's desire to build a nation, a 'people,' becomes more visible when we examine the institutional work involved. This is not to devalue local enthusiasms, or locales where 'hockey is bred in the bone' – there is no doubt that community fervour for hockey goes back to the game's beginnings (Gruneau and Whitson 1993). Our point here, rather, is that the dialogical relationship between community and local culture, on the one hand, and the interests of the nation-state (and national culture), on the other, are worth examining. *HNIC* telecasts have long appealed to individual communities, most of which have native sons who play(ed) professionally, and who are interviewed between periods. But at the same time as it reflects these local interests, the CBC is constructing a national community through its broadcasts, thereby merging the communal and the national within a mass-mediated frame.

Hockey in Canada thus provides an occasion for analysing the ways in which the state uses cultural activities for purposes of nation building. Cultural and national identity is being built, and the most important institution mediating this relationship has been the CBC, the broadcasting arm of the Canadian state. That hockey is an expression of Canadian culture and a symbol of Canadianness (or of Québécoisness) is something many Canadians take for granted, though explicit tensions, and potential identity crises, have threatened to disrupt the significance and status of the game.

In the past these tensions had to do with the supposed threat posed by Americanization and commercialization, which to worried Canadian nationalists were interchangeable terms. The claim was that American business interests were a threat to how Canadians related to and played the game (Kidd and Macfarlane 1972). This perception was consistent with the Canadian cultural nationalism of the day, as encountered also in the fears expressed by Canadian artists, writers, and intellectuals that American imperialism was having a negative impact on Canadian cultural identity (Edwardson 2008). Perhaps more significant for the collective well-being were the rising challenges to Canadians' self-proclaimed hockey 'supremacy' – challenges that included the 1972 Canada–USSR showdown, the 'Summit on Ice.' That series was more than a bitterly fought sports event; it was framed politically, and it touched on nation-state conflicts – most obviously capitalism versus communism and Canada's threatened status as a superpower in its own game. Prime Minister Pierre Trudeau saw the 1972 series as an opportunity to open dialogue with the Soviets as well as to unite Canada after the October Crisis in Quebec (McKinley 2006). (It is notable that despite all this baggage, the games were televised not on the CBC but on its rival network, CTV.)

Hockey ethnocentrism prevented the Canadian side from taking the Russian team seriously at first. For example, the Canadians failed to see the point of some of the Soviets' pre-game drills, viewing them as 'merely technical and quite automatic' and as representing an inferior collectivist approach (Kennedy 2009, 50). The Soviet team was not taken seriously until it beat the Canadians handily (7 to 3) in the first match, played in Montreal. The emotionally intense series would come down to the eighth and final game, which Canada won with Paul Henderson's now-iconic last-minute goal. That victory ended a long and humiliating international hockey drought for Canada (McKinley 2006; Kennedy 2009). The CBC's *HNIC* website stated in 2011 that 'Sidney Crosby may have the golden goal, but Paul Henderson will always have Canada's greatest goal.'

The 1972 Hockey Summit, played five years after Canada's Centennial celebrations, can be regarded as a coming-out party for Canadian national sporting pride. Canada could boast about being the best in the world in hockey. It was also an important moment in the development of Canadian identity. Besides being a touchstone moment, the encounter with the (Soviet) 'other' produced an awareness of identity that has become part of Canadianness and has been enshrined in Canada's hockey memory (Kennedy 2009). However, as Kennedy argues, a much-changed, post-1972 Canada must deal with the 'other' in more complex ways. Multiculturalism posed a challenge to unitary conceptions of identity and made it uncertain that hockey would continue to have the cultural resonance (i.e., among new Canadians).

Tensions around Canadian hockey identity were also created by the influx of European players into the NHL (e.g., Borje Salming and Inge Hammarstrom of the Toronto Maple Leafs), which began in the early 1970s with league expansion. Salming now enjoys legendary status among Leafs fans, a testimony to the 'multiculturalization' of the game but also based on his excellence as a long-serving Leaf defenceman. In the early days, however, Salming's foreignness generated taunts and threats from opposing players (especially Philadelphia's 'Broad Street Bullies') as well as scepticism from his Leaf teammates (Salming 2007). Significantly, the early influx of these players coincided with the worst days of 'goon' hockey. That style of play was a consequence of the NHL's expansion, which had diluted the pool of talented players, encouraging a more aggressive physical style of play by many teams to counter the more established teams, which had more skilled players. The era of the Big Bad Bruins and the Broad Street Bullies was known for its flagrant on-ice intimidation tactics and bench-clearing brawls.

As the NHL recruited more and more European players, arch-Canadian hockey nationalist Don Cherry expressed his dismay. Foreign players who avoided physical confrontations came to be known as 'chicken Swedes.' Canadians became aware that their game was different – that it was much more physical and that it included fighting. This was evident during the Summit Series, which the Canadians won in part because Bobby Clarke (one of the Broad Street Bullies) inflicted a vicious slash on the Russian star Valeri Kharlamov, fracturing his ankle and eliminating him from the seventh game. The high emotions during that series made it clear how seriously many Canadians took their hockey. Indeed, Clarke's deviance – anathema to good sportsmanship – could be viewed as an act of sacrifice for the greater good: Canadian national self-esteem. The Canadians' dirty play generated opposing views: some decried it, while others supported the win-at-any-cost tactics (McKinley 2006). John Ferguson, an assistant coach for Team Canada, had encouraged Clarke to take aggressive action against Kharlamov. Sociologists would refer to such actions as 'deviant overconformity,' referring here to the ways in which individuals overconform to the sports ethic as a demonstration of their commitment. This overconformity suits the institutional structure of hockey and allows some players to obtain jobs up the institutional ladder (Coakley and Donnelly 2004). Ferguson had been regarded as the league's heavyweight champ during his years playing for Montreal in the 1960s; after his playing days, he would become a coach and general manager in the NHL. Clarke went on to become Philadelphia's general manager.

Responding to those who disliked Canada's violent play, Ferguson said: 'Hell, these guys can't know much about the game . . . That's the way it's been played for the past fifty years, and that's the way it'll be played for another fifty. Has hockey ever been anything else but a street game? After a century, we're going to change it to suit the fine arts crowd?' (McKinley 2006, 217). Ferguson's comments reflect the famous dictum of Maple Leafs owner Conn Smythe: 'If you can't beat'em in the alley, you can't beat'em on the ice.' Comments like these point to conflicts of culture and class with regard to Canadian orientations to hockey. While the implication is that the 'fine arts' crowd is ignorant of hockey, the framing is extreme and sarcastic – perhaps a dig at this crowd's softness. Besides assuming a split between high culture and popular culture, opinions like these leave out the possibility that other Canadians, including middle- and working-class Canadians, might well object to violence in hockey. These conflicts of Canadianness continue in the open. For example, Don Cherry champions aggressive hockey and fighting and expresses disdain for groups that disagree with him, including journalists, 'left wing pinkos,' and Dr Charles Tator, a neurosurgeon who has criticized Cherry's support of aggressive play because it contributes to player concussions. The CBC is uneasy with its relationship to Cherry. Too often for the corporation's liking, he does not represent the CBC's views, and he has been castigated for some of his comments. Nevertheless, as we discuss later in this chapter, Cherry continues to do important work for the CBC *and* the state.

Intimidation and violence persist in hockey. But broader societal changes seem to be exposing hockey violence for what it is – an institutional survival that the game does not need, whatever traditionalists might claim. Public concerns about hockey violence and (in particular) brain-damaging headshots have reached levels that are unprecedented in NHL history. Sidney's Crosby's concussion following a headshot in the 2010–11 season sharpened this debate quite suddenly. The NHL had never in the past taken concerted action with respect to rules that would reduce the incidence of concussions and other serious injuries (Cole 2011; MacGregor 2011b; Pearce 2011). This now seems to be changing: the league's new Vice-President of Player Safety and Operations, Brendan Shanahan (a former NHL star), has altered the rules governing headshots in order to reduce their presence in the game.

Fighting in the NHL seems a more stubborn problem. While fighting is part of the 'sentimental spectacle,' it has also clearly served utilitarian purposes in teams' quests for victories. Although the Philadelphia Flyers teams of the 1970s (the aforementioned 'Broad Street Bullies') were notorious for their intimidation tactics, it was perhaps the Montreal Canadiens who institutionalized bullying by calling up Ferguson, who had been a renowned pugilist in the American Hockey League. The Canadiens' management was concerned about how the team had been pushed around in the 1963 playoffs, so they brought Ferguson on board for the 1963–4 season, and the team won the Stanley Cups in the two seasons that followed. Ferguson's physically aggressive play was an important component of those victories (McKinley 2006, 195). This utilitarian approach to violence has since been institutionalized (Robidoux 2001). While players in the past had to defend themselves, since the 1970s teams have found it necessary to employ 'designated fighters' (Dryden 2011a). The persistence of violence in hockey requires discussion as a feature of mass entertainment and sports spectacles, of Canadian culture, and of male socialization processes.

We asked at the beginning of this chapter what hockey had to do with the state. Certainly, hockey is an expression of Canadian culture. But sports and violence also relate to the state and state formation, not just to culture. States themselves are cultural entities, developed and sustained within particular symbolic environments; they are subject to and take part in historical civilizing processes (Elias 1978). In our discussion here, we treat hockey as it pertains to state/culture dynamics: hockey is an expression of Canadian culture and at the same time is used by the state for nation-building purposes. Thus it is worth reflecting on hockey violence not only in relation to the game and attitudes toward it, but also in terms of state orientations and responses to it. It will be instructive to draw from sociological and cultural theory to consider these interrelationships.

In his ground-breaking work on the civilizing process, sociologist Norbert Elias (1978) discusses the historical and societal forces that link members of society to state formation. In doing so, he sheds light on how manners, habits, personalities, and attitudes are linked in their development and how these developments generate norms and constraints. Significantly, he argues that state development works through the micro or interactional level: the two levels are not separate. Civilizing processes engender 'habituses' – that is, structured habits and dispositions that come to characterize collectivities in particular historical and social contexts – and states are shaped by these same processes.

Elias also discusses how culture comes to designate self–other differences – that is, how it becomes a way for groups to self-consciously construct and enact a sense of identity. Culture, as it comes to signify a group's identity, becomes a way for groups to consciously differentiate themselves. In this chapter's context, hockey has helped foster Canadians' self-conscious orientation to identity, through claims of possession –the 'national game,' 'our game' – but also by signifying Canadianness. This is evident in the game's relationship to the environment – hockey as play/culture has developed in relation to climate and geography but also through formulations of national identity and character.

Elias has also written extensively about sport's relationship to civilizing processes. Sport is a mimetic activity that allows contests and aggression to take place, imitating warfare but in a way that regulates expressions of aggression and violence. Like other aspects of social life, sport and contests undergo civilizing processes and have assumed an important place in modern societies. As sports undergo these processes, physical violence and death become increasingly unacceptable features of them. Elias (1986) has coined the term 'sportization' to refer to the implementation and enforcement of rules, the increasing orderliness of games, and the emphasis on self-discipline rather than sheer physical force. Sportization is a feature of civilizing processes and allows for the regulated expression of aggressive emotions. The debates surrounding hockey violence and concerns about the concussions being inflicted by dangerous headshots reflect the ongoing sportization of hockey. The violence and injuries that have long been part of the game are being more closely scrutinized. The result is likely to be that new rules will be implemented to reduce unnecessary expressions of violence on the ice.

Elias views the 'quest for excitement' in sport and leisure as complementary to the overt control of emotionality in everyday life that is a consequence of civilizing processes. Sport provides excitement in 'unexciting societies' in which civilizing processes have restricted the venues for direct contestation. Sports provide an institutional outlet not only for

emotions but also for a 'socially approved arousal of moderate excitement behaviour in public' (1986, 65). The effects of civilizing processes
on sports and games relate to both participants and spectators. Sports
spectacles involve the expression of emotions; they allow for a controlled
decontrolling of emotions. Sport both produces and contains tensions
and is a mimetic activity – one that imitates real-life situations and that
provides safe forms of activity without risks.

Let us now contrast Elias's sport-excitement formulation with the critique of entertainment expressed through the 'bread and circuses' argument. One version of this argument is that circuses are ideological
(similar in meaning to Marx's adage that religion is 'the opium of the
people'). Put another way, circuses deflect people's gaze from social in-
equities, from organized forms of dominance and oppression, and from
the mechanisms whereby their daily bread is produced and distributed.
Another version is that the populace needs bread *and* circuses and that
sport responds to human social needs by organizing individual and collective emotions (Elias 1986). The controlled decontrolling of emotions
thus has relevance for state formation as well as for constructs of nationalist identity. We suggest here that hockey serves both versions of
the bread and circuses argument: it draws from and expresses collective
emotions, providing a genuine form of enjoyment for fans, while also
being used for statist projects.

In their sociological analysis of hockey in Canada, Gruneau and Whitson (1993) comment on the significance of Elias for an understanding ·
of modern sports; but they also caution against the 'quasi-evolutionary'
aspect of his work (193), pointing out that factors such as capitalism and
social conflicts must also be considered. Furthermore, when we draw
from the idea of civilizing processes, we are referring to sociological processes that include practices of social control but we do not assume that
these processes are necessarily good or desirable. Rather, our interest
lies in analysing the sociological processes that shape Canadian institutions, identities, and dispositions.

The concepts of civilizing process, habitus, and culture aid our understanding of the ways in which hockey figures as a cultural object in
Canada, and the ways in which the game relates, not only to members'
socialization, but also to state and national identity formation. Hockey is
symbolically significant for Canadian civilizing processes insofar as these
processes are marked by struggles to define Canadian nationhood and
identity. Furthermore, the relationship of sport to civilizing processes

helps us understand the place of and tolerance for violence in modern societies.

Civilizing Projects

Civilizing processes relate to historical projects of constructing Canada and its citizens. Social conflicts are a feature of those processes. The concept of civilizing processes is a useful one, not only because it points to broad cultural developments, but also because 'Canadianization' projects (such as the Massey Commission) have had an explicitly civilizing mission. This section examines how civilizing projects have been enacted by various institutional actors. Historical projects of Canadianization are thus civilizing projects insofar as their goal has been to produce and shape Canadian identity. An ongoing feature of these processes has been the notion that Canada's identity is distinct from that of the United States. In hockey, constructions of identity have taken place not only through international tournaments (including the Olympics), but also in terms of concerns about the commercialization – read 'Americanization' – of the game and the belief that hockey violence is something that *American* fans want (Dowbiggin 2008). Hockey has provided Canada with a *brand* – that is, with a cultural object that it can use internationally as a marker of its status and cultural identity.

Certainly the 1972 Summit Series mentioned earlier celebrated nationalistic differences through sports. The ongoing Olympic contests have long done the same thing. Medal counts in the Olympics have come to be a source of national pride (or embarrassment). If there were any lingering notions that the 2010 Winter Olympic Games in Canada were about the international celebration of athletic prowess, the push to 'own the podium' made it clear that the point was in fact to win as many medals for Canada as possible. Perhaps what was most significant about the Summit Series was that for Canadians, hockey represented a sacred value, a core identity that generated collective emotion. That hockey continues to hold this power is demonstrated by those people who decry the use of foreign players and who defend, if not essentialize, the style of play of good Canadian boys. This perspective is an institutional survival. Hockey is still ardently held to be 'our game' – by announcers on CBC hockey telecasts and by advertisers and Canadian writers – yet the game itself is international. In fact, the Summit Series can be regarded as a watershed event in the globalization of hockey, for other hockey 'cultures' became visible – certainly to Canadians, if not internationally – and foreign players began migrating to the NHL. As a result, it became important, from the point of view of defending 'our game,' that Canadian hockey be characterized by a particular style of play so that Canadians could claim they were guarding the essence of the game. A defence of violence thus became important to the defence of Canadianness.

A discussion of hockey allows for reflection not only on cultural and national identity, but also on violence, as hockey is the site of a particular kind of institutionalized Canadian violence. Violence is related to civilizing processes for particular nation-states. Put another way, attitudes towards, state responses to, and uses of violence are *socialized*. In Max Weber's terms, the state has a legitimate monopoly on the use of force (violence); but by the same token, states themselves embody dispositions towards violence that have been shaped by civilizing processes (Elias, 1978).

We can contextualize this understanding by examining differences between Canadian and American attitudes towards guns and gun ownership, and differences in terms of state uses of violence (such as capital punishment) against citizens. Violence as a cultural phenomenon is shaped in terms of collective dispositions through civilizing processes. In this regard, hockey violence is a marker of significant tensions confronting Canadian culture and identity, for such violence runs counter to our international reputation as peacekeepers, a reputation that is rapidly diminishing. The peacekeeping reputation has been eclipsed by the role of the Canadian military in Afghanistan and by the efforts of some high-ranking military officials, such as Rick Hillier, to transform Canada's orientation to the military. With respect to the military and other issues, Lawrence Martin, columnist for the *Globe and Mail*, discusses this rebranding of Canada under the Conservative government:

> Canada is [now] a country that venerates the military, boasts a hardened law-and-order and penal system, is anti-union and less green. It's a government that extols, without qualms of colonial linkage, the monarchy, that has a more restrictive entry policy, that takes a narrower view of multiculturalism, that pursues an adversarial approach to the United Nations. In a historical first, Canada's foreign policy, its strident partisanship in the Middle East being a foremost example, can be said to be to the right of the United States. (Martin 2011)

According to Martin, Canada is shifting from 'a country of Ken Dryden values to one closer to those of Don Cherry.'

Surveys by pollsters such as Michael Adams (2003) indicate that Canadians have become less deferential to authority over time. We suggest, however, that deference to authority persists in a statist desire. Peace, order, and good government have been inscribed as implicit ideals in Canadian society, and this has underpinned attitudes towards the state and its legitimate monopoly on the use of force. This is demonstrated in the symbolic threat the gun poses to Canadian society, in contrast to the United States, where many individuals feel it is their right to arm and protect themselves. There has been some resistance in Canada to gun control, mainly in rural regions where hunting is part of the culture (as evidenced by the debate over the long-gun registry), but this resistance does not signify the same culture of committed gun ownership found south of the border, where ownership is tied to political-cultural values of self-defence and to constitutional rights.

From a Canadian point of view, violence is the prerogative solely of the state, and individuals do not have the right to use it *against* the state. This is supported by opinion polls taken after the police response to protests at the G20 meeting in Toronto in 2010. According to those polls, about 73 per cent of Torontonians and 66 per cent of other Canadians felt that the arrest of hundreds of protesters and the use of rubber bullets and tear gas were appropriate in order to maintain order (Gillis 2010).

Returning specifically to hockey: in the wake of tragedies such as the broken neck suffered by NHL player Steve Moore and the death of junior player Don Sanderson in a hockey fight, debates concerning the place of fighting in 'our game' have intensified (Simpson 2009; MacGregor 2011c; Brady and Gordon 2011). Concerns about fighting are couched in terms of how hockey might change if violence were eradicated from it. (Would the game be radically changed for the better or worse? Would it appeal to Americans?) Those same concerns, however, also point to questions about how non-violent Canadians actually are, given that generally speaking, Canadians are not considered to be violent people. In this regard, it is worth reflecting on how the objectives of peace, order, and good government are achieved in Canadian society. This raises a question: What methods of governing are utilized in attempts to domesticate the population and insinuate the state into Canadian pleasure and versions of identity? Peace and order may be ideals in Canadian society, but they are not sacred in professional hockey, where violence has been institutionalized. (We point out that there is, however, the Lady Byng Memorial Trophy, awarded by the NHL to the player showing the most sportsmanship and gentlemanly conduct, i.e., for being the 'nicest guy on the ice.' Note the gender influence here, and the concern for 'gentlemanliness.' Also, the less well-known Bill Masterton Memorial Trophy is awarded to the player who best exemplifies the qualities of perseverance, sportsmanship, and dedication to hockey. That trophy is named after the only NHL player to die as a result of injuries sustained during an NHL game. In 1968, he had been knocked unconscious by a body check; he died two days later.)

With the Lady Byng trophy, named after the wife of a Canadian war hero, Lord Byng of Vimy, and the Stanley Cup (previously the Dominion Hockey Challenge Cup), named after Lord Stanley of Preston, the Governor General of Canada from 1888 to 1893, we see traces of how influential state representatives have embedded themselves in the development of Canadian hockey, and of how the state has formally intertwined itself with an important facet of Canadian culture. Perhaps, too, we see how hockey has become 'elevated' as a result of contact with state representatives.

There are other examples besides these of hockey, and hockey players, being sanctioned by the state apparatus. Lord Stanley during his tenure as Governor General built an ice rink outside Ottawa's Rideau Hall and helped popularize the game as a national pastime. Former Montreal Canadiens captain Jean Beliveau turned down an offer to be appointed Governor General in 1994. Frank Mahovlich, a star for the Toronto Maple Leafs and Montreal Canadiens during the 1960s and 1970s, was appointed to the Canadian Senate, where he continues to serve. Former Montreal Canadiens coach Jacques Demers has also been appointed to the Senate. Ken Dryden, a long-time goalie for Montreal, was a prominent Toronto Liberal MP until he lost his seat in the 2011 election. The Stanley Cup itself has been put to state use; for example, it toured Afghanistan twice, in 2007 and 2008, as a morale booster for the Canadian troops serving there, and came under missile attack during the first of those tours. In 2009, when the cup visited Nova Scotia, the home province of hockey superstar Sidney Crosby, as part of the Stanley Cup celebrations, Crosby was flown in to Halifax harbour by military helicopter, and hoisted the Cup on the deck of the warship HMCS *Preserver*. During that event, Crosby met members of the military and their families and expressed his wish to share the Cup with them (CBC 2009h). The jersey worn by the Winnipeg Jets features a fighter jet above a red Maple Leaf within a roundel. This was inspired by and pays homage to the Royal Canadian Air Force. When the jersey was unveiled, four Jets players walked down the ramp of a Hercules CF-18 jet at 17 Wing Winnipeg Canada Forces base. The historical relationship between hockey and the state continues, most noticeably on *HNIC* telecasts. But where Lady Byng had civilizing projects in mind with her trophy, CBC hockey broadcasts are a frame and a forum for civilizing-cultural conflicts, with the telecasts largely complicit in the culture of hockey violence.

The issue of concussions received strong media coverage during the 2010–11 season, and awareness is growing that some retired players are now suffering from brain trauma as a result of years of head hits from fights and checks (Cole 2011; Maki 2011). In 2008, the Center for the Study of Traumatic Encephalopathy at Boston University was established to study 'chronic traumatic encephalopathy, a degenerative brain disease caused by repeated head trauma' (Spencer 2011). A number of deceased National Football League players have had their brains analysed at that centre, and some high-profile NHL players have donated (or will donate) their brains to help medical science understand the implications of blows to the head. Those players include Bob Probert and Derek Boogaard (both deceased) as well as Keith Primeau and Kerry Goulet (retired). Boogaard was an active player with the New York Rangers and was, like Probert, an enforcer. He was living with the effects of a fighting-related concussion during his last NHL season, and was found dead at the age of twenty-eight in his apartment after the season ended. The medical examiner ruled that the cause of death was a mix of alcohol and oxycodone (a powerful painkiller) (Maki 2011).

The 2010–11 post-season was not kind to the NHL.[2] After Boogaard, two more players died – Rick Rypien and Wade Belak. Rypien was about to start a new assignment with the Winnipeg Jets. Belak had just retired from hockey and was set to start a career in hockey broadcasting. Both players were enforcers, and both were said to be dealing with depression. These deaths seem coincidental (Rypien and Belak were suicides); even so, they offer a significant glimpse into the dark side of pro hockey culture, where painkillers flourish and emotional and physical problems are hidden 'backstage' (Gordon and Maki 2011). Don Cherry's world view seems to come at a high cost, especially for those players he champions most, the tough guys and the fighters (Laraque 2011).

Scientific findings about brain trauma and the 'links between chronic pain and depression – and between depression, head injuries and acute stress' (Gordon and Maki 2011, S1) – will contribute to the sportization of hockey and other professional sports. Ken Dryden has weighed in on the issue, arguing that headshots should be eliminated and that future generations will regard today's tolerant attitude towards hockey violence as stupid (Dryden 2011b). But in the case of NHL hockey, the findings of science will have to contend with the traditionalists who celebrate aggressive play. Bruce Dowbiggin suggests that *HNIC* gave 'short shrift' to Boogaard's death. In discussing the responses of Cherry and his sidekick Ron MacLean to the topic, Dowbiggin (2011a) notes:

> Thankfully, Don Cherry – you can count on him for this, at least – had the decency to note Boogaard's passing and try to give some dignity to a player who did the dirtiest, most dangerous job in hockey. A moment MacLean did his best to diminish by noting that two of Boogaard's brothers were in law enforcement. MacLean then put on his grave look and said, 'Three great policemen in that family.'

While issues of ethnicity and gender have been thrashed out on *HNIC*, though not explicitly, in the interplay between Ron MacLean and Don Cherry and in panel discussions, changes to the culture of hockey violence have been slow, as the commentary on *HNIC* and persistence of fighting both attest.

Significantly, and in relation to values such as 'good sportsmanship,' social class enters into conceptions of hockey's place in Canadian culture, especially in relation to the persistence of violence. Dowbiggin (2008) distinguishes between what he takes to be the 'Tim Hortons' and the 'Starbucks' demographics in Canadian society, and relates these to differences between rural and urban Canadian life. Left out of his account is any explicit discussion of social class. In their sociological analysis, Gruneau and Whitson (1993) point to the ongoing importance of social class in discussions about hockey's appeal and about fighting in the game. The values of good sportsmanship are drawn from middle-class attitudes and relate to how sport has traditionally been seen as a builder of character. Good sportsmanship thus relates to explicit civilizing projects, whereas 'rough hockey celebrates a hard man's approach to life, which has a long tradition in the history of Western popular cultures and is particularly understood and appreciated among working class fans' (189).

Our discussion sees in hockey – and especially in the CBC's relationship with the NHL – another means to shape Canadian desire, that is, a vehicle for Canadian socialization. In doing so it points to the ways in which the state is implicated in civilizing processes, which include the socializing of emotions at the family, community, and national levels.

A number of books about hockey and socialization feature father–son relationships: Dryden's *The Game* (1983), Roy MacGregor's *The Home*

Team: Fathers, Sons, and Hockey (2002), Martin O'Malley's *Gross Misconduct: The Life of Spinner Spencer* (1988), Walter Gretzky's *On Family, Hockey and Healing* (2001), and Wayne Gretzky's *Gretzky: From Backyard Rink to the Stanley Cup* (1985). Films depicting hockey and father–son relationships include Atom Egoyan's film version of *Gross Misconduct* and the CBC film *Waking Up Wally: The Walter Gretzky Story*. The mass-mediated socialization of many boys into the 'national community' has included the ritual of *HNIC* telecasts, described by Gruneau and Whitson (1993, 1–7) in *Hockey Night in Canada*. We also note in this context Don Cherry's dispensation of hockey-playing wisdom 'to all you young kids out there' in episodes of 'Coach's Corner.' Certainly, the values of good sportsmanship and teamwork have been passed down from fathers to sons, and Wayne Gretzky, Mario Lemieux, and other players have openly criticized fighting in hockey. But traditional conceptions of masculinity are also passed down, and are collectively sustained in communal hockey settings, including minor hockey (192). After a string of 1970s-style violent outbursts during the 2010–11 NHL season, violence and dangerous play became serious issues for young players and their parents: one concern was 'whether allowing body-checking in youth hockey opens the door to NHL-style bad behaviour' (Pearce 2011, A16). The issue of socialization is thus important for considering themes such as hockey violence and the ways in which Canadian masculinity is performed.[3] How does violence relate to the issue of state–culture dynamics?

Representations of and concerns about violence in hockey can generally be considered in terms of Canadian civilizing processes – processes that are observable in CBC broadcasts. The CBC, as we have discussed in this book, plays a symbolic and administrative role in Canadian nation-building and civilizing projects. The corporation's support of fighting is evident in the signifiers that the CBC uses as lead-ins to *HNIC* telecasts. Those telecasts begin with Elton John's 'Saturday Night's Alright for Fighting,' sung by the popular, generic Canadian arena-rockers Nickelback. The accompanying visuals show checks and fights. During the game, fights are given camera coverage and Don Cherry's hockey fight videos are promoted:

It's in Canada don't forget, where the highest media priests who defend fighting reside. And not only in Canada, but on the CBC. As if Don Cherry were not already the country's leading cheerleader for fisticuffs, the CBC went out and hired the worst general manager in the past 20 years, Mike Milbury, as an 'analyst.' He quickly joined Mr. Cherry in trotting out the old

clichés about the indispensability of fighting as an outlet for aggression. He
then added his own denunciation of 'pansification' in hockey, for which he
had his knuckles rapped. (Simpson 2009, A19)

Simpson's comments remind us of the spokesmen the CBC has chosen
to represent hockey to Canadians. There is, admittedly, a countervailing
force in the person of *HNIC* host Ron MacLean, who regularly articulates
a middle-ground – one might say politically correct – perspective that is
more in keeping with the CBC's position as the state's socializing agent.
Yet as Simpson makes clear, the CBC is not against hockey fighting. Also
noteworthy here is the sexuality (and not just gendering) of hockey as
uttered by Milbury – a sexuality that points to the domain of hockey as
the arena of traditional, and aggressive, masculinity. Milbury's comments
and Cherry's defence of fighting can be taken as defensive responses not
only to challenges to hockey traditionalism but also to social changes
that threaten the place of traditional male values in the larger society.

Indeed, part of Cherry's agenda seems to be the policing of Canadian
masculinity, at least as it should appear in the realm of hockey: players
should be tough on the ice and polite, modest, and well groomed off of
it (Allain 2010). If the aggression and violence of hockey represents an
untamed masculinity and is to be valued for this, proper comportment
off the ice points to the values of good Canadian civilization. Gruneau
and Whitson (1993, 192) suggest that 'the proposals to take the fighting
out of hockey do not really threaten the game itself, despite what is often
said in public forums. The ultimate threat, the threat that produces a
recalcitrance to change, is the perceived threat to the maleness of the
game, and beyond this to the place of traditional masculinity in a changing economic, cultural and gender order.' We take it that the signifiers
of 'pansification' might include anything that is perceived to soften the
code of the ice and, more broadly, the institution of professional hockey:
the political left, women, gays, perhaps even doctors.

Canadian cultural identity has been and continues to be built through
hockey. This is a feature of nation building, which by definition is a
nationalistic project carried out under the auspices of the state. That
hockey has become a recognizable icon of Canadianness is due in great
measure to the CBC's broadcasting of *HNIC,* which is itself a brand, besides being a statement on the place of hockey in Canada. Those broadcasts began on radio in the 1930s through the now classic play-by-play
of Foster Hewitt, who announced the earlier General Motors Hockey
Broadcasts and Imperial Oil Hockey Broadcasts.. The CBC aired its first
televised *HNIC* game in 1952. *HNIC* telecasts became 'CBC-ized' (to use

writer Scott Young's term) as the network gained greater control over telecasts in the early 1990s. This included, among other things, the announcers donning CBC blazers and the corporation acquiring greater power to muzzle announcers who did not toe the CBC broadcast line (Young 1990).

If *HNIC* is a brand, the CBC has succeeded in merging itself with the telecasts. The corporation has used hockey to build and disseminate Canadianness, in keeping with its official mandate. An early example of this was the hockey broadcasts during the Second World War: 'The Canadian government had allowed the league to operate during the war as a morale booster, and national radio broadcasts of games on the Canadian Broadcasting Corporation were often subtly linked to patriotic themes and messages' (Gruneau and Whitson 1993, 103). Since the 1990s hockey coverage has become a more prominent component of CBC programming, and in the playoffs, hockey coverage dominates the schedule, pushing news programs out of their normal time slots. As with the CBC's use of the popular reality-contest genre discussed in chapter 1, the increased coverage of sports – and of hockey in particular – has been a consequence of financial pressures and the need to bring in more viewers and dollars. In hockey the CBC has the perfect vehicle for attracting large audiences and carrying out its mandated task of building the nation.

In the second decade of the 2000s, the CBC is facing competition from a growing variety of sources, including specialty channels such as Leafs TV (which is dedicated to all things Leaf, including broadcasts of games from the past). Meanwhile, the corporation has expanded its hockey coverage into more 'cultural' forums, such as the *Hockey Day* and *Hockeyville* telecasts. Also discernable is a project of Canadianization, complete with tensions related to civilizing processes, within the CBC hockey broadcasts themselves. In his analysis of the various Canadianization projects of the twentieth century, historian Ryan Edwardson (2008) eschews any discussion of hockey in order to focus on the arts, the media, cultural policy, and those individuals and groups who have featured prominently in Canada's 'Quest for Nationhood.' Yet even Edwardson recognizes that he needs to explain the absence of hockey from his discussion. Our own discussion here stresses hockey's important role in Canadianization and brings to light the tensions related to the civilizing project produced by the use of hockey in building Canadian cultural identity.

Civilizing projects, especially as they were formulated by the Massey Commission (see previous chapters), have been of central concern in Canada. By the time the commission conducted its work, hockey was being broadcast on the radio, although the Massey Report did not mention this in its discussion of radio content and culture. In the early 1900s, Canadian elites were seeking to preserve the amateur status of various sports against the developing forces of professionalism and commercialization, and it was largely the middle class that participated in hockey (Rutherford 1993). However, Canadian cultural elites in the 1920s and 1930s and into the Massey era of the late 1940s and early 1950s were concerned about the strong attachment to sports and entertainment among the unpolished members of society, in no small part because these signified threats from American and lowbrow culture (Gruneau and Whitson 1993; Rutherford 1993).

Watching *Hockey Day*

The ninth annual Tim Hortons *Hockey Day* – a 'celebration of all things hockey' – was televised on the CBC on 21 February 2009, perhaps to help Canadians endure the bleak February winter. This telecast of *Hockey Day* was based in Campbellton, New Brunswick; like previous *Hockey Days,* it featured three hockey games between Canadian teams. The day, named in allusion to *HNIC,* was part of the broader hockey–Canadian socialization phenomenon also found in the *Hockeyville* contest.

Hockey Day moves to different Canadian sites each year; clearly, the program wishes to be inclusive and to reflect the country's geographic diversity. These programs provide an opportunity for Canadian towns to gain recognition in Canada, not only for their hockey traditions and related claims to fame, which are played up in the broadcasts, but also through their mass mediation. They appear on the CBC and thus take part in the mediascape that helps 'collect' Canada.

Programs of this type contribute to the identity of the communities where they are set by celebrating them as hockey towns. For example, the town of Antigonish, Nova Scotia, was invited to compete in Kraft *Hockeyville* 2011. Schoolchildren in all grades were brought out of classes to the afternoon rally and were invited to wear hockey jerseys, shake boxes of Kraft Dinner, and make as much noise as possible. (The Kraft Dinner was then donated to the food bank.) Kraft promised the winning town $100,000 to renovate its local arena, as well as an NHL pre-season game and an *HNIC* broadcast from that arena. The winner of the *Hockeyville* contest – that is, the town that showed the strongest commitment to hockey – would get bragging rights as well as recognition in the Canadian mediascape. The towns in the contest become objects for the

Canadian (CBC) viewing audience, with the community members performing for the camera in the attempt to embody this spirit.

Hockey Day is an 'annual celebration of excellence and our game.' In 2009, Ron MacLean uttered these words as he began his duties as master of ceremonies. The lead-up showed MacLean walking along the banks of the Restigouche River in showshoes, finally settling on a spot where he read a passage from David Adams Richards's book *Hockey Dreams*. As the show began, the viewers heard Joni Mitchell's song 'River,' which includes the line 'I wish I had a river to skate away on . . .' The show presented itself as an exuberant celebration of 'our game' and of the town that had been selected to host the *Hockey Day* festivities. The 2009 program included satellite locations, all of which demonstrated some hockey theme. The locations that year were Plaster Rock, New Brunswick (home of the International Pond Hockey Championships), Toronto (where there was a street hockey game with Leafs alumni and, later, a Toronto Marlies game that hosted Don Cherry's 'Salute the Troops Night'), Windsor, Ontario (home of the National Street Hockey Championships), Carlyle, Saskatchewan (home of Dallas Stars captain Brendan Morrow), and Cold Lake, Alberta (home of a Canadian Forces Base, where Calgary Flames alumni played a game against Canadian military personnel). We see here an interest in geographical diversity, with the CBC seeking to include and represent communities across Canada. *Hockey Day* moves to different Canadian sites each year, and *Hockeyville* pits different towns from across Canada against one another.

A Canadian history and pedagogy are also taught on *Hockey Day*. In 2009, along with the nationalistic framing, there were themes of the state and lessons about diversity. The nationalism was apparent in the merging of hockey with national identity and in the repetition of the term 'our game' throughout the broadcast. Writer David Adams Richards, on hand as literary-hockey Canadian, declared that 'we are one unified nation when we drop the puck' – the puck implicitly collecting and symbolizing the we-ness of the nation. (Sports writer Bruce Dowbiggin's book *Puck* [2008] also draws from the presumed cultural significance of this vulcanized piece of rubber when pointing to how hockey explains the meaning of 'modern Canada.')

In terms of diversity, during the 2009 broadcast we saw and heard Willie O'Ree, the 'first black in the NHL,' who entered the league in 1958. We also learned about hockey's material culture through the display of a very early hockey stick, found in Cape Breton, used by one 'William Moffatt.' There was also a discussion about whether the Mi'kmaq were the first to

craft a hockey stick. In terms of diversity, and of Native people's con-
tributions to hockey, we also learned about Fred Saskamoose, the 'first
full-status native in the NHL,' who played a key role in the development
of Indian hockey in Saskatchewan. A lesson presented throughout all of
this was, as Ron MacLean put it, 'How hockey teaches diversity' (Mac-
Lean 2009).

Through this sort of explicit pedagogy, a game that is agonistic – often
brutally so – becomes tamed, or at least is placed in the service of a multicultural agenda that is supposed to teach Canadians about the ethnic
other. It seems that hockey is in some way becoming domesticated – at
least, it is being put to work domesticating the nation. Let us be clear,
though: while professional hockey is becoming more diversified, hockey
itself does not teach diversity – Black players are still subject to racist slurs
on the ice, as are Native and French Canadian players and referees (Dowbiggin 2008). As suggested earlier, it is more likely that in recognizing
hockey, immigrants become Canadians. Some immigrants view hockey
as a means to integrate themselves, and the effects of multiculturalism
in Canadian society are visible in the growing popularity of hockey in
the Punjabi community, and in the drafting by the Toronto Maple Leafs
of Muslim player Nazem Kadri (Anderssen 2009).[4] If hockey 'teaches
diversity,' it is through a pedagogy uttered by CBC spokespeople such as
MacLean for the state's own purposes.

The year 2010 saw the tenth broadcast of *Hockey Day*. Since its first
broadcast in 2000, 'the CBC has criss-crossed the country, taking the show
to blue-collar places like Red Deer, Alta., Stephenville, N.L., Iqualuit,
Nunavut, Winkler, Man., and Campbellton, N.B' (CBC 2010a). The CBC
clearly considers it important to visit and celebrate 'blue collar' Canada,
and this link with social class is made clearer still on the *Hockey Day* website: 'One thing *Hockey Day* does is allow people who drink the working
man's champagne to get up close to MacLean and Cherry, two celebrities
who they have invited into their living rooms for decades through *Hockey
Night in Canada*' (Ibid.). MacLean and Cherry are Canadian celebrities
because of hockey. In any case, they are state celebrities as CBC employees
and spokesmen for some version of Canada. As testament to Cherry's
celebrity status in Canada, in 2010 the CBC aired a two-part docudrama
based on his life. Predictably, that miniseries scored high ratings. This
sort of treatment of a Canadian amounts to recognition – at least by the
CBC – that the subject is an important and influential Canadian. It also
contributes to the creation of certifiably Canadian objects, and thus to
nation building. It is noteworthy that Cherry placed in the top ten in the
CBC's *The Greatest Canadian* contest, alongside politicians and scientists.

Perhaps to link hockey with other Canadian traditions, or to inject some 'high' culture into representations of our game, *Hockey Day 2010* took place in Stratford, Ontario, the home of the annual Shakespeare Festival. The theme of this *Hockey Day* was 'team.' The show opened in a theatre with Don Cherry in royal garb, complete with crown, reciting verses from *King Lear*. Given Cherry's past conflicts with the CBC and his unpolished diction, the image of Cherry as Lear was incongruous, but also fitting, given the recognizable status he had by then achieved in Canada through *HNIC* and Coach's Corner. However, one can wonder if the CBC was offering a joke to the viewers by casting him as Lear, with a Masseyite wink to those who knew their Shakespeare. After all, the king is ultimately foolish and impotent.

Ron MacLean then entered the scene, and dispensed a story about Howie Morenz, the 'king' of Stratford, a player for the Montreal Canadiens, who, we were told with a reminder of tragedy, 'died from a broken heart.' In this way, the program brought together Stratford's 'hockey and Shakespearian' traditions: popular culture meeting high culture. As with the previous *Hockey Day*, the broadcast suffered no shortage of nationalistic hyperbole. MacLean declared Hockey Day as 'the greatest day of our year.' Hockey was thus merged with 'our' – Hockey Day is Canadian, it is ours, and apparently it is more Canadian than Canada Day. It is the greatest day *because of* hockey. Throughout the telecast, the iteration of hockey with Canada was constant. The game was referred to as 'our great sport' and as 'what Canada does best' (CBC 2010a). On the CBC *Hockey Day* website, Maclean told us: 'All Canadians are core rink rats. They all know what it was like to fire that last puck into the snow bank. They have a great humble disposition that makes them great. The people are enthusiastic because of their love for the game' (Ibid.).

In keeping with all this, *Hockey Day 2010* included a variety of CBC celebrities, including an iconic Canadian, news anchor Peter Mansbridge, honorary chairman of *Hockey Day in Canada* (Ibid.), who took the viewer on a tour of Stratford's William Allman Memorial Arena. At the Ottawa location on the frozen Rideau Canal, host Evan Solomon talked about how 'new Canadians are learning how to skate.'

All of the CBC's annual *Hockey Days* seek to celebrate community and to that end encompass satellite locations across the country. During the 2010 broadcast, the CBC hosts discussed the significance of Hockey Day for communities. The Mayor of Windsor, Nova Scotia, site of the first *Hockey Day*, talked about how the broadcast had been a big moment for the community and the most important event in her term as mayor. According to the hosts, *Hockey Day* 'galvanizes' communities. The CBC website states that *Hockey Day* has 'become a real highlight for every community that hosts it,' that 'it has become a tradition with Canadians from coast to coast to coast, and [that] it has become common for Canadians to pay tribute to the game they hold close to their heart' (Ibid.). The day thus finds the CBC at work building communities, building traditions, and building a nation. For these purposes, hockey is a tool.

As with the *Hockeyville* reality contest, there is a strong focus on inclusion – in particular, the inclusion of small towns, which are offered a chance to celebrate their hockey history. The electronic mediation of the local community arena links to the national arena, where it is possible to say that the local and the national exist at the same time – an imagined community where the local authorizes national and national authorizes local. Community hockey is celebrated through its mediation, and also in the ways it is utilized to support the CBC nation-building mandate. As CBC media representations, *HNIC, Hockey Day in Canada,* and *Hockeyville* conflate all time and space into the 'arena' of hockey. All of Canada (in spite of diversity) is Hockeyville. Hockey, according to the CBC, is 'our national theatre' (Ibid.).

To Fight or Not to Fight

With the continued existence of fighting in the NHL, we have ample evidence of the sporting desire to beat the crap out of the other, because the fans 'just love it' and because it is part of the hockey 'code.'[5] This desire is entrenched uniquely in hockey, the only sport that continues to allow it (Simpson 2009). 'We have (fighting) because we like it. We like fighting. We like it when a player gets hit and knocked down and his teammate comes and gets immediate retribution in the nose . . . We love it when teams stand up for themselves' (Milbury, quoted in Brady and Gordon 2011, A16). Here we encounter an emotional response to the game that seems to resist any pedagogy: the fighting generates as much fan excitement as a goal, if not more. There is an apparent conflict of positions embodied in the utterances of Ron MacLean (the forces of middle-class CBC civilization) and Milbury and Cherry (the latter the bombastic patriarch, spokesman for the working class, and lead supporter of the gladiatorial world view). How could fighting be a lesson about our relation to the state? We find a clue to the answer in Don Cherry's popularity.

Dowbiggin (2008) notes Cherry's popularity and credibility in Canadian hockey culture and 'how he saturates the debate on hockey in Canada at every level' (131). Indeed, Cherry's popularity extends beyond the cultural arena of hockey: he is a pitchman for countless products on TV and radio (beyond his own series of hockey fight videos), and he has even served as a pitchman for politicians. He publicly supported Conservative MP Julian Fantino's campaign bid in a by-election in the riding of Vaughan, Ontario, and he was invited to speak at the swearing in of Toronto Mayor Rob Ford. True to form, Cherry, dressed in a bright pink patterned silk jacket, proclaimed that Ford was going to be 'the best Mayor this city has ever seen' and expressed contempt for the 'left wing pinkos' who inhabit the city: 'I'm wearing pinko for all the pinkos out there that ride bicycles and everything' (Rider 2010).

As has been noted, it would not take much to eliminate fighting from the game (Simpson 2009). The International Ice Hockey Federation has already banned fighting and deliberate attempts to injure from its games, including the Olympic Games. Brady and Gordon (2011) remind us that 'while academics and former players might argue that fighting is red meat for the fan base, consider that the three most-watched hockey games in history were played under rules that strictly ban fighting: the 1980 Olympic semi-final (the U.S. 'Miracle on Ice'), the 1980 gold medal game, and the 2010 Olympic final in Vancouver' (A15). Some of the more recent disturbing examples of hockey violence have involved the old-fashioned goalie fight. Goalie fights rarely occur now in the NHL, reflecting the fact that 'the incidence of fighting has been cut in half since the peak season of 1987–88' (A16). However, there were outbreaks of extreme violence in the 2010–11 season, including goalie fights. In one of these, New York Islanders goaltender Rick Dipietro suffered facial fractures and was sidelined for a fair portion of the season. Goalie fights still happen at more junior levels. They typically involve the goalies skating towards each other and brawling, alongside their less equipment-burdened teammates. They are comical to watch because of their ritualistic nature. Goalie fights are a pure expression of team solidarity – the goalies, of course, have to skate across the ice to meet each other. Another disturbing example involved Jonathan Roy, son of famous NHL goalie Patrick Roy, who was charged with beating up the opposing team's goalie during a junior game in Quebec.

In the Roy episode, watching this relic – Roy's thumping of the other goalie, who didn't want to take part and who had no interest in meeting Roy halfway, and Roy's moronic victory address to the crowd – one can only make sense of it as hockey dramaturgy. Roy seemed to believe that this 'performance' was desirable and that the hockey crowd accepted it and indeed wanted to see it. His violent display provides a good case for eliminating fighting (except that the pro-fighting crowd would say that the other goalie should have skated to centre ice, met Roy, and duked it out). In the past, hockey fights were not prosecuted in Quebec if no serious injury was inflicted (CBC 2009i). Roy, however, was charged with assault, to which he pled guilty, receiving an unconditional discharge. The court had decided it did not want to set a precedent by issuing a criminal charge (Brunt 2009).

Headshots may be another matter: the Quebec Crown Prosecutor's office has laid a criminal charge (assault causing injury) against Patrice Cormier, a player with the Rouyn-Noranda Huskies of the Quebec Major Junior League, for his violent 'elbow to the jaw' of Quebec Remparts player Mikael Tam (Canadian Press 2010). The assault left Tam convulsing on the ice. The NHL has raised headshots as an issue of concern but has yet to do anything serious about them (Cole 2011; MacGregor 2011b). However, since the sidelining of NHL superstar Sidney Crosby as the result of a headshot concussion during the 2010–11 season, the issue of headshots – and violence in the NHL more broadly – has reached a flashpoint. Mario Lemieux, former NHL superstar and owner of the Pittsburgh Penguins (Crosby's team), has questioned, publicly, whether he wants to continue to be part of an NHL that supports the persistence of fighting and violence in the game.

Diversity has become an ongoing issue in CBC hockey commentary. Ron MacLean contends that 'hockey teaches diversity,' while Don Cherry has been strongly against diversity. Certainly, nationalism has become a fraught issue now that support for the game is shifting in particular ways. Fans' emotional attachment to teams and players, and to the game itself, complicates the issue even more. In the 2011 Stanley Cup final series between the Vancouver Canucks and Boston Bruins, there was debate among Canadians about which team to pull for: Vancouver was the Canadian team in that series, but the Bruins had more Canadian-born players. Other tests of hockey nationalism have included the trade of Wayne Gretzky from the Edmonton Oilers to the Los Angeles Kings and the move of Canadian teams to the United States. For example, the Winnipeg Jets moved to Phoenix, though Winnipeg once again has an NHL team. During the Toronto–Vancouver game shown during the *Hockey Day* telecast that featured the return of former Maple Leafs captain Mats Sundin (a Swede) to Toronto after his absconding to the Vancouver Canucks, Cherry noted that while the Leaf fans gave Sundin a standing ovation, they booed former Leaf Brian McCabe – a Canadian – when he returned for a game in Toronto. Cherry did not understand why a non-Canadian got an ovation (here he was dwelling on nationality rather than years of exemplary service as Leaf captain). His conclusion: 'Canadians don't like Canadians' (Cherry 2009a). Durkheim articulated the ways in which membership in a collective is primary and emotional: in Cherry's comments, we witness the ways in which, from the perspective of the fans, a player's nationality is secondary to sacrifice for the team, as well as how the local (devotion to one's 'home team') supersedes the national and how fan pleasure derives from player performance rather than place of birth. We suspect that Cherry's lament – heard often in various forms in the Coach's Corner segment of *HNIC* telecasts – reflects a 'Canada' that his arch-nationalist, rock 'em sock 'em value system does not comprehend.

Similarly, criticisms of hockey fighting are apparently incomprehensible to Cherry, who defends the idea of hockey honour, which has its own 'code.' That code is what has made it possible for him to market his *Rock'Em Sock'Em* videos, which are advertised by and sold through the CBC. And Cherry is not alone – many players and commentators continue to defend fighting in hockey. An example is the aforementioned Mike Milbury, the former Boston player and coach turned commentator, who has voiced concern about the 'pansification' of the game (gay groups took umbrage at the use of this term) (Simpson 2009). The NHL's pro-fighting contingent, which continues to have its way on the fighting issue, demonstrates its 'masculinist moral capital' within the institution (Stempel 2006). NHL players whose 'job' is to be enforcers or fighters have continued to keep their jobs and have come out against proposals to eliminate fighting from the game. Some retired enforcers, however, such as Georges Laraque, Stu Grimson, Chris Nilan, and Jim Thompson, have opened up about the toll that fighting takes on players, as well as about the possible links between fighting and emotional problems, alcoholism, and addiction. Characteristically, Cherry lambasted Grimson, Nilan, and Thompson in a Coach's Corner episode at the beginning of the 2011–12 season, calling them 'pukes,' 'turncoats,' and 'hypocrites.' Unhappy with Cherry, the three demanded an apology. They got it, but Cherry did not back down on his pro-fighting stance.[6]

Not all hockey commentators endorse fighting. That said, the almost all-male hockey talk itself perpetuates masculinist hegemony in terms of the values that shape the sport and the public's relationship to it. Van Krieken (1998) notes that 'one of the most important features of violence in Western societies is its profoundly *masculine* character, both

among active participants in sports and leisure activities and among
spectators' (159). It is interesting to consider the CBC's reality contest
Battle of the Blades in the context of masculinist hegemony in hockey. The
contest celebrated the joy that Canadians take in skating, and it brought
men and women together on the ice surface. It also presented professional hockey players in a new and seemingly less traditional masculine
role: the male figure skater. Several of the participants had reputations
as hockey tough guys. Wade Belak, the just-retired player discussed earlier, was rehearsing for the program when the news of his death spread
through the Canadian media.

Since *Battle of the Blades* is related to CBC hockey, Don Cherry takes
part in the presentation. It is amusing to imagine the CBC deciding to
temper the macho discourse of people like Milbury and Cherry by tele-
vising the program – 'taming the tough guys.' The potential 'Canadian'
appeal of the show is no doubt what prompted the CBC to televise it, and
it turned out to be very popular among viewers. The show was inspired
by the popular American reality show *Dancing with the Stars*. It is noteworthy that within two weeks of the end of the program's first season, Brendan Burke, son of tough-talking Toronto Maple Leaf general manager
Brian Burke, announced publicly that he was gay. In televised interviews,
Brian Burke supported his son all the way. He also participated in the
International Day Against Homophobia and Transphobia at Toronto's
City Hall, and he was critical of the lack of media coverage of the event.
To date, no gay NHL players have 'come out.' However, NHL 'bad boy'
Sean Avery publicly declared his support of gay marriage ('marriage
equality') while he was with the New York Rangers, thus challenging the
traditional masculinist culture of professional hockey. While Avery's position has received support, Bruce Dowbiggin (2011b) points out that
'the irony in the debate is that hockey remains the most closeted of the
pro sports. While former NBA, NFL and MLB players have come out,
no NHLer of any description has ever confessed to being gay. Brendan
Burke, the gay son of Toronto GM Brian Burke who died in 2010, was as
close as the sport had to an outing.'[7]

Perhaps the masculinist world of hockey is changing. This is certainly
a worthwhile topic for those interested in the sociology and culture of
sport. Since *Battle of the Blades* is a CBC presentation, it is also worth
examining how the CBC responds to and represents gender issues in
relation to nation-building projects. In the context of issues of danger,
violence, and gender, it also is worth noting that the hockey players who
participated in *Battle of the Blades* extended their status as warriors into
their role as ice dancers. The female skaters on that show were trained

figure skaters, and thus the 'experts' in this sport, yet they were offered up to the hockey players to be thrown into the air or swung upside down with their skulls grazing the ice surface. Part of the show's entertainment value had to do with the less than polished movements of the hockey players and the risk of serious mistakes and falls. The risk of serious injury fell primarily on the women partners.

The hockey 'code' is precisely what makes it difficult for women, regardless of skill, to embody this sport. Certainly, women's hockey has risen to prominence in Canada. This has been occasioned by the success of the women's international teams and by the creation of the Clarkson Cup in 2005 for Canadian women's hockey. (The cup is named after Adrienne Clarkson, the second female Governor General of Canada.) Also, female commentators, such as former Canadian national team player Cassie Campbell, have been added to *HNIC* telecasts. It remains to be seen whether the expanding place of women in amateur and professional hockey will affect the masculinist traditions and discursive framings of hockey in Canada. Certainly the 2010 winter Olympic Games demonstrated the symbolic difference between men's and women's hockey. While the Canadian women's Gold Medal win was highly valued, the men's game against the United States was the culminating spectacle of the Olympics, ending hours before the closing ceremonies. The street celebrations coast to coast in Canada showed that the men are still Canada's symbolic national warriors. If there is a code in women's hockey, it is not the code of men's hockey. Thus, the code not only signifies a set of norms for how social order is produced and negotiated on the ice, but also signifies a set of norms for the doing of masculinity – norms that, as suggested earlier, have shaped the institution of men's hockey and (more broadly) perceptions of and emotional attachments to hockey in Canada.

The CBC continues to use hockey to build and maintain Canada's national identity – that is, to deliver its statist message. This is so even while hockey's 'code' is increasingly contested by society at large. An interesting nationalist-statist configuration is thus being shaped. The nationalism of hockey, of 'our game' – the 'our' being asserted, assumed – in short, the unity of the nation behind the dropping of the puck, has been placed alongside the teaching of diversity. Hockey is construed as pedagogy, as teaching a version of 'our.' As we have been discussing, we cannot overlook the CBC's role in this as the state broadcaster and thereby as the creator and articulator of nationalist sentiments. We also point out that a commitment to the state (which is a legal-rational entity, i.e., an entity governed by laws and rules) is abstract and dry and that what mobilizes citizens' collective commitments is not the state as bureaucratic, legal-rational entity, but rather objects that are cherished because they have an emotional value. The semiological presentation of hockey during the CBC broadcasts is rooted in its emotional appeal; for example, *HNIC* broadcasts, as they begin, celebrate the game with fast and furious clips of goals, checks, and plays, images of cheering fans, and the playing of the hockey anthem.

This chapter began with a discussion of play and the pleasures derived from the spirit of play. The pleasures of hockey emanate from its particular structure as a game. However, Canadians' attachment to it, predicated on tradition, emotion, and ongoing socialization, is at the same time built within the national arena. Canadians link the pleasure of the game to their ability to recognize themselves as Canadian. Canada is officially multicultural, yet issues such as ethnicity and race, and also gender, sexuality, and social class, are being contested within this arena. The framing of threats to the game is constructed by those who *define* the game – that is, by hockey's opinion leaders – whether those threats have been conceived as foreign invaders (such as the early European NHL players) or as various types of unhockey-like characters, who have included the 'fine arts crowd,' 'pansies' and even French Canadian players who wear visors.

Is it possible, then, to think of hockey fighting along the lines of national defence, or at least to highlight the values that underlie both? We are thinking here of the hockey fighter as a warrior who guards the nation's boundaries, which must be defended from perceived threats. It is useful to again invoke Durkheim, who demonstrated how collectivities and institutions are underpinned by feelings and values that need to be ritually enacted. Collective identities are supported and sustained by these enactments (in terms of the state and nationalism, for example, consider national anthems and state holidays and important dates that stimulate collective adherence). Collectives thereby come to represent themselves as different from other groups. These rituals contribute to the making and sustaining of collective identities, as well as, for better or worse, representations of self/other cultural differences. As an institution and as a form of ritual, the hockey fight is a prominent and dramatic feature of the pro-hockey culture 'code,' one that enacts a particular set of values and a particular type of identity. Indeed, not only hockey, but also the hockey fight itself, is a Canadian 'collective representation,' to use Durkheim's language ([1912]1965, [1895]1982). Players, commentators, and fans support this collective representation in discourse.

Don Cherry has got into trouble at the CBC in the past for his disparagement of various groups, including foreign and French Canadian hockey players. Yet he does important work for the state and the CBC. He represents a version of Canadian identity through the kind of hockey he supports – a male, hockey-loving, working-class identity – and the language he uses betrays his formal education level. In his early days as a CBC broadcaster, the CBC admonished him for his language (e.g., for his habit of dropping his g's) (Young 1990). This no longer seems to be a problem for the CBC, now that Cherry has become a Canadian icon and a huge ratings draw for *HNIC* telecasts. CBC's sports website even offers 'The Don Cherry Lexicon,' which characterizes Cherry as 'colourful' and 'straight-shooting' (CBC 2010b). This lexicon includes Cherryisms like 'left-wing pinkos' and 'chicken Swedes,' mispronunciations of 'foreign' (including Québécois) names, his unique grammar ('youze guys,' 'aint,' 'anyhows,' 'anythinks' and 'dat deres'), and his support for the Canadian military and for tough players. Generally, his commentary is framed in terms of the notion that there are many things that viewers think that are not allowed in public speech. Cherry has become a spokesperson for the silent 'majority,' and he often begins his comments with a phrase like 'I'm gunna get in trouble for this.' From this rhetorical position he says what is outside 'politically correct' official discourse. In one segment he reminded the 'kids out there' that Christmas is about 'baby Jesus' birthday' and not just 'Santa,' a clear shot at the secularization of Christian holidays. Yet Cherry defends a notion of code both on and off the ice (and he makes a clear distinction between on-ice and off-ice behaviour). Hence, he criticizes players – as well as their handlers – for poor language, dress, and comportment.

Nevertheless, we suggest that while Cherry seems to talk outside the box of official CBC language and opinion, he is also an important ambassador for the state. As instalments of Coach's Corner have demonstrated, the topic of hockey has often taken second place to the memorializing of Canadian soldiers who have died in Afghanistan, or of police officers who have died in the line of duty. On 3 January 2009 it was 'Canadian Forces Appreciation Night' at the Air Canada Centre. In the Coach's Corner segment of the *HNIC* telecast, Don Sanderson, who died in a hockey fight, was honoured. Two dead Canadian soldiers were also honoured.

In supporting the troops and their families and making sure that each dead soldier was given recognition, Cherry gave Canadian soldiers recognition in the eyes of hockey fans who might not have otherwise paid close attention to the Canadian military's position in Afghanistan. In the recent *Hockey Day* celebrations, for example, there was a greater positioning of the war in CBC hockey presentations.[8] As a former coach, Cherry explains that the players are like soldiers: 'As Napoleon said, "If you don't have morale, you've got nothin"' (Cherry 2009b).

Conclusion: The Arenas of Violence

To return to the hockey fight and its defenders, Gruneau and Whitson (1993) point out that what is being guarded is a version of hegemonic masculinity. In the context of this discussion, this hegemony is linked to larger issues of nation and identity, in that social attitudes and dispositions are socialized and connected to civilizing processes. As Elias discusses, sport is not an epiphenomenon of culture. Rather, it demonstrates and reflects civilizing processes and connects with broad issues of national identity and state formation. In Canada, hockey in particular demonstrates and collects themes of nation building and statehood. *Hockey Night In Canada* is popular culture, but this does not detract from its uses as a Canadianizing force, one that is put to use for projects of national identity. While the positioning of the state in relation to hockey can be traced back to the game's early days, the place of hockey in strong projects of Canadianization began in the 1950s, through the mass mediation of games through the CBC radio network (Rutherford 1993).

As mentioned, the Summit Series was a pivotal event in Canadian national and hockey consciousness and had an impact on the cultural nationalism movement of the 1960 and 1970s. That movement was to a great extent supported by cultural producers and elites in Canada who were concerned about threats to Canadian cultural identity and sovereignty (Edwardson 2008). It was during those decades that the emphasis on hockey as national cultural product and symbol became discernible. Perhaps it was also during those decades that explicit cultural conflicts around hockey began to appear. Beginning with the Masseyist high-cultural conceptions of Canadianness and continuing into the phase of cultural nationalism, Canadian elites attempted to hold off the pernicious effects of American mass culture. Hockey cannot be described as a high-cultural tool for building national identity and uplifting the Canadian masses; but perhaps, for those worried about the threats posed by American popular culture, a Canadian sport is better than an American one when it comes to building cultural nationalism.

Through the CBC, hockey has become a civilizing project – a popular cultural support of Canadian nationalism. As we have been discussing in this book, popular culture has been, and perhaps *must* be, utilized more and more for national projects that have to compete with centrifugal pulls away from national and cultural identities. Yet the CBC's role in popularizing hockey exposes some of the cultural tensions that have surfaced in relation to competing conceptions of Canada. The interactions between Cherry and MacLean represent some of these tensions as they talk hockey (and, in Cherry's case, affairs of state) under the watchful eye of their employer. Cherry's socially conservative, 'lunch pail' sensibilities may conflict with the CBC's 'official' sensibilities, which express the cultural position of the educated middle class; but the state has been supported through Cherry's nationalist positions, including in terms of the air time he devotes to military issues. Cherry deplores the elites (whom he considers to be 'left wing') and what they want to do to hockey, so there are (apparent) conflicts about hockey and the kind of Canadian identity 'we' want. The CBC provides a vehicle for the conflicting positions, even while seeing their utility for nation building.

If there is moral uplift, perhaps it exists in the dramas of character, both individual and collective, that are presented during the telecasts. Here we find not only the glorification of the hockey gods but also the romanticizing of the Canadian player-warrior. We might well ask whether this last figure is outside of society, given that fighting steps out of accepted norms of interaction. But as attitudes and orientations towards violence are socialized, we can consider the enforcer or 'goon' as a deviant *over* conformer in the institution of professional hockey. Is the hockey fighter a sacrifice of some kind – he certainly is an entertainer – risking a bloody face for a particular version of identity?

Hockey is both a commercial product and a spectacle, and there is no doubt that hockey violence is part of the product. The retention of fighting, including staged fighting, rather than an outright ban on it, points to the ongoing entertainment value of the hockey fight and of the fighters ('performers') themselves. If the hockey fight is symbolically ordered by the hockey 'code' – a position supported by Cherry – there is also the popular view that fighting provides a safety valve for both players and fans. In social scientific terms, this is the 'catharsis theory' (Blake 2009). Perhaps Cherry himself is a 'safety valve.' According to how Canadians view themselves, Cherry is in many ways an anomalous Canadian – loud, brash, rude, and bossy. In the early days of Coach's Corner, he was notorious for verbally bullying Ron MacLean. Cherry isn't afraid to stand out in a crowd, as evidenced by his loud opinions and louder clothing. His presence has prompted some people to consider him a clown (recall the 'Don Cherry Lexicon' on the CBC website), but this is a clown that many hockey fans take seriously. From the position he has carved out for himself, Cherry can walk the line between the serious and the non-serious and voice 'unofficial' arguments and opinions; thus his views cannot easily be dismissed, as his influence attests.

We are interested in *why* hockey provides an arena of violence – an 'outlet' (and one in which the law has rarely intruded). But we can also ponder the role that Cherry plays on the CBC and his significance for Canadianness. CBC employees have complained that the corporation has allowed him a soapbox, which can be seen as a violation of the principles of objective reporting (Dowbiggin 2008). His main base of support is the diehard hockey fan who embraces aggressive hockey. And perhaps this is where the elites come in, and where we see elite and popular interests coincide: the elites use hockey for state purposes (nation building), while vocal supporters of hockey violence actually contribute to the containing and state use of violence by condoning it in the arena. Violence is thereby legitimized, but in a way that serves the state's purposes (e.g., going to war). The soldier sacrifices self for the national-political collective; the hockey fighter sacrifices self for the fans, for the values that endorse this version of hockey and hockey character, and for the social identities these values buttress.

Even those who might be expected to condemn Cherry have to acknowledge and accept him, especially if the CBC employs them. The CBC's house comedian, Rick Mercer, is gay, yet he cavorts with Cherry on *The Rick Mercer Report* (on one occasion, he helped Cherry choose fabric for his famously gaudy, tailor-made blazers). Similarly CBC's resident scientist and environmentalist, David Suzuki, uses Cherry to promote his causes (even though Cherry has for years called him a 'left-wing weirdo'). Cherry, being an icon, must be taken up by these people if they hope to legitimate their own status on the Canadian media landscape.

If contemporary forms of regulated sport 'have come to serve as symbolic representation of a non-violent, non-military form of competition between states' (Elias 1986, 23), the persistence of violence in Canadian hockey – and of fighting in particular – is sociologically significant. The acceptance of violence within the arena not only points to the 'decontrolled controlling' of emotions (for players and fans), but also links it to Canadian civilizing processes and state formation, since the state could step in to ban fighting outright if it so decided. The state has decided not to civilize the game with respect to on-ice violence, but this does not mean that 'civilizing' is not occurring. It *does* mean that hockey, as well as the hockey fight, continue to be resources used by the state to build Canadian cultural and national identity.

But perhaps there is an even more direct relationship between hockey violence and the state. Let us return to Brunt's question, which we used to open this chapter: 'At what point does the state have a place in the rinks of the nation?' Put another way, how far can hockey violence be allowed to go before the police are called onto the ice to enforce assault laws? And, for that matter, how can this question be answered? The role of the state in the bedrooms of the nation seemed clear by the late 1960s; the role of the state in the hockey rink remains complex. In symbolic terms, by entering the rink the police would be violating a sacred space that has rules unique to it. The ice, as it is currently understood, is a sanctuary for legitimated violence (though only, of course, when hockey is being played). Similarly, the arena of symbolic violence (the soapbox of Coach's Corner) is a sacred arena within this arena of state. It is protected, not by the right to freedom of expression, but by the right of the state to represent itself. It is also protected by its difference from the 'official,' middle-class culture of the CBC. This apparently beleaguered voice of the ordinary Canadian, as embodied by Don Cherry, seems to stand in contrast with the state line on diversity, multiculturalism, and even the place of violence in society. But Cherry does not argue for violence in the broader culture. He argues for its containment and celebration within the symbolic world of the state. So while Ron MacLean embodies the oversocialized Canadian, deferential and polite, Cherry embodies the socialization of violence. He suggests that violence is good (in its proper place), that is it not out of control, and that it is working towards collective ends. He has 'colourful' names for those who imagine that the state is not an arm of violence, both symbolically and literally. Like stacking Russian dolls, the state's authority to exert itself is put into Coach's Corner, which is stacked into *Hockey Night in Canada,* which is stacked into the CBC. At the heart of all these stacked social locations is the ice surface itself as a unique site of violence in Canada.

In this sense, violence is inherent to Canadian hockey, but not to hockey itself. In a culture that often claims to be non-violent, this violence does much work for nationalist and statist ends. It is even, counter-intuitively, part of the civilizing process in that it contains, organizes, and ritualizes violence towards an enactment of state authority. It is a form of domestic (at home) violence both in the sense of being local and in the sense of being protected by norms of non-involvement. As feminists have pointed out regarding violence in the family home, it was until recently considered by police and the broader public to be a private problem (albeit illegal) that should not be managed by the law. Common sense shored up this protection of violence by claiming there was something unique about romantic relationships, the nature of men, and the nature of women. Common sense, in the form of Don Cherry, argues that there is something about men and hockey that makes this game inherently violent. We suggest that there is something inherent in the symbolic role of hockey in Canada that makes it our unique arena of domestic violence. Interestingly, as it displaces violence into a contained arena (with a second discursive arena inside it), this violence is domesticated (in the sense of being contained or controlled) as well as domestic (unique to us and our sense of self). In that it is true of all nation-states that they must assert their right of force over citizens, it is always best, from the point of view of the state, that citizens defend and enjoy this right. Both in the stacking of cultural sites into one another, and in the naturalization of violence, the state appears and disappears within collective identity and pleasure.

As Canada's longest-running TV program (Scherer and Whitson 2009), *Hockey Night in Canada,* a national tradition, has been an important builder, communicator, and representative of Canadianness. Through the broadcasts, we see the merging of the spectacles of nation with those of entertainment, and the place of violence in the production of Canadian identity. Hockey is 'our game': an ongoing source of national identification and the arena of a uniquely domestic and domesticated violence.

4

Peace, Order and Good Gambling

An institution, after all, cannot take it on the lam; it must pacify its marks.

Erving Goffman (1952)

Making money is great, but winning it is even better.

Super 7 Lottery slogan

Thus far, stereotypical ordinary Canadian pleasures have been discussed in this book – the CBC, Tim Hortons, hockey. To be sure, gambling is not a topic that represents Canadianness like the CBC and hockey. And while coffee drinking is not uniquely Canadian, we have shown how Tim Hortons has succeeded in generating a kind of Canadianized coffee culture – or better, in creating and branding a consumption space that represents Canadianness as a feature of its commercial interests. Gambling is important for our overall discussion, not because there is anything uniquely 'Canadian' about gambling, but for the way in which the state is explicitly invoked in terms of the organization of that activity, and the significance of this organization for Canadians. If the state appears in various guises in relation to our earlier topics – explicitly (if contestedly) in terms of the CBC, tangentially in terms of Tim Hortons, and directly and indirectly in terms of hockey – with gambling the state looms large, albeit in a curious way. Legalized gambling in Canada seems here to stay for the foreseeable future, and with some exceptions, it will continue to be a state-owned activity. Nevertheless, it is curious that governments have come to govern citizens through mechanisms such as electronic gaming machines (slot machines and video lottery terminals) and more generally by being the 'house,' quite willing to accept the various kinds of bets legally available to citizens. In the past, governments would have been the regulators of gambling, not active market participants and beneficiaries. This has all changed, especially since the early 1990s.

The legalization and expansion of gambling in Canada has followed a general trajectory similar what we find in other countries. This story is actually a global one: many countries have legalized gambling and opened up gambling markets, though there are significant differences in terms of legal and commercial organization and the policy rationales for particular arrangements. In Canada, the various provincial governments have organized gambling primarily as government-owned monopolies. It is true that many countries have government-run lotteries; some also have government-owned casinos (such as the Netherlands, Sweden, and Canada), as well as government-owned sports betting schemes and electronic gaming machines (EGMs). The fact that gambling in Canada has been organized as a state (government) monopoly points to a version of Canadianness that can be analysed as a strong example of the state's relationship to pleasure. This is also significant because the state's involvement signifies an interesting shift in its conduct towards and relationship to Canadian citizens.

It is worth mentioning again the importance of Bill C-150. That bill resulted in the legalization of certain sexual activities (e.g., homosexual sex) as well as gambling. Legalization implies a liberalization of activities, which in turn suggests the state's withdrawal from the activity – as in Trudeau's pronouncement that the state has no business regulating sexual activity between consenting adults. Strangely, however, legalization has paved the way not for the state's withdrawal from gambling, but for its takeover of gambling. That activity has been legalized – adults can now participate in it, but only insofar as the state owns the venues for it and extracts any benefits. This is how legalized gambling has played out in Canada. The bill allows federal and provincial governments to conduct lotteries. Since the federal government handed over gambling regulation to the provincial governments (in an amendment to the Criminal Code in 1985), the provinces have generally taken full advantage of the opportunity to expand gambling, well beyond the relatively harmless realm of lotteries. What does this story say about how the state orients to and induces the pleasure of Canadians?

The phenomenon of legalized gambling in Canada provides an opportunity to reflect on the state's relationship to pleasure, in that the state has used its legal powers to change gambling's illegal and deviant status for the purpose of exploiting it for revenue purposes. The development of legal commercial markets has brought gambling out of the shadows and made it visible. This in turn has produced gambling behaviours, which have become subject to shaping, in much the same way that other forms of consumption are shaped to generate expenditures.

More than the other topics discussed in this book, and for several reasons, gambling makes explicit the problem of desire. First, unlike contests, coffee drinking, hockey, or comedy, gambling in Canada until quite recently had the dubious distinction of being an officially undesirable activity. Gambling has been subject to state concerns about vice and illegality and, aside from horse racing, bingo, and church raffles, was prohibited until the passage of Bill C-150 in 1969. As a previously illegal activity, today it speaks to the ways in which states govern citizens' 'deviant' proclivities. But it also points to the state's desire to collect revenues from illegal or shadow economies, as well as to how an activity's status can come to be redefined as legal and socially acceptable. Thus, forms of deviant desire can be examined in terms of how they are defined – legally and morally – by the state. Second, if the history of gambling has long been one of moral condemnation, this relates not only to religious proscriptions against it but also to the excesses it can produce. Profligacy and loss affect the life of the gambler and those around him/her; in addition to that, gambling has been framed as a threat to societal values. Specifically, gambling has been a threat to Protestantism, the values of 'producerism,' and the religious and societal conceptions of the relationship between work and reward (Ramp and Badgley 2009). As we discuss, the relationship between work and reward is now being sundered and exploited by state-owned gambling enterprises. Early critiques of gambling as unproductive, profligate, immoral, or deviant are largely put to rest when gambling can be made economically productive, especially for the state, which has the means to exert moral and legal suasion.

The profligacy and loss related to gambling have now been cast in medicalized terms – specifically, as 'pathological' gambling (a term that appeared in the Diagnostic and Statistical Manual of Mental Disorders IV [DSM-IV] in 1980). Now that they have legitimized gambling and taken 'ownership' of it, governments have had to orient themselves to these framings of excessive desire. How, then, are gambling behaviours being shaped in order to make gambling a legitimate business enterprise for the state? This relates in part to the way the state conducts gambling as a business, which raises the issue of how the state should act in relation to civil society.

This chapter, like the others in this book, has as its theme the shaping of desire. That said, gambling is the most explicitly problematic of the topics this book specifically addresses. In legalizing and expanding gambling, the state is taking the risk that excess will percolate into Canadians' everyday lives. As we will discuss, this threat needs to be managed – that is, defined and ordered – and our discussion of that will bring into relief aspects of how Canadian desire is shaped in relation to the state itself.

Provincial governments in Canada have at times justified their gambling revenues on the premise that gambling is 'what the people are going go do anyway.' For example, the Nova Scotia Gaming Corporation's Social Responsibility Charter (2006) begins its section 'Our Five Pillars of Social Responsibility' with this statement: 'Gambling has become a widely-enjoyed entertainment option for adults in most parts of the world . . . More than 89% of Nova Scotia's adult population gamble each year.' But this claim obscures the ways in which gambling markets have developed in Canada. The *state* has been the major developer of the market for gambling; it has legalized and indeed promoted that activity. And it has done so through a monopoly model that allows governments to be the main beneficiaries of gambling enterprises (Cosgrave and Klassen 2009). That many Canadians have easy access to gambling venues is a direct consequence, rather than cause, of public policy. That 'people are doing it anyway' is a consequence of the state's role in legalizing, legitimizing, and promoting gambling in Canada.

With the expansion of state-run commercial gambling, new social groups have been introduced to the activity – women, seniors, and youth – and those groups are being encouraged to participate. While people under eighteen cannot gamble legally ('at least 18 years of age in the case of lottery and bingo, and 19 years of age in the case of gaming,' according to the Ontario Lottery and Gaming Corporation website), it is difficult to enforce laws prohibiting them from, for example, buying 'gaming' products in the corner store. Gambling, both legal and illegal, is now easily accessible – in fact, it is now 'normal' for Canadians.

A small percentage of Canadians gamble on the Internet, although this number will surely increase. The moral objections relating to Internet gambling have been overcome, just as Canadian provincial governments have overcome their reluctance to move into that arena. The Ontario provincial government has announced that it plans to join British Columbia in the online gambling fray. This will attract some gamblers from 'illegal' sites provided that the choices, odds, and payouts presented by the government sites are a better deal for gamblers. It will also attract new online gamblers who might otherwise have shied away from illegal sites. It is significant, however, that governments have forgone a regulatory interest concerning Internet sites it deems to be illegal, and instead has opted to join them and compete for market share. In announcing its intentions, Ontario Lottery and Gaming Corporation chairman Paul Godfrey said: 'Across Canada and around the world, online commerce is part of our everyday lives and OLG is excited to start the consultation process for online gambling and growing its marketplace in the future' (*Globe and Mail* 2012). But what alibi do governments really have for their participation? With their interest in gambling revenues, and with their direct participation in gambling consumer markets, governments appear to be indistinguishable from corporations and to be willing to accept the potential for harm to individuals that may accrue. If gambling is now just like other forms of 'entertainment' – in other words, another consumer product – it seems that there is no reason not to get involved in the sale of *any* product. Ontario will, of course, offer a 'socially responsible' product, and those willing to gamble through its online offerings will no doubt be encouraged to be 'responsible gamblers.'

Canadians have no legal choice but to gamble in the state-owned enterprises. The state's role in gambling enterprises is thus instructive for what it says about aspects of Canadian culture and about the social organization of Canadians' everyday lives. There are, here, two related issues to be explored: first, how the state stimulates gambling desire and legitimizes its own conduct as it does so; and second, how gambling activities are ordered and governed. In our discussion of Canadianness, we take it as significant that the state, through the process of stimulating the desire to gamble, frames gambling as another example of the desire for the state.

Legal gambling is now embedded in Canadians' everyday lives. It is ubiquitous, easily accessible, and promoted heavily on television. The state insinuates itself into everyday life in many ways: by promulgating and enforcing laws; by developing infrastructure; by fostering cultural projects such as the CBC; and so on. In that context, gambling strikes us as a strange form of insinuation. Unlike other forms of 'entertainment,' it is a 'contested moral activity' (Magendanz 2003). Nevertheless, it has become part of the state infrastructure, in the physical sense of casinos and technologies such as electronic gaming machines. More important, it has become a form of state conduct, in the sense of being both a revenue-generating vehicle and, more broadly, a relationship or orientation to civil society. As we discuss in this chapter, gambling as a form of 'entertainment' requires that citizens' desires be shaped.

We begin our discussion by extracting several items about gambling from a Canadian newspaper, the *Globe and Mail*. The first of these reported on the B.C. Lottery Corporation's decision to raise its betting limits. This item included as a sidebar 'Gambling Facts and Myths' (also provided here), the content of which was disseminated by the B.C.

Partnership for Responsible Gambling. The second item we provide below is a comment on the first, taken from the *Globe and Mail's* online 'Comments' section. The third is a short excerpt from a newspaper series on gambling in Canada, also published in the *Globe and Mail.*

Item #1

The British Columbia Lottery Corporation says its decision to markedly increase its weekly play limit was primarily designed to meet the demands of players, but it has been met with criticism from experts and government opposition.

'It's another cash grab by [a] government that's very anxious about its budget situation,' said NDP MLA Shane Simpson.

Starting today, BCLC's PlayNow website will allow British Columbians to set their weekly play limit at nearly $10,000. The previous limit was $120.

The provincial government currently faces a deep budget deficit, but BCLC, a crown corporation, said the decision was based on demand and business considerations.

'This is definitely an independent decision of the corporation,' BCLC spokeswoman Susan Dolinski said.

The corporation said it arrived at the decision to increase the weekly limit after experts in its responsible-gambling program indicated that allowing people essentially to set their own limits helps them take responsibility for those choices.

Rich Coleman, the minister responsible for overseeing gaming in the province, was not available for comment yesterday.

The province's website lists revenue from commercial gaming in B.C. at nearly $2.61-billion in 2008–09, most of which it says went to prize payouts, operator commissions and operating and employment costs. The province received about $1.08-billion in net gaming revenue.

And, according to the government, Internet gambling is growing at a rate of 20 per cent a year. The industry is estimated to be worth $12-billion a year and that's expected to rise to $21-billion by 2010.

Ms. Dolinski said there are probably more than 2,000 websites available that have no gambling limit, and it was time for BCLC to catch up.

'An industry standard has been set,' she said. The weekly limit is now capped at \$9,999.

Mr. Simpson said to increase the weekly limit with no consultation and analysis was irresponsible. He said people are more susceptible to Internet gambling than other forms of gaming, and the government should have been cautious about making changes.

'It creates potentially greater hardship for people,' he said.

A gambling expert calls the corporation's move an attempt to catch some of the legal online gaming revenue.

'This is their play to begin to capture some share of that,' said Colin Campbell, criminologist at Douglas College.

Dr. Campbell said that while it is strategic for the corporation to do so, it will have an impact on online gamblers who play in isolation.

He said in traditional casinos, there are programs to help people who may have a gambling addiction, but in the online world, the problem is less detectable. Dr. Campbell said online gambling particularly appeals to the younger generation – kids who were raised on non-gambling video games who are now old enough to have their own credit cards.

Irene Tang, a gambling-addiction counsellor, said her clients who gamble online tend to be younger. BCLC's increased weekly limit will pose a challenge for those already at risk of exceeding their personal limit, she said. In the 2008–2009 fiscal year, 25,000 new players signed up on PlayNow with the total players registered at 115,000.

'Don't bet on it'

According to B.C.'s Partnership for Responsible Gambling website, many people mistakenly believe they can beat the odds and win big. It lists the following myths and misconceptions about gambling:

MYTHS

Gamblers have flamboyant, carefree personalities. (Some are, but others are quiet, introverted and serious-minded.)

Gamblers enjoy risks in all areas of their lives. (Some are big risktakers, others are conservative in personal habits and work.)

If you don't gamble daily, you're not a problem or compulsive gambler.

You can't be addicted to an activity. (Gambling can change one's mood by affecting the biochemistry of the brain much the same way as alcohol or drugs.)

Gamblers are thieves and criminals. (Not true, but some gamblers may resort to criminal behaviour in desperation.)

A compulsive gambler will bet on anything. (Problem gamblers generally have preferences and are not tempted by every type of gambling.)

All compulsive gamblers want to lose. (Most are addicted to the act of gambling – they would rather lose than be out of the action.)

Compulsive gamblers are weak-willed, otherwise they would simply stop.

MISCONCEPTIONS

Gambling is an easy way to make money.
Gambling is the solution to my problems.
I believe I can beat the odds.
Borrowing to gamble is okay.
I can always win it back.
This machine is ready for a large payoff, or it's my turn to win.
My lottery number is bound to come up if I consistently play the same numbers.

(Bhamra 2009)

Item #2

The following is one of the responses to the above article, taken from the 'Comments' section following the article on the Globe and Mail website:

Lotteries are nothing more than a tax on people who are bad at math.

If governments really want some more money, maybe they should implement a tax on illiteracy too.

What really kills me is that we make so much of our progressive and humanitarian tax system that effectively takes money from people who have way more than they need and redistributes it to people who don't.

What does a lottery do? It takes money from a lot of people who don't have enough for the express purpose of creating a very few people who will have way more than they need!!

It's the complete antithesis of 'Canadian' values! (*Globe and Mail* 2009b)

We have included this comment for its conception of Canadianness, which appears to be challenged by the apparently anti-Canadian lottery form of taxation. The themes it points to are taken up later in the chapter. The final item is a short excerpt from a *Globe and Mail* series examining 'Government's Gambling Addiction' and refers to a case where an individual, Mr Isaacs, is suing the OLG and Falls Management Company over the 'financial disaster' that followed from his gambling addiction. The excerpt is from the statement of defence for the defendants.

Item #3

> 'Casino gambling is a form of entertainment,' says the statement of defence. 'Casino patrons pay for that entertainment through their wagering, just as theatre patrons pay for a ticket to a play or sports fans pay for a ticket to a game. Mr. Isaacs's wagering was an expenditure, not a loss recognized at law.' (Priest 2009, A10)

As depicted in Item #3, commercial gambling is often represented now as 'entertainment,' so it is worth considering how gambling has come to be framed in this way, since unlike other forms of legal entertainment, some forms of gambling carry serious risks. These items raise a number of issues, particularly in relation to the stimulation and governing of gambling desire.

Let us look more closely at the BCLC article. In it, gambling is being 'liberalized' through the limit increase. The gambler is now less constrained by the state's protective hand; but at the same time, the state is providing a list of gambling 'Myths' and 'Misconceptions' as a form of pedagogy. That list is from the B.C. government's Partnership for Responsible Gambling website – the journalist is merely reproducing it. Also, that list is being presented as 'facts,' well within government language. Nowhere are the myths and misconceptions it contains discussed or challenged. The author's voice has thus become the voice of the BCLC Gambling Partnership, and this serves to close any gap between journalist and state authority. By some definitions, including that of Jürgen Habermas (1989), a democratic public sphere must cultivate debate between citizens (as supported by a free press), outside of state influence. Otherwise, the public sphere becomes a place for 'a staged form of publicity' by the state (201). The embedded list in Item #1 is a good example of such staging. Presumably, the hope here is that gambling myths and misconceptions will be dispelled by being communicated. The assumption is that citizens lack knowledge of how gambling really affects behaviour and that they must be educated. The betting limits have been increased, but at the same time, ignorance apparently prevails and education is required.

One critic of the B.C. government's act says that increasing the limit without consultation and analysis is 'irresponsible.' This raises a number of issues. First, this type of move – without consultation, and certainly without public input – has been typical of gambling expansion in Canada. The B.C. government is acting unilaterally and on the assumption that the action is legitimate, a form of paternalist statism. Second, such an act may well be irresponsible for a state institution whose *raison d'être* is 'responsibility.' As the criminologist referred to in the article points out, online gamblers – including young gamblers – are more at risk of encountering gambling problems.

To quote again from Item #1: 'The corporation said it arrived at the decision to increase the weekly limit after experts in its responsible-gambling program indicated that allowing people essentially to set their own limits helps them take responsibility for those choices.' In other words, gamblers need to learn responsibility *by gambling* and the BCLC will help them do so by raising the spending limits. One wonders why the BCLC responsible-gambling program exists: clearly, it is not to protect the players from themselves, or from harm. Instead, the limit is being raised in order to 'help' them learn responsibility.

By this reasoning, there is no need for the state to intervene in the desire to gamble. Yet a pedagogy and rhetoric of responsibility is at work here. Morality is being individualized. Just as we find in other publications about responsible gambling disseminated by Canada's various lottery and gaming corporations, the state seems to have abandoned the realm of moral sanction and instead is enjoining the individual to act on him/herself in terms of becoming responsible – that is, to learn about the risks of gambling. Put simply, irresponsibility is the new immorality.

We thus see how 'responsibility' works in the official discourse of state-owned gambling. That term is displayed in a neoliberal frame: the state makes market-based decisions, its 'experts' say the individual will learn 'responsibility' through choices (including excessive ones), the official agencies provide after-the-fact gambling knowledge, and the limit increase is thereby somehow rendered acceptable. Besides being obviously paternalistic (the experts espouse responsibility and know how individuals will learn it), the morality here is of a state that has withdrawn from its relationship with citizens, except that (1) it provides the gambling venues through its policy decisions, and (2) it provides individuals with the conditions for responsibility to be learned, even while creating the conditions for the gambling-related risks to increase. The state reserves the right to expand and benefit from gambling opportunities. State moralism, however, has thus far forbidden private corporations from owning gambling enterprises, while self-governance for individuals ('responsibility') is advocated in the face of risks the state is largely responsible for introducing.

The B.C. government denies that the limit increase is a response to serious budget deficits. Instead, it frames the move in terms of 'business' – as a market-driven response to player demand and to competition from online markets (where many sites have no betting limits). Some provincial gaming corporations answer directly to the finance ministry, and this, owing to public health concerns about problem gambling, produces tensions with the health ministry (McKenna 2008). The underlying assumptions to be noted here include the following: gambling is normal; consumers choose to gamble; players desire more access to gambling (i.e., higher limits); and a role of government is to supply gambling entertainment. The government's market orientation demonstrates its corporate objectives. The government, in its gambling enterprises, is no different from a corporation (it is, after all, the B.C. Lottery *Corporation*), except for its apparent commitment to responsibility. That claim to responsibility, though, is the same that many corporations make on the Corporate Social Responsibility pages of their websites. The B.C. government here is presenting itself as a market player and as a provider of a consumer product (gambling experience), and it is catering to consumers in terms of their increasing desires.

There are three relevant issues here in terms of our general discussion in this book. First, how are the risks associated with gambling contained and managed so that it can be offered as a legitimate entertainment activity (given that it was once illegitimate and deviant)? Second, how do states that legalize gambling and that benefit from it frame their participation in gambling markets to avoid moral criticism, conflicts of interest, and the accusation that they are involved in the production of social harms (i.e., all the negative consequences that flow from gambling addiction)? In the case of state-run gambling, the first issue is subsumed by the state's direct involvement in legalizing and legitimating gambling in order to benefit from gambling markets, and all manner of gambling-related risks (i.e., to gamblers due to participation, and to the state in terms of legitimacy) require management. Third, how are we to understand this orientation of the state as a provider of pleasure and stimulator of desire, and how does that orientation affect how Canadians go about their everyday lives?

The Legitimation of Gambling and the Canadian State

Historically, many cultural activities and forms of entertainment and consumption have been considered dangerous or threatening – the mass media, expressions of sexuality, and alcohol and drug consumption have been heavily regulated by the state. The bureaucratic responses to such 'dangers' – CanCon regulations to counter debased American mass culture, pasties and G-strings to prevent outbreaks of lustful masculinity, obscured windows on bars in Ontario, large sums spent on drug enforcement – have been heavy-handed. The presumed dangers reflect assumptions about who the citizen is and how his or her desire works. Powerful groups – governments, cultural elites, and moral entrepreneurs like the Women's Christian Temperance Union – have organized themselves around 'protecting' various groups who have not asked for protection. Dangerous or threatening activities have been subject to state forms of moral regulation, based on the state's interest in the moral behaviour of its citizens. Somehow, the reasoning goes, ways must be found to moderate such activities and behaviours, if not outright prohibit them.

Unlike alcohol consumption, drug consumption, prostitution, and pornography, gambling has been legalized by the Canadian state expressly as a revenue generator. The state owns and promotes gambling enterprises and directly collects the revenues generated by player losses. Certainly, governments collect tobacco and alcohol taxes, and in most provinces, alcoholic products are permitted to be sold only in state-controlled venues. These products are still taxed as 'sin taxes,' the assumption being that they are inessential, pleasure-based indulgences. In other words, the very reason for their being taxed is historically connected to their semi-deviant status as illicit pleasures. Admittedly, government-run liquor stores have evolved from stark, prohibitive environments into attractive stores and boutiques that promote alcohol consumption, but the justification for their taxation remains the same. The taxation of tobacco has been accompanied by the reverse treatment: the sale of tobacco is now heavily restricted in terms of its display, promotion, and advertising. Today, tobacco companies are even forbidden to sponsor sporting and high-cultural events. (Interestingly, governments are now resorting to such sponsorships to sell their gambling products.)

Prostitution provides an interesting contrast here. It is legal, but certain activities surrounding it – solicitation, operating a common bawdy house, and living off the avails – are *il*legal. This legal ambiguity may reflect moral ambivalence among governments and lawmakers. All of this has resulted in unsafe working conditions for prostitutes, who cannot get off the street and operate their own houses without fear of legal reprisal.[1]

How does the state construct these dangers? How is a version of morality transmitted through constructions of danger? Questions like these arise with gambling, whose dangers are now imagined as lying within individuals in terms of their proclivities to excess and 'pathology.' The liberalization of desire that we find with legalized gambling, in tandem with liberalized attitudes towards other activities, has diminished the importance of the very idea of vice – an idea that clashes with the notion of the individual's freedoms. Furthermore, gambling has been destigmatized and sanitized for mass consumption. This new, 'free' citizen may be allowed to participate in certain activities or consume certain products, but the state nevertheless maintains the right to invoke its own moral parameters.

It is tempting to say that gambling in Canada has been liberalized and that Canadian morality has moved beyond its Protestant and Victorian heritage (at least in English Canada). This 'liberalization,' though, has been only partial. Gambling has been liberalized insofar as the state can control it and benefit from it, which is a 'selective liberalization' (Abt 1996; Cosgrave 2009). This liberalization has manifested itself as a state monopoly, which further depends on a moral monopoly. This means that the state has the power to define a cultural activity and how it will be organized. In this case, it has come to pass that there is no wholly private ownership; instead, the state has from the outset shaped the gambling field. This is a moral framing of a cultural activity – the state has become the owner of gambling enterprises, and Canadians have tacitly agreed that this is the way things should be. This represents a Canadian political-cultural and moral value that private industry should not be the owner and beneficiary of gambling activities. But it also points to the ways in which statism has been implicated in the Canadian cultural imaginary. This moral monopoly has allowed the state to expand gambling enterprises, including electronic gaming machines (EGMs), at a rapid pace, with attention paid to citizens' concerns about harms only after the fact. This bureaucratic and regulatory statism demonstrates what we call state moralism: a conception of the public good that implies that the state should own gambling enterprises and that assumes or rests on the state's definition of the public and cultural good. Significantly, however, while Canadians may have tacitly accepted this state of affairs, government policy has not corresponded with the views of Canadians on gambling expansion in Canada (McKenna 2008; Smith et al. 2011). Canadians have been allowed little input into government decisions about gambling policy, including policies that are legalizing previously forbidden gambling formats (Osborne 1989; Azmier 2001; Smith and Wynne 2004).

In contrast to the contested place of the CBC in the cultural and everyday life of Canadians, the state's use and definition of gambling demonstrates a statist orientation, in that gambling has largely been imposed on Canadians without public input. At the same time, however, the administration of pleasures and desires is organized in such a way that the state becomes a major component of pleasure itself. While the state *appears* to withdraw from a moral and regulatory approach to gambling, it provides opportunities for gambling consumption in its enterprises, and in doing so, conducts itself in ways that shape desire in the direction of the state.[2] This defining and organizing of gambling is an example of what French sociologist Pierre Bourdieu refers to as symbolic violence: the ability of institutions to impose categories of thought and perception on dominated subjects, who come to take these modes as right. In this way, power and legitimacy are naturalized.

Gambling has been legalized to enable state activities – the revenues generated thereby can be put to use for social purposes. This declared objective has certainly helped legitimate the state's involvement in gambling enterprises. This monopoly model relies on cultural/moral values that could be described as collectivist (e.g., the revenues do not end up in the hands of private profiteers) but that also reveal statist interests. Yet the form of gambling ownership that results does not necessarily equate with the public interest. We could just as easily say that gambling as it has been organized in Canada serves the state first and not necessarily the interests of gamblers themselves, or of communities, or of the public at large. If collectivism is a Canadian value – over and against individualism, for example – it is important to distinguish varieties of collectivism. Canadian collectivism is increasingly *state* collectivism rather than *communal* collectivism. This is demonstrated through the state's use of gambling for charity purposes and through how gambling money is distributed to communities (discussed later in this chapter).

One argument for legalized gambling is that it benefits the gamblers themselves – that individuals get to enjoy a particular type of activity or consumption experience without fear of legal reprisal. It should, though, be pointed out that the monopoly model restricts this benefit by eliminating competition. If gamblers are now to be seen as consumers, they may not be getting the best value for their gambling dollars. Campbell (2009) notes that 'there are few initiatives that seek to address the fundamental fairness of proffered games such as the odds or rates of return paid by EGMs, which are overwhelmingly advantageous to the gaming operator' (85). For example, the Pro Line Sports betting system forces parlay wagering – a clear advantage for the house. Parlay wagering requires a single bet placed on multiple events (such as a minimum of three hockey games in Pro Line), and the wagerer must get all events correct to see a payout. A wagerer who wins three events out of four as separate single bets is doing very well; a parlay wager with three out of four events correct gets nothing. This is an example of how gambling is organized to benefit the state rather than gamblers. Gamblers would get much better odds and payouts gambling online or through bookies. Thus, the disadvantages to the gambler in the state-run system actually encourage participation in illegal gambling. The state's system exploits those citizens who participate by excluding fairer odds (e.g., allowing betting on one game only) and by capitalizing on gamblers' ignorance. It can do so because it is the only legal sports betting game on the scene. The 'benefit to the gambler' argument also assumes the existence of gamblers who *want* to have access to legal gambling venues – that there is a demand-side desire for supply. But this argument does not fully address that, from the supply side of the equation, the state is 'making' gamblers by creating gambling markets and by seeking to stimulate the demand for various gaming products. Which leads to these questions: How are desires shaped by marketing forces? And how are the risks related to gambling participation to be managed? This includes the ways individuals' behaviours are shaped and the ways people are encouraged to think about and orient to their gambling.

Now that gambling has been legalized and commercialized, the providers – be they the state or private industry – are increasingly having to address demands for consumer protection – that is, ensure that the environmental and behavioural factors for 'safe risk' are in place (Gephart 2001). Gambling – here referring to its venues, its environment, and its technologies – must be organized to ensure integrity as well as conformance with standards set by governments. (The OLG boasts on its website that 'we are not required to conduct 90,000 tests on our slot machines. But we do it anyway' [OLG 2010a].) Some of the risks that have been related to gambling must be seen to have been removed: dangers such as dodgy neighbourhoods, shady characters, swindlers and criminals, and the risk of arrest. Paradoxically, however, risk has also *increased* as a result of the state being the 'only show in town.' In effect, the state has positioned itself to tell us how to measure and weigh the risks of our own behaviour. All sides of gambling-related risk have been subsumed within the same organ – the state – which now enjoys a monopoly on the construction and framing of risk.

Regarding this idea of 'safe risk,' the risks of addiction are now being framed in particular ways. As a risk management strategy both for gamblers and for providers, the latter seek to communicate and inculcate responsible gambling. In addition to that, addiction itself is being managed through the government's own treatment programs for those who feel they cannot control their gambling. Since the consequences of gambling addiction can be devastating, the government must be able to claim that it is concerned about pathological and problem gamblers and that it is providing treatment for them. It must provide opportunities for problem gamblers to 'get help' if they choose. Government involvement in gambling has produced individuals who gamble excessively. That same involvement has made the problem gambler visible in society by producing discourse around gambling problems. One result of all this has been that the provincial governments have placed themselves in positions of legal liability, as demonstrated by recent lawsuits in Canada against various gaming corporations.

The history of gambling in Canada has been ably recounted by Suzanne Morton (2003), who focuses on the years 1919 to 1969. Also, the development of legal gambling markets has been discussed by Canadian gambling scholars. So only those historical features that pertain to our discussion will be recounted here. The focus in this chapter is on how the organization of legalized gambling speaks to state/culture dynamics. This in turn prompts questions about how desire is generated and regulated. How are activities that have been considered vices, or that are morally questionable, or that potentially generate excessive consumption, shaped as features of state/culture dynamics and in relation to state conceptions of the desirable and the desiring citizen? How are desires socialized in relation to the interests of the nation and the state? How are those desires governed as moral projects conducive to state interests? *How* desire is shaped is a question faced by all nation-states.

Until the last third of the twentieth century, except for bingo and horse racing, most forms of gambling were illegal in Canada. The past forty years have seen a rapid expansion in legal gambling, especially since the early 1990s, after 1985 amendments to the Criminal Code allowed provincial governments to enter the casino and electronic gaming industry in earnest. The first Canadian lotteries followed from a state objective: the funding of the Montreal Olympics in 1976 (Campbell 2009). We also point out here the state's funding of athletics in the service of the state-nationalistic goal of Olympic honour. Governments have gone from peddling the relatively benign lotteries, where the cost of 'imagining the freedom' and the intensity of the gambling experience are low, to being the main beneficiaries in the spread of casinos, electronic gambling, and sports betting. With gambling liberalization, not all gambling has been rendered legal: your friendly neighbourhood poker den is illegal, and the Canadian provinces have been slow to legalize Internet gambling and colonize it for revenue purposes.

TV commercials for early lotteries such as 'Wintario' – Ontario's first lottery (started in 1975) – showed a community setting with local residents dropping by the corner store to pick up a ticket and chat with the store owner. The lottery draws took place in Ontario communities, and community members took part in the festivities. Relatively speaking, this was good, clean, wholesome fun for Ontarians. But much has changed in the Canadian gambling environment, especially since the early 1990s. We note the increase in the number of lotteries (Wintario went defunct in 1990), as well as the significantly larger jackpots. Wintario jackpots were a maximum of $500,000; today, Lotto 6/49 and Lotto Max jackpots reach into the tens of millions of dollars, with Lotto Max capped at $50,000,000. These lotteries and their promotion in the media have contributed to the ubiquitous gambling environment; they also speak to the increased role of lotteries in state and government financing and to changes in state conduct. McMullan and Miller (2009) studied hundreds of lottery ads from Atlantic Canada and found that they made 'little reference to actual odds of winning' and were 'enticing people with the prospects of huge jackpots, attractive consumer goods and easy wins, showcasing top prize winners, and providing dubious depictions that winning is life-changing' (291). In late-capitalist societies, where employment is often precarious, direct correlations have been found among unemployment levels, low income, and lottery ticket expenditures; this, even though ads often present participation in terms of consumption and leisure. State-owned gambling in general is a regressive form of taxation, with the poor spending a higher percentage of their income than the wealthy (Vaillancourt and Roy 2000).

Governments are now promoting and benefiting economically from riskier forms of gambling. We are referring here to continuous and experientially intense forms of gambling, such as EGMs, which include video lottery terminals (VLTs) and slot machines. The term 'riskier' here refers to the greater probability that an individual will develop a gambling problem and encounter its consequences: bankruptcy, family conflict and breakdown, mental health problems, criminal activity (fraud and theft), and suicide.

The old Wintario ads focused on community interactions. We might well wonder, then, how conceptions of community are changing under conditions of ubiquitous gambling. We also point to the ways in which state-run gambling has affected community forms of gambling such as horse racing and bingo. It is significant that both these forms of gambling have been in decline, in part because newer generations of Canadians have little interest in those gambling forms, and in part because of competition from newly legalized forms of gambling such as casinos and EGMs. The newer generations of gamblers have been socialized in an environment that is saturated with legal gambling, and they have easy access to many forms of gambling, from scratch-and-win tickets and sports betting at the corner store, to casinos (often a short drive away), to various forms of Internet gambling, which can be accessed from the comfort of home or even by cell phone. The neighbourhood card game and the illegal poker den still exist in their communal forms; contrast this with the rationalized and anonymous setting of the casino, and with highly individualized forms of gambling such as EGMs, now that gambling has been legalized and expanded in Canada.

One of the more controversial aspects of gambling expansion has been the rapid spread of electronic gaming. This form has generated the greatest concern among community and anti-gambling groups, who are protesting it. It is a significant societal development that EGMs are now the most common and widespread form of gambling. That this is so speaks to the ability of these machines to generate revenues at much lower costs than table games, which require paid employees to run them. It also speaks to how the gambling market is being shaped as well as to what people view as 'gambling' (though some would refer to this type of activity as 'gaming'). EGMs are considered to be the riskiest form of gambling in terms of their propensity to stimulate excessive gambling (i.e., gambling addiction; see Smith and Campbell 2007). Unlike table games such as blackjack and poker, where play takes place with others, and where interaction, even a 'social order,' develops (Marksbury 2010), EGM gambling is a solitary activity that requires no links to friends or to community, or to anyone at all. The gambler's desire is mediated directly by these machines, which have become increasingly complex and technologically sophisticated.

Critics of the spread of this form of gambling point to the behaviour-shaping capabilities of these machines. Peter Adams (2007), an Australian who has written on the threats to democratic systems posed by gambling expansion and by the reliance of governments on gambling revenue, refers to EGMs as 'gambling supply consoles' comprising an electronic as well as a psychological technology (6). Fellow Australians Charles Livingstone and Richard Woolley (2007) offer that 'gamblers are not powerless to resist the enticements of EGMs, but EGM games have been scientifically developed to attract gamblers, reconfigure their agency, and maximize their expenditure. Excessive levels of harm production are in our view a concomitant of this' (369). While the type of addiction related to these machines – stimulated by operant conditioning – is nothing new, the machines differ from older slot machines in terms of their technological sophistication, in that they provide 'an unsafe mode of rapid and expensive consumption' (369).

Emile Durkheim argued that the two most dangerous qualities of modern society were 'anomie' and 'egoism.' *Anomie* refers to the notion that individuals who do not experience the constraints of collective norms have no capacity to set limits on desire. In other words, the meaning of any success or 'win' depends on the broader social context in which it appears. When we see others getting more and more without effort, it makes hard-won successes (such as money gained through wage labour) less rewarding. Similarly, the value of a small sum is relative to the moneys accruing to others around us. *Egoism* refers to the increasing tendency for people to live outside the bounds of deep group affiliations that would give them identity – family, kin group, local community, religion, profession, trade union, and so on. We are increasingly isolated individuals. In Durkheim's terms, anomie involves a lack of limit or regulation of desire, whereas egoism involves a lack of integration into community. Taken together, nothing better describes the effect of EGMs, in that they are expressly designed to stimulate desire and isolate the player. As we will discuss later, gamblers are encouraged by state agencies to enjoy EGMs without losing control. The difficulties of locating satisfaction and limit are, however, designed right into these machines.

Hence a behavioural desire is being shaped and configured as a form of entertainment, and governments are willing to exploit that desire. While some Canadian provinces confine their EGMs to casinos, others allow them more liberally, in bars, lounges, and airports. This is contributing to 'convenience gambling.' Governments are aware of the harms these machines generate but are unwilling to ban them – they are too important a revenue source (McKenna 2008; Cosgrave 2009). This individualization of gambling can be contrasted with how various social programs and community projects are funded. We might well ask about the effects on communities of easily accessible gambling, and further point out that state-owned gambling is in effect not much more than a revenue (tax) circulation system, in that it transfers money from individuals to various governments, with the EGMs and casinos acting as the collectors.

Significantly, the state has responded to the threat posed to the horse-racing industry by the spread of other legal state-owned gambling forms by inserting itself into horse-racing venues. Those venues have been transformed into 'racinos' by installing slot machines at them, the argument being that this will help bring patrons to the tracks. But this has also allowed the state to spread its gambling reach by colonizing privately operated venues, thereby increasing its own gambling revenues. We see here the state's interest in acting like a commercial provider and in gaining a competitive advantage as a result of its legal power to monopolize a particular consumer market. Provincial governments have been responsible for the spread of slot machines and VLTs in Canada, in casinos and racinos and – in some provinces – in convenient settings such as bars, lounges, and airports. It is a curious phenomenon that governing is now being 'done' through slot machines and other electronic gaming devices.

Who Is the Gambler-Citizen?

All of this points to the effects of state gambling policies on communities, and also to the ways in which community and citizen are conceptualized. The charity model of gambling has largely been colonized by the state. In Ontario, for example, privately operated roving charity casinos have been made illegal, and the state has taken over this gambling form, replacing those venues with stationary charity casinos, such as the Brantford, Thousand Islands, and Great Blue Heron casinos. Also, the use of gambling moneys to fund social programs, projects, communities, and charities has shifted the generation and distribution of charity money to state control. Groups seeking funding for their projects apply for it to the distributors, such as Ontario's Trillium Foundation. One effect of this arrangement has been to extend state power by making the state the definer of charity and the controller of charity money. This extension of state power has resulted from the extension of the state into gambling enterprises in the first place. Thus the state – rather than the individual, the church, or the community – has been placed in the position of defining 'charity' and deciding who deserves it. Provincial governments have no problem dispensing charity money derived from gambling, but some recipients wrestle with the ethical issues raised by accepting money from this source, and indeed, some have turned it down (Ramp and Badgley 2009). Those who do accept it are, in effect, legitimizing this structure of dispensation. In this way, communities and charity groups are brought into the gambling revenue economy, thereby reinforcing the state's own definition of community and charity.

Gambling is no longer explicitly morally objectionable in broad cultural terms, and arguments for its prohibition no longer hold any real force. That said, we must recognize the role the state has played in transforming the moral status of gambling in Canada. Not so long ago, gambling was a 'sin' to the religious believer and a 'vice' to the government official, the law enforcement officer, and the law-abiding Canadian citizen. As Suzanne Morton points out in her 2003 study, the approach to gambling in Canada for many decades demonstrated attitudes of unofficial tolerance and official condemnation. For example, the Irish Sweepstakes were highly popular but also illegal, though law enforcement did not closely monitor ticket sales. There was significant covert gambling throughout the twentieth century prior to the period of liberalization, but gambling activity remained morally questionable and contentious. As discussed earlier in this book, lottery schemes became legal in the late 1960s as part of a Liberal omnibus bill that also liberalized divorce, abortion, contraception, and homosexuality. In 1985 the Criminal Code was amended further to give provincial governments control over lotteries (in return for payments to the federal government) and also to allow the provinces to operate lottery schemes through a computer, video device, or slot machine (Campbell 2009). This amendment has paved the way for the rapid spread of electronic gaming in most Canadian provinces. It has also, along with the stimulatory provincial gambling promotions, fostered the conditions for the cultural normalization of gambling in Canada.

Clearly, the state has played an important role in the moral transformation of gambling. Here we see particular state/culture dynamics at work. Gambling legalization also speaks to the role of religion in Canadian culture. In English Canada, gambling legalization had to wait for the waning of Protestant values and for the church to lose its grip on the definition of morality. The situation has been different in Quebec, where the dominance of Catholicism has meant a more tolerant attitude towards games of chance. A feature of the Protestant world view is the equation of hard work with merit (i.e., reward follows diligence). The reliance on chance is irreligious; gambling has thus been objectionable to ascetic Protestantism. Consider next the slogan once used in an ad for the (now defunct) Super 7 lottery: 'Making money is great, but winning it is even better.' Consider also the 'Imagine the Freedom' campaign for Lotto 6/49. Imagine the freedom to buy, and the freedom from drudgery. Through their gambling enterprises, governments are promoting the validity of chance and are helping undermine the belief that reward follows diligence and that diligence is its own reward.

In this era of legalized gambling, moral discourse does not appear to frame gambling as inherently wrong. We should qualify this: some gambling activities in Canada *are* stigmatized – illegal poker dens, for example – and governments are now finding it expedient to destigmatize Internet gambling. But in those cases, the issue is not the activity itself but rather the lack of state colonization. Being a gambler, or going gambling, does not seem to entail the same shading of deviance that it did not too long ago. This is not to say there are not social conflicts over gambling, as we have seen in those provinces with VLT gambling. As noted earlier, the negative impacts on communities and citizens are implied by the lawsuits against lottery corporations. Lawsuits have been lodged in Ontario, Newfoundland and Labrador, and Nova Scotia; and Loto-Québec has reached a tentative agreement to compensate thousands of addicted gamblers. That is an out-of-court settlement, however, which means that no legal precedent is being set for similar cases (*Globe and Mail* 2009c). We mustn't, here, underestimate the state's efforts to legitimize its gambling activities through TV ads, the use of gambling money for sponsorship purposes, and 'for the social good' arguments. Gambling seems to have become accepted, at least tacitly, although public opinion is often critical of or opposed to gambling, as we discuss below.

These developments raise questions about the moral framing of behaviours that the state (and not only religion) once prohibited. In earlier formulations of gambling behaviour, the desire to gamble was desire gone wrong. It entailed a desire to have things you don't deserve. In the religious formulation, gambling was sinful; in modern secular terms, it was a vice. Gambling was socially condemned in moral terms. Now, the undesirable aspects of gambling exist only as by-products of the activity itself. Imagine a day when gambling could exist without risk. *That*, in some ways, is the ideal of the providers, notwithstanding that problem gamblers are the best customers. On that day, there would be nothing wrong with the desire to gamble. The moral connection between work and reward would be cut, and in keeping with the ethos of consumer society, gambling desire could be incited, stimulated, and exploited without repercussions.

Paradoxically, while governments are promoting the chance ethic among the citizenry, it is a feature of the organization of legalized gambling in Canada that its revenues be made productive. That is, gambling should not result in sheer unproductive expenditure, and gamblers' losses should not line the pockets of private industry. It is tempting here to see a residual Protestantism in this shaping of gambling in Canada. Certainly, this is evidence of the value that Canadian society places on the state. The moral discourse here has been transferred from the gambler (now that gambling itself has been legitimized) to the beneficiary – the private sector doesn't deserve this revenue. The revenue itself is 'clean,' as is the practice of gambling. The transference to the provinces' coffers in effect means that the moral discourse now revolves around the 'positive' uses of the revenues – which reflects the state moralism already in place in Canadian political culture. Problematic gamblers are in effect throwing a wrench into the circulation of gambling revenues. On the one hand, they provide a significant portion of the revenues (which for them, of course, are losses). On the other hand, they become a cost to the system, either through prevention and treatment campaigns or through legal claims (as discussed earlier).

Regarding the productive uses of gambling expenditures, we are reminded of the moral orientation to profits of the early Protestants as discussed by Max Weber in *The Protestant Ethic and the Spirit of Capitalism* ([1905]1958). The Protestant believer solves the moral problem of profit by reinvesting it, for profit should be thought of as a possible sign of salvation and not as a sign of worldly success or as a means to personal pleasure. The recirculation of profit back into work ritualistically removes it from pleasure and indulgence. The notion of community served by this reinvestment is as abstract as the Protestant God – a semiotic puzzle that involves the incessant circulation of signs. If it is not necessarily a

Protestant framing to link the proscriptions against pleasure and indulgence with contemporary exhortations against excessive gambling (one should be a 'responsible' gambler), the excessive or problem gambler nevertheless is evaluated or framed by rationalistic conceptions of an autonomous, sovereign subject who should have self-control (Reith 2007).

This role of the state in gambling enterprises situates the state in a contemporary consumer culture, where pleasure and the immediate satisfaction of desire are reigning values, rather than hard work, thrift, and the prospect of future rewards. In this gambling-friendly climate, the individual is mobilized to pay tax in part through voluntary participation in gambling, which requires heavy advertising to stimulate the desire. It also points to the individualization of taxation, for imposed taxes are unpopular in neoliberal economic climates. Neoliberalism, which privileges the idea that social and economic relations – including the state's relationship to citizens – should be conducted as market relations, challenges purported Canadian collectivist and social-democratic values. This seems to be the gist of the response to the BCLC article in the comment included earlier in the chapter. The state is using gambling as a revenue generator, thus enacting a market solution to taxation even while imposing further statism through its control of gambling enterprises. In their advertising and annual reports, the various lottery corporations point out to us the social good those gambling revenues are doing. An example:

> Ever wonder where the money goes? OLG generates $3.8* billion annually in economic activity in Ontario.
> Contribution – 1.9 billion to the province includes:
> $110 million – Gaming proceeds distributed through the Ontario Trillium Foundation to local and provincial charities
> $10 million – Support for amateur athletes through the Quest for Gold program
> $1.8 billion – Hospitals, health related programs and other provincial priorities
>   (*based on the period April 1, 2008 to March 31, 2009) (OLG 2010b)

Apparently one is to conclude that gambling is good for Canadians.

The state monopoly form is found in other countries. Even so, we can learn something about *Canada*'s state and culture and about its state/culture dynamics by examining the way legal gambling has been structured and socially organized here. The story of gambling in Canada since 1969 and into the twenty-first century is not just about its liberalization, legalization, and expansion; it is also about how the state is using gambling as a political-economic vehicle. The legalization and organization of state-owned gambling is a performance of state conduct and an expression of Canadian political culture. State-owned gambling is an approach to governing citizens – or, more accurately, *consumer*-citizens, given that the state desires that citizens takes part in gambling consumption. But state-owned gambling is also an act of symbolic violence, one that reproduces Canadian statism. Thus it offers us an opportunity to reflect on the construction of what could be called 'Canadian risk.'

In what way is state-run gambling an expression of Canadian culture and an example of the shaping of Canadian desire? Through the example of gambling as a cultural activity, we can see how orientations to vice and to risk are shaped by the state and how this shaping reflects cultural values and attitudes.

Problem and pathological gamblers pose a problem for state-run gambling. Where gambling activities have been destigmatized, it is gamblers who cannot control their gambling that become a problem, not only for themselves and their families, but also for the legitimacy of state involvement in gambling enterprises. Gambling desires, then, must be shaped, and this is accomplished through initiatives such as 'responsible gambling,' but also through the framing of the social good that gambling revenues serve. In terms of shaping individual desires, responsible gambling is supposed to help prevent the onset of gambling problems, but it is also a strategy for deflecting criticism of readily available gambling away from the owners (the provincial governments) and onto the gamblers, who must learn to become responsible in their gambling conduct. In this way, governments lay gambling risk onto the individual – except that, where they offer programs to help problem gamblers (thus admitting to creating the problem through gambling-friendly policies), they set themselves up for liability. Besides the lawsuit against the OLG mentioned in the article excerpted earlier, there have been a number of others against provincial lottery corporations, including a $3.5 billion class action lawsuit against the OLG for the apparent failings of its self-exclusion policy. The OLG had previously settled nine self-exclusion cases, but it had not faced a large class-action lawsuit such as this one.[3] With gambling, risks are offloaded; gambling casualties are a risk of doing business, and the money directed towards problem gambling is the official solution.

Gambling liberalization and legalization suggests a socially laissez-faire approach to gambling and even a weaker state, in that states no longer have to police an illegal activity. But the neoliberal state does not signify a reduction in the range and scope of state interventions; rather, it involves market colonization or the culling of activities that produce revenue. In other words, the neoliberal state moves into an activity that requires a market approach and corporatization. Gambling liberalization in Canada has brought with it an increase in state powers, especially as the state has taken on a central and active role in building gambling markets. This increase in the state's powers occurs not only through its expanded albeit conflicted role as revenue seeker and gambling regulator, but also through its interest in knowing the effects of gambling on society, which in turn requires that research institutes and projects be funded. The state develops and manifests itself corporately through its gambling market interests; meanwhile, it takes an interest in gambling behaviours by funding institutes such as the Ontario Problem Gambling Research Centre and the Alberta Gaming Research Institute. The production of gambling knowledge is also generated by programs devoted to gambling addiction research, such as McGill University's International Centre for Youth Gambling Problems and High Risk Behaviours.

We suggest that this marks a significant transformation of the Canadian state: a shift away from the welfare state towards the risk-managing neoliberal state, but in tandem with the ongoing phenomenon of Canadian paternalistic statism. Furthermore, as we have been discussing, the state appears to govern through the procurement of pleasure, but this too must be viewed in terms of how the desires and pleasures of Canadians must, in effect, orient themselves to the state's versions, or at least not pose a threat to them.

The state not only culls a cultural activity for its own revenue purposes, but also expands gambling, builds and shapes the gambling market, and defines gambling in its legal forms. That process of defining includes legitimizing gambling as an acceptable activity for state involvement. Furthermore, because the state plays a central role in gambling markets (as the provider of 'entertainment' to generate revenues), it has a vested interest in gambling behaviours. Thus it seeks to maximize revenues while simultaneously managing the risks that arise as a result of participation in gambling. The state stimulates gambling behaviours through advertising even while funding research into gambling behaviour. It governs gambling through its direct role in consumer markets. TV viewers watch advertisements, many of them shown during prime time (sometimes back to back), that variously (1) promote some form of state-owned gambling, such as a lottery or casino, (2) warn against the dangers of gambling, and (3) celebrate the benefits of gambling revenue to communities. In Ontario, all of these ads are paid for by the Ontario Lottery and Gaming Corporation – in other words, through the revenues generated from gambling in Ontario.

The state's direct involvement in consumer markets goes beyond regulating them: it is the state that *owns* the gambling enterprises and that sells the 'gaming experience.' This places the state in a conflict of interest, a conflict that is risk-managed through the framing of the revenue uses (social programs and the public good) as well as through the notion that the individual's involvement in gambling is one of consumer choice. Yet the individual must be *responsibilized* in this choice, as the article included earlier implies.

Since the proceeds of gambling are intended to be used productively, a portion of gambling revenues are cast as a form of 'charity.' Yet at the same time that these revenues are used for communities, these communities are home to problem and pathological gamblers and to individuals who are 'at risk' of becoming so (i.e., who are in need of the proceeds of gambling as a result of gambling too much). The Canadian state has colonized or culled a cultural activity (Cosgrave and Klassen 2001), and in doing so has generated new forms of risk. But because that risk is productive for the state (i.e., it generates revenues), it is important for Canadians to understand the ways in which the state is developing and exploiting gambling markets. Furthermore, while the legitimized notion of state-owned gambling has produced glaring tensions and contradictions (Smith and Campbell 2007), that notion is also being eroded by deals with foreign gambling operators as well as by the challenges of Internet gambling.

Through sleight of hand, the state has made gambling seem like a *fait accompli*, as if it really was in the public interest. Gambling is touted by lottery and gaming corporations as a revenue generator for social programs. Yet the proceeds from gambling that go into social programs have come out of the pockets of the same people and communities that *need* those programs. Legal gambling has also led to suicides.[4] The public good in this is surely debatable.

With gambling, the state has become a utilitarian risk manager, drawing upon a Canadian-brand (statist) moralism that allows it to monopolize gambling for the public good. (By 'utilitarian' we mean a broad political philosophy – made famous by British philosopher Jeremy

Bentham – that argues that the public good is simply whatever provides the most pleasure for the most people. It is a form of consequentialism by which the value of any action or policy is measured by its effects rather than in terms of the moral quality of the act itself.) Perhaps the problem is the state's definition of the public good, especially when, as in the case of gambling, the public has not been consulted. In these circumstances, the state will shape its version of peace, order and good gambling in such a way that gambling risks can be controlled and the public good will be served. With gambling, however, we have a neoliberal form of state conduct that makes taxes difficult to generate. We note of course two things: that the state often does not consult the citizens, and that it is capable of paternalistic moves that seek to protect citizens from harm to themselves or other citizens. With gambling, though, this sort of paternalism is amoral. In its approach to framing the citizen, it resorts to neoliberal utilitarianism, and for an alibi, it claims to be generating revenues that will serve the public good. As citizens are oriented to as individual consumers (who are encouraged to consume the state's gambling products and accept the legitimacy of those enterprises), democratic systems are degraded (Adams 2007).

When it comes to gambling, then, the state generates revenues through the market and acts like a corporation selling a product to the public. State-run gambling is heavily promoted on television, even though tobacco ads are banned and alcohol cannot be shown to be directly consumed. When it comes to promoting 'vices,' the state clearly has an advantage with its products. In promoting gambling, the state has withdrawn from its responsibility for protecting citizens by introducing risk and opening the potential for harm, which the individual is then encouraged to manage. As the earlier articles indicate, they must learn to be *responsible* gamblers. The state will help the problem gambler by providing treatment, but this is *after* the money has been pocketed. It is significant that in Canada, funding for treatment and for various programs aimed at problem gamblers came *after* the spread of state-run gambling, and all the while, the provinces have been happy to collect revenues from problem gamblers. A clearer example of neoliberalism would be harder to find: the state has shed its social welfare obligations.

The issue of social problems – problem gambling in particular – did not arise as a concern when the state was launching gambling enterprises – after all, gambling was going to be framed and sold as 'entertainment.' This oversight was due either to ignorance or to expediency (i.e., there was knowledge of gambling problems but the revenue interest prevailed). Whichever was the case, we should now be questioning whether the authority of the gambling providers is legitimate. The point here is that statism has prevailed – for 'the good of Canadians.'

The state has legitimized its involvement in the gambling market in part by funding studies of problem and pathological gambling. This is meant to show that it is addressing the problem scientifically. The founding of the Ontario Problem Gambling Research Centre in 2000, by the Ontario Ministry of Health and Long-Term Care, amounts to an admission by the Ontario government that its policies have generated problem gamblers. This admission is also tacit in the Loto-Québec lawsuit. The apparently after-the-fact problems generated by gambling expansion can be dealt with by applying science to them – that is, by counting and measuring problem gamblers, making them visible, and providing education and treatment programs. In other words, gambling problems have become fodder for risk management. Problem and pathological gamblers, who account for a significant proportion of gambling revenues, are deemed not to pose a threat to the legitimacy of state involvement in gambling.[5] Regardless of where we locate the source of gambling problems arising from excessive gambling, addiction or gambling pathology is embedded in the gambling economy. It is an object of study, and problem gamblers, instead of exposing the state's complicity in their plight, have been integrated into the legal and legitimate gambling economy (Cosgrave 2010).

State-run gambling seems to rely on two perceptions: that the state is benign, and that gambling is 'entertainment' and can be put to work for social purposes. However, the conflict of interest involved brings to light the utilitarianism of the state and points to the moral question of how a state should relate to its citizens. The state, having become the 'house,' collects gamblers' losses. It is also involved in creating social harm, however small the number of problem gamblers may be. Instructive in all of this is how the gambling example brings into clear relief contemporary practices of state power: the state, if not hiding under the cover of the benign, obscures its interest in shaping citizen conduct in particular directions. Think here about how the state reifies itself, that is, takes on a particular shape and form for the citizen through gambling – as the provider of fun and excitement, perhaps in an otherwise dull world, or as a response to the rationalization of everyday life. On this point, the lottery ads are telling – 'imagine the freedom' to buy whatever you want. And, as mentioned, there is also the denigration of the work ethic, demonstrated in the Super 7 ads, which featured characters such as 'Relaxo' and 'Two Weeks Notice Man' – 'Because you can!' Insofar as gambling has been legalized, the state continues in its role as regulator of enterprises and activities. However, what we have been discussing points to an interesting and significant conception of the state: it demonstrates its power by offering pleasure, as the provider of 'safe' risk. It governs through the cultivation of desire. Perhaps the state as the 'house' is more than just a metaphor. Maybe the state *is* the house. And what is the Canadian public in this?

In Canada, the apparently benign interest in 'peace, order and good government' is seen in relation to the control and management of 'vices' by the state; but with state-owned gambling enterprises, the interest in order and the regulation of gambling together reveal a patronizing, utilitarian, and morally problematic orientation. The state's conflict of interest with its ownership of gambling enterprises reveals that the state has the power, even in neoliberal contexts, to define the gambling situation: not just to regulate it but to exploit it for its revenue interests. Put differently, the conflict of interest indicates that the state has come out on the side of its market and corporate interests; the conflict of interest 'goes away' once we understand the interests and orientations of the neoliberalized state.

If public opinion does not really support the government's gambling policies, it doesn't matter – the state has implemented gambling under the assumption that Canadian desire is desire for the state, even if the state is no longer the welfare state it once was.

'Cooling the Mark Out'

The work of Erving Goffman, a Canadian-born sociologist, is useful in this context. Much of Goffman's work demonstrated that the strategies found in deviant social locations are very similar to those found in legitimate ones. In 'On Cooling the Mark Out' (1952), he argued that the strategies used by con men to cool out or placate the victim of the con (the 'mark') are similar to those used in the workplace, in courtship, and in business. In other words, co-workers, spouses, and customers are handled like marks. Workers who are being demoted or fired, romantic partners who are being dumped or divorced, and customers who feel dissatisfied or disrespected are handled so that they come to feel that their loss is not really a loss at all. They are 'cooled out' and made to feel good about what has happened to them. The loser becomes the winner, at least to some degree, as the situation is redefined. As Goffman says, his study is about the 'sugar-coating . . . and not the pill' (18).

Goffman's work is highly relevant here, for the social proximity of illegal con games (gambling) and the legitimate world becomes even closer when the state becomes the 'house.' The con artist must manage the mark so that the latter does not run to the police; similarly, the state must manage the gambler/citizen so that its legitimacy is not questioned. As Goffman puts it: 'An institution, after all, cannot take it on the lam; it must pacify its marks' (9). In the case of gambling, the state must manage the risk of being seen to be like the illegal con artist who profits from rigged games and unfair strategies. Next we look at some of the educational and promotional campaigns that are shaping our understanding of gambling in Canada. As noted earlier, the roles of educator, protector, benefactor, promoter, and house are all rolled into one agent – the state. This provides great flexibility when it comes to cooling the mark out.

The first type of government campaign we will consider involves those whose aim is to educate the gambler/citizen. On the face of it, such campaigns are intended to provide information about the realities and risks of gambling so that the gambler can make better decisions about gambling. But considering the remote likelihood of a big win, the state must manage the gambler's education in ways that both encourage gambling and control it. In one such campaign, the OLG invites those who visit their website to take a quiz to measure their gambling 'I.Q.' (OLG 2010c). Of course, the notion of IQ is used very loosely here. It is not based in the Stanford-Binet notion of IQ, where scores are evaluated relative to the general population. There are ten questions. Each question provides four choices, three of which are patently incorrect. The correct answers that will reward you with a perfect score (and the assurance of the high 'I.Q.'), are plainly set out in the choices. Here are two of the ten questions on the quiz:

When playing Roulette, it might be a good idea to:
a) Wait until you have a 'gut' feeling about your chances of winning.
b) Figure out a strategy to beat the odds.
c) Set a budget of how much you want to spend and stick to it!
d) Wear your 'lucky' t-shirt.

Notice the punctuation that accompanies two of the wrong answers. Both 'gut' and 'lucky' are put in scare quotes, making answers 'a' and 'd' clearly bad choices (as they involve superstition). Now only 'b' and 'c' are left, increasing the odds of a 'win.' Only 'c,' the correct answer, speaks emphatically to the reader with an instruction about spending (not 'losing,' by the way). Here is another question:

> Responsible Gaming Resources Centres are a good place to find information about:
> a) Problem gambling help and resources.
> b) How gambling works.
> c) Tips to keep gambling fun.
> d) All of the above.

Clearly, 'd' is the correct answer. If a Responsible Gaming Resources Centre is a 'good place to find out information,' presumably it provides lots of information of various and relevant kinds. It also must emphasize that gambling should be fun because the gambler must understand himself or herself to be a 'winner.' Finally, in terms of cooling this mark out and making everyone a winner, the end of the quiz generates the message: 'Congratulations! You got an x out of 10 correct.' (Even if x equals zero).

Goffman would have pointed out that this quiz is not intended to educate as much as to cool the mark out – that is, to allow us to feel good about ourselves and our gambling savvy. As Goffman explains: 'In many cases . . . the mark's image of himself is built up on the belief that he is a pretty shrewd person . . . and that he is not the sort of person who is taken in by anything' (4). This quiz marries the pleasure of a quiz/game with the reward of success. But easy success and rigged gaming are the hallmarks of the con. They are not supposed to be embedded in a quiz that aims at education. In other words, while the questions in the quiz suggest that we are learning about the real odds of winning, what we are actually learning is to trust the legitimacy of state gambling. Either the form of this quiz undermines the goal of education (as it is hard to imagine someone so lacking in common sense as to not recognize the correct answers), or the goal is actually to con and cool out the mark. The test is designed to let us feel competent in the face of gambling.

Another OLG lesson comes in the form of a video that explains the odds involved in slots games: 'The Slot Machine: What Every Player Needs to Know' (OLG 2010c). At first glance this video takes its audience far more seriously than the IQ quiz. It explains how the odds work when playing slot machines. It goes into detail about the way many people apparently think of the machines – which is, as a conveyer belt with marbles moving forward. In this analogy the player imagines incorrectly that the odds of winning improve as play moves along. This faulty analogy sets up the 'trap of playing beyond your limit.' The video explains that the correct analogy would be a huge cylinder filled with marbles. After a marble has been selected (with each spin of the slot machine), it is reloaded into the cylinder before the next spin. The odds of a big win (about 1 in 1,000,000) remain the same with each spin. This is a forthright and clear explanation of how odds work in this type of game. But after providing this explanation, the video cools out the mark. For example, it suggests that understanding and bearing in mind the *correct* analogy will protect against the traps that arise with the *incorrect* analogy. After the odds are set out, the video discusses strategies of risk management that will actually keep the gambler returning to the slots. Given that these machines are expressly designed by experts in behavioural psychology to encourage addictive behaviour, it does not discuss the odds that these strategies will succeed. In other words, it does not discuss the isolation, mechanization, and anomie that have been designed into these machines quite intentionally. Instead the 'Seven Habits for Problem-Free Gambling' are presented: (1) set a limit on spending, (2) don't bring a cushion of extra money, (3) plan a departure time, (4) avoid ATMs, (5) cool down (go to the lounge), (6) recall the odds, and (7) picture the cylinder. Finally, the viewer is told to 'maximize enjoyment and reduce risk.' This again returns to the isolating and mechanized nature of this machine. Such machines are designed to prevent interaction with others, so that the only possible enjoyment arises from actually using the machine. To reduce risk, one would have to reduce play. What would the pleasure of using these machines look like if the possibility of winning were not present? It would certainly not involve pleasures such as interacting with others, displaying skill, winning or losing with grace, developing a reputation of some kind, sharing stories about past communal play, working within a complex etiquette, or any of the other challenges and pleasures that accompany, say, poker games among friends or in the gambling den. Again, the citizen-gambler at a slot machine becomes a mark, and the video is prepping him to think he is not one. According to Goffman,

> a second general solution to the problem of cooling the mark out consists of offering him a status which differs from the one he has lost or failed to gain but which provides at least a something or somebody to become. Usually the alternative presented to the mark is a compromise of some kind, providing some of the trappings of his lost status as well as with some of its spirit. (11)

We see this strategy in government campaigns that promote gambling explicitly. They do this by invoking some of the notions apparently dismissed by the educational campaigns – such as luck. Take, for example, this account of the 'Super Player's Club' winner:

> On the night she won her major prize, she was supposed to be babysitting for her son while he and his wife went to a movie, which happened to be sold out. So instead, Judith went out to play Bingo and ended up winning $43,338 playing the Late Link!
>
> A stay-at-home mother of four, Judith has been playing Bingo for over 10 years. She feels that the people at the hall are her second family and she loves the anticipation of winning. She plans to share her winnings with her family and buy flowers for her yard. (OLG 2010d)

Here is it suggested that 'as luck would have it' the movie was sold out and family obligations were lifted, allowing Judith to get back to the bingo hall and win that night. It suggests that if she had not attended bingo that night she would have 'missed' the win intended for her (just the type of thinking that the OLG claims not to encourage). Judith is blessed with luck. She is a winner. Moreover, this website extends the notion of 'winner' to anyone who can demonstrate that they spend time in the casino – the more they swipe their Super Player's card with the purchase of bingo cards, the more prizes and rewards they earn. Caesars Windsor Casino features the 'Progressive Multiplier,' which increases rewards up to twenty-five times if swiped four consecutive weeks. Loyalty cards also describe their uses as 'winners' – for example, 'Winner Circle Rewards.' In other words, by gambling more, patrons become more economical and sensible gamblers. In fact, they 'earn' these points and rewards. Here luck mixes with *earning* or *deserving* (working for) one's rewards. The old Protestant work ethic is being invoked to assure the consumers that they are acting in a rational and calculating way. Essentially, this mark is being cooled out by the assurance of inclusion. Goffman explained that the mark may be cooled out by way of compensation. Although the mark is not a 'winner' in the literal sense, he or she is included in the 'winner's circle.' Goffman comments that

> sustained personal disorganization is one way in which a mark can refuse to cool out. Another standard way is for the individual to raise a squawk, that is, to make a formal complaint to higher authorities obliged to take notice of such matters. The con mob worries lest the mark appeal to the police. The plant manager must make sure that the disgruntled department head

does not carry a formal complaint to the general manager or, worse still, to the Board of Directors. (13)

As we have discussed, the problem gambler is one social type who has raised a squawk.

The third broad type of government campaign is aimed at the consequences of problem or pathological gambling. Right off the top, Goffman might recognize a general cooling of the mark (as citizen) in the state's general assurance that 'something is being done' or 'we take this problem very seriously' even while it continues to control and expand gambling. In Nova Scotia this campaign uses the image of the yellow warning flag. In these ads the problem gambler suffers social isolation as he or she disappoints friends, relatives, and roommates. In other Yellow Flag ads, life-sized bottles of beer or VLTs appear the day after an indiscretion to reveal all the details that the gambler or drinker would rather keep hidden. These ads play on powerful human fears of rejection and humiliation. They also imply that our pleasures are themselves a form of surveillance. They tell on us or leave traces that will come to haunt us. The tag line for the ads is 'It sticks with you.'

These ads do not seem to set up or cool down the mark. They do, though, raise questions that would interest Goffman, who in his 1952 essay writes that status is the most important thing for anyone and that the loss of status is avoided at all cost. In fact, the mark must be cooled down in most situations, including the workplace and romantic life, because of the devastation caused by the public loss of status. That the legal state-sanctioned VLT will take your money one day and then act to discredit you publicly the next day is certainly a powerful threat. Goffman would warn that trying to counterbalance 'winner' talk with 'loser' talk is socially dangerous and may not have the desired effects. He would, nevertheless, recognize the many examples of cooling the mark out at work in these campaigns.

Conclusion

All states posit a version of their citizens and their desires. Thus we ask how the state imagines, administers, and cultivates a version of citizens and their desires. The regulation of desire is central to the state; and as discussed in earlier chapters, one version of desire and its cultivation is through the manufacture of nationalism or national identity. In a liberal, consumer, individualist culture – indeed, in a neoliberal milieu, where market relations are the model and where the notion of vice is no longer part of discourse – citizens are addressed through their individual desires. And as discussed, the teaching of risk management techniques is a way in which the state regulates, or governs, citizens' desires. But what versions of the public and of the public good are being produced and reproduced by the state in this imaginary?

Gambling is the ideal cultural site for examining that question because it allows the promotion *and* management of risk. Gambling is the quintessential site of both the individualist-consumer and the object of surveillance, calculation, and administration. The stakes are high in terms of thrill, possible loss (even of life), and hence the need for control (the legitimization of the state as the house). The rational-legal nature of administration seems to take the risk out of risk – it is now calculable. The citizen can enjoy risk (perhaps orienting to it as chance, luck, or the mystified) but also needs the state's help when it comes to understanding and estimating risk. The citizen is posited, as the 'Myths' and 'Misconceptions' make clear, as the naive gambler who needs help but who also can be easily 'taken' when high on Luck. The final moment – ritual cleansing of the profits, which are going to public good – is necessary in the formula. That last moment shifts emphasis away from the interaction in the gambling moment to the collective outcomes. Here we find a version of Canadian collectivism, except that this collectivism reproduces the statist interest. Unlike other forms of collectivism cherished by Canadians (such as universal health care), state-owned gambling is a form of governing citizens through individualizing them: the desire for the collective good is hollowed out as the state orients itself to the citizens, who are asked to risk-manage their now legitimate gambling proclivities. The dispensation of revenues to communities (the public good) both depends on this relationship to citizens and submits communities to this state method of dispensation.

All of which raises the question of how the citizen is supposed to desire the state. Is the state the protector or an enabler? Does the citizen-gambler gamble against the state/house (perhaps also by seeking out illegal forms), or does the gambler accept the house odds and submit his or her losses to the state's goodwill? With the example of gambling, we cannot say that the gambling-friendly state protects its citizens in the welfare state sense. Provincial governments follow the tradition of Crown corporations by owning gambling enterprises, but this organization of gambling makes apparent a less benign form of statism. The neoliberal state is a risk provider and risk manager, and its morality is utilitarian.

The legalization and expansion of gambling, starting in the late 1960s, coincided with the third form of Canadianization, which we have referred to in terms of statist/industrial orientations to culture. Earlier versions of Canadian culture (e.g., Masseyist [high], and cultural producer [nationalist]) have given way to the quantitative conception of culture, where what counts is industrial product – the sale of Canadian goods on the international market (Edwardson 2008). Utilitarianism and the bureaucratic interest in quantitative measures of 'value' define the state's relationship to culture. This utilitarianism is found in the state's orientation to gambling and in its revenue interests, as well as in its orientation to the casualties of its gambling policies – the problem gamblers.

The claim that gambling is being put to collective uses relies on Canadian statism and allows the state to exert its power in Canadian culture – that is, its power to define a cultural activity, legalize it, and expand in such a way as to enable its own conduct. This statism may be a continuation of the Canadian political cultural tradition of state fetishism; however, we must point out the shift that has occurred. We are no longer dealing with a seemingly benign welfare or guardian state, but rather with one that is utilitarian in its orientation to citizens and that responds to taxation pressures – brought on by globalization and neoliberalism – not by acting to constrain corporations but by exercising power on individuals and by asking them to be the risk managers of their own voluntary engagement in gambling, the latter of which is the consequence of top-down policy decisions.

Perhaps we can entertain a non-rational interpretation of gambling itself. Unlike the quantitative risk-management orientation of the state, which entails (among other things) generating prevalence rates of problem gamblers as percentages of gambling populations, and which also governs the casino's orientation to chance – that is, leaving nothing to it – the gambler who orients to luck is not abiding by, or perhaps is rejecting, the rationalized, probabilistic orientation. Jean Baudrillard (1990) proffered that gamblers don't believe in 'risk,' but rather in Luck. This is a kind of defence against the legal-rational and statistical logic of administering the citizen. But the state nevertheless has to manage this desire in a (legal-)rational and statistical fashion. While gamblers seek the excitement of action (Casino Rama's slogan is 'We Deal Excitement – Big Time!'), the heated passion of gambling (including the excesses to which it can lead) has to be cooled down, but not too much if it is to be a form of commercial mass consumption activity. It is possible to conceive a form of resistance in the gambler. Nevertheless, as we have seen, the gambling citizen is also the mark to be cooled out – to be flattered and redirected in ways that ensure that the state's many (conflicting) roles and interests do not come to the fore.

Peace, order and good gambling means this: the state should own and benefit from gambling enterprises, and the people should order their gambling activities and habits – they should become 'responsible gamblers,' managing their gambling risks so as to not be a 'cost' to their families or to the state.

It may be old-fashioned to accuse the contemporary state of being in a conflict of interest, as discussed earlier. At any rate, we must be alert to the ways in which government and state conduct is increasingly corporate in orientation – in how it is mobilizing citizens as consumers as it involves itself directly in markets in search of tax revenues. We posit here that the state, to accomplish its ends, has embedded itself in everyday life as a shaper of citizen desire and, more and more, as a procurer of pleasure. To be sure, as we have discussed here, the state has its utilitarian interests and objectives; but rather than standing outside the phenomenon of pleasure (and merely regulating or suppressing it), it acts on the *basis* of it: not just to give citizens pleasure, but rather as a means to organize allegiance and enable its own conduct.

However we might think about this, there is the paradoxical or perhaps 'Canadian' expression at work here: gambling is ubiquitous, but there is no legal 'free market' in gambling pleasure. The state's utilitarian orientation represents a shift in morality away from the earlier Protestant disdain for gambling and the conception of gambling as vice. The state can offer gambling as entertainment as a legitimate commercial activity, and it appears to refrain from interfering in gamblers' choices. However, those choices are already shaped by a market that is dominated by the state's enterprises; morality is evident in the tacit assumption that the state should own gambling and in the efforts to shape the gambler's conduct. If Canadians could think of their gambling merely as entertainment – 'just as theatre patrons pay for a ticket to a play or sports fans pay for a ticket to a game' – risk would be eliminated: we would have peace, order and good gambling in Canada.

We move next to a less controversial type of entertainment, but one where the state is still present, albeit in ambiguous ways, as provider: CBC television comedy.

5

The Funny State Apparatus

Canadians sure are funny folk.

CBC

We must remember that popular can be meaningful . . . programs deliver important social messages through humour.

Robert Rabinovitch, President and CEO of CBC

While I admit I am not a journalist, I do play one on TV . . .

Rick Mercer

Perhaps the most complex topic to be raised in this book is that of humour and the state. After all, there is nothing funny about the state, at least from an official point of view. Given its power and mandate, it cannot take itself as an object of humour or even offer up humour without risking its sober authority. A classic *Monty Python's Flying Circus* skit nicely explores the problem of the state and humour. During the Second World War in England, a civilian writer (Ernest Scribbler) inadvertently discovers a joke so funny that it kills. After reading his own joke, he begins to laugh so hard he falls over dead. His wife enters the room and to her horror finds her husband. She picks up the piece of paper, reads it, and also dies laughing. The British military quickly seize on this joke as a weapon. They translate it into German and use it against the enemy. Soon the Germans realize that they will have to develop a killer joke of their own. On the German side, this project becomes an object of state interest (as there is nothing outside the state). Hence, a nervous white-lab-coated writer brings his joke to an officer. He reads the joke and the unsmiling officer promptly shoots him, saying 'we'll get back to you.' When the man falls to the ground, the viewer sees the pile of white-lab-coated joke writers who have fallen before him. Why is this funny? It is ridiculous that an officer would be in charge of deciding what is and is not funny. It is funny also because we imagine that this officer cannot possess humour (at least in his capacity at work). The failed joke writers are killed – perhaps a bureaucratically sanctioned feature of the job itself. What would be officially funny in this context?

But, if the state has no sense of humour, it certainly can become an *object* of humour. Indeed, the more the state extends itself (ultimately into judging what is funny), the funnier it becomes itself. According to Rudolph Herzog (in Crossland 2006), who has recently written on humour during the Nazi period, 'political jokes weren't a form of active resistance but valves for pent-up public anger. They were told in pubs, on the street and this suited the Nazi regime which was deeply humourless.' The newspaper article about this book goes on to explain that 'the Nazis banned criticism of the regime, but court cases usually resulted in a warning or a fine. By the end of the war, however, a joke could get you killed.' As the war proceeded, naming one's dog or horse 'Adolph' became officially less funny. What is strange about the Nazi response to humour is the power they seemed to grant it to subvert; Herzog gives it far less power in his analysis.

As discussed in chapter 1, the Canadian state takes responsibility for managing the content and form of much cultural production, but deeming what is or is not funny does not fall directly under its cultural purview. There are a few exceptions to this rule. Recently the Human Rights Commission has been called upon to investigate the offensive nature of a stand-up comedian performing in a British Columbia nightclub. Presumably, the commission must try to distinguish between humour and offensiveness. Is it possible, then, that a joke can be offensive *and* funny? (If failing to be funny itself becomes an offence, many stand-up comedians will be in serious trouble.) The Ministry of Heritage offers many notions of Canada, but it does not offer national or regional jokes as a part of cultural heritage. Hence, it is not a part of our official heritage to tell jokes about even our apparent politeness: 'How do you get a bunch of Canadians out of a hot tub? – You say, "Please get out of the hot tub." ' You can, however, find such jokes on the CBC. This displays the difference between the CBC and other arms of the state. In spite of its earnest mandate, discussed in chapter 1, laughter and humour are a large part of its work (especially, as we will discuss, on television). The CBC's relationship to the state, however, remains ambiguous. While there are many targets of CBC humour, the state itself has some protections – even, as we will discuss, some advocates. As the quote at the beginning of this chapter shows, the CBC approaches humour as official work – that is, as delivering 'important social messages.'

The following is the television line-up for the CBC (Tuesday, 22 February 2010) during prime time, from 8 to 10 p.m.:

8:00 – *The Rick Mercer Report*
8:30 – *This Hour Has 22 Minutes*
9:00 – *Kids in the Hall – Death Comes to Town*
9:30 – *Halifax Comedy Festival*
10:00 – *The National*

This Tuesday night schedule is comedy heavy and is capped with the national news. It is a significant slice of the CBC's TV comedy programming – which has included the long-running *Royal Canadian Air Farce* (on radio also), *CODCO*, and in its later years, *SCTV*. CBC comedy programming goes back to the Wayne and Shuster radio broadcasts of the 1940s. Those two comedians would later become staples of CBC TV from the 1960s to the 1980s, with their monthly comedy specials. Wayne and Shuster were Canadian icons, and as testament to their popularity, they also appealed to American audiences, appearing on the *Ed Sullivan Show* more than any other guests.

Why the use of comedy programming by the state broadcaster, going back to the early years of the CBC? The development of CBC programming was constrained by its official mandate to build nation and culture on the one hand (with the "high culture" intent of the Massey Commission), and by economics and the need to maintain audiences on the other. Thus, popular American shows were imported and broadcast alongside Wayne and Shuster and NHL hockey (Edwardson 2008, 59–60). As discussed in chapter 3, *Hockey Night in Canada* (first broadcast on CBC television in 1952) has come to be an important signifier of Canadianness. If a comedy program such as *The Wayne and Shuster Show* (which was first broadcast on CBC Radio in 1946 and moved to CBC TV in 1954) features in the project of nation building as an early example, it shows some of the difficulties inherent in this project. The CBC provided a venue for Canadian talent, indeed, it had to draw upon that talent (with the comedians being among the first Canadian media stars) in order to offer programming to Canadians that would come to be known later as 'Canadian content' (Edwardson 2008). Furthermore, and blurring the distinction between high and popular culture, Wayne and Shuster's comedy was characterized as 'a unique brand of literate farce' (Rutherford 1990, 210) (the duo often incorporated Shakespeare and Latin into their skits), one that appealed to a mass Canadian as well as American audience (Ed Sullivan referred to the duo as his "Canuck egghead comics"). The team's comedy could, in retrospect, be thought as a kind of 'accessible Masseyism' for Canadians. Salutin (2011) notes that 'Wayne and Shuster never did much political humour. They were too focused on what you could call cultural nation-building.' But if the CBC used certain types of programming (such as comedy) in an effort to differentiate and develop a 'Canadian' taste in relation to the more commercial fare being transmitted from across the border, the popularity of Wayne and Shuster in the United States (and the popularity of imported American shows in Canada) points to the difficulties in asserting 'national' content, even in an early mass-mediated television environment. Wayne and Shuster themselves were influenced by American comedians, including the intelligent comedy of Sid Caesar. And Rutherford (1990, 211) notes that the team was concerned with their TV production values: 'Wayne claimed . . . that he watched a lot of American variety, (but rarely Canadian), to see what the opposition was doing.' We nevertheless see from the early days of CBC TV the institutionalizing of comedy as part of its nation-building mandate. We might well ask, however, whether such institutionalizing has had cultural consequences for the possibility of a strongly political humour on television in Canada, and for subversive and deep satirical work, as distinct from parody and a comedic sensibility that largely refuses to cross the line.

In this chapter we explore the comedic treatment of Canadian objects, especially on popular CBC comedy programs. The objects we examine have become recognizable as *Canadian* through their mass mediation. The early self-referential style of Canadian comedy, which aimed at recognizing everyday experience through myriad media representations, was found in Wayne and Shuster's parodies of TV commercials, and most explicitly in *SCTV*, a mock TV network that parodied all things television.

What role does comedy play on the CBC? Like other forms of entertainment, whether drama, music, or sports, comedy programming is part of the CBC's national-cultural mandate. As we discuss, however, comedy is also a mode of address to Canadians – that is, it draws not only from

Canadian things, people, and events, but also on the way these things have been constituted by the media (CBC) as recognizable Canadian objects. This is not to say that the relationship between such shows and the CBC has always been smooth. Famously, *CODCO* struggled with the CBC over issues of offensive content, and *SCTV* was told, when the CBC finally picked it up, that it was short on Canadian content. The *CODCO* group suffered internal strains trying to maintain their artistic integrity while staying on the air; by contrast, *SCTV*'s Rick Moranis was in a position to parody CBC regulations (see chapter 1) because *SCTV* was then at its height of power, having been picked up for a ninety-minute weekly show on the American NBC network.

Are there certain generic features to Canadian comedy? Is there a detectable Canadianness in the humour, or are there at least certain themes that signify a Canadian sensibility? When it comes to humour, famous signifiers of Canadian sensibility are suggested by the work of Stephen Leacock. In addition, academics – especially those influenced by a postmodern perspective – have referred to the ironic stance of Canadians, who, they say, demonstrate such things as a scepticism towards icons, myths, and authorities (Hutcheon 1990; Rukszto 2005). Leacock (like Mark Twain, Oscar Wilde, Groucho Marx, and Mae West) was a wit. He was also an academic, and this made his style of humour doubly attractive to intellectuals, for it affirmed their own cleverness. In a 1916 essay, however, Leacock explained that academics usually do a terrible job of trying to understand humour. In typical Leacock style, he made quick work of the academic pretension to explain humour, reducing their complex theories to silliness:

> Kant . . . has said that in him everything excites laughter in which there is a resolution or deliverance of the absolute captive by the finite. It was very honourable of Kant to admit this. It enables us to know exactly what did, and what did not, excite him.

Sociologist Herbert Spencer received similar treatment:

> Herbert Spencer tells us the thing called a laugh is a sort of explosion of nervous energy, disappointed in its expected path, and therefore attacking the muscles of the face. Admirers of Spencer's scientific method may find in this plausible statement a pleasing finality, though why the explosion in question should attack the face rather than other parts of the body still seems a matter of doubt. (Leacock 1916)

With the ghost of Leacock lingering, we nevertheless press on. We take from him the point that academic work is itself often unintentionally funny. In his classic study *Crowds and Power,* published in German in 1960, Bulgarian-born Swiss writer Elias Canetti (1984) formulated the characteristics of various national and cultural groups through his discussion of crowds and 'crowd symbols.' Here are a couple of examples, which are inadvertently funny in retrospect. Clearly, there is great potential to poke fun at national groups, either in stereotypical or absurdist terms:

> Everyone knows what the sea means to an Englishman; what is not known is the precise form of the connection between his relationship to the sea and his famous individualism. The Englishman sees himself as a captain on board a ship with a small group of people, the sea around and beneath him. He is almost alone; as captain he is in many ways isolated even from his crew . . . His life at home is complementary to life at sea: security and monotony are its essential characteristics. (Canetti 1984, 200)

> The crowd symbol of the Germans was the army. But the army was more than just the army; it was the marching forest. In no other modern country has the forest-feeling remained as alive as it has in Germany. The parallel rigidity of the upright trees and their density and number fill the heart of the German with a deep and mysterious delight. To this day he loves to go deep into the forest where his forefathers lived; he feels at one with the trees. (Canetti 1984, 202)

One can only imagine what Leacock or Freud would have done with those rigid, upright trees whose impressive girth and count apparently so pleasure the German heart, or with this pre-social English seaman. It is probably politically incorrect now to make these kinds of claims and to engage in national stereotyping (note how the Englishman or German is every Englishman/German, embodying all the attributes of Englishmen/Germans). Yet the construction of collective attributes is not simply a feature of certain types of jokes – it is also a way in which cultural groups persistently evince self/other differences. And this also happens *within* countries, as regions and locales poke fun at their purportedly dim-witted or backward neighbours.

Newfoundlanders have traditionally been the targets of ethnic humour in Canada. The island's distance from the mainland, its Catholic, hinterland culture, and its late and ambivalent union with Canada (in 1949), made Newfoundlanders easy targets for humour about their apparent backwardness. But these jokes did not originate from the mainland. Like the Irish humour from which it derived, this self-effacing and locally produced humour played on notions of innocence, isolation, stupidity, and immoral habits like drunkenness, adultery, and dishonesty. Many played off contrasting the worldly character of the 'American' ('Yank') or 'Torontonian' – who are almost interchangeable here – with that of the 'Newfie.' Certainly these jokes could be circulated and enjoyed by 'mainlanders' to denigrate Newfoundlanders, but their local origins betrayed that more was at work than reinforcing the secondary status of the Newfie. Often these jokes drew a moral conclusion about the pitfalls of arrogance and ambition. For example, take the following joke about a man from Newfoundland who goes to the mainland to study law. He returns to practise law in Newfoundland so that he can be a powerful and impressive figure. When his first client walks into his office, he pretends to be on the phone to Toronto, engaged in hard-nosed negotiations with references to large sums of money and the Supreme Court. When he hangs up he finds out the man in his office is there to hook up the phone. Clearly, this joke plays on the notion of the Newfie as foolish around technology; but it also sends the message that arrogance and pretence make fools of us all. This outcome puts him back in his place (both socially and geographically) and reminds him that a real Newfoundlander would not engage in such superficial posturing.

Other jokes that seem to play on backwardness and innocence similarly undermine the pretences of financial success and modernity. Take, for example, the joke about the American golf star Tiger Woods, pulling into a gas station in his impressive new car in rural Newfoundland. While he is gassing up his car, a couple of golf tees fall out of his pocket. The Newfie gas station attendant asks what they are called and what they are for, and Woods explains that they are for holding up his balls when he is driving. The Newfie comments that these new cars have everything. Obviously this joke is about the body, particularly about male genitalia. It is also, however, about the silliness and excesses of wealth and all its trappings. From the point of view of the Newfie in this joke, it is fully plausible that a wealthy, famous American would have such a ridiculous luxury item because he comes from a culture without limits. The non-Newfoundlander is what Durkheim called anomic – self-centred, unlimited by communal norms and traditions, and suffering from limitless desire. Those who come from the outside bring socially and morally disastrous values.

These types of ethnic jokes are for the most part semi-legitimate. Jokes like the hot tub joke provided earlier are *more* legitimate because they invoke the entire group as both teller and object. In other words, the 'national joke' is an official way we talk about ourselves as Canadians. In fact, being funny, is a national trait, at least according to the CBC. But this point is itself serious. Canadians often characterize themselves as polite, quiet, ironic, funny, tolerant, and deferential to authority, though not as deferential to authority as they used to be. Some of these characteristics are the *product* of social science surveys and polls that seek to tell Canadians who they are (Friedenberg 1980; Adams 1998). We can see the potential here for humour, absurdity: '9 out of 10 Canadians say that they are funny.' But we can also see how nationalist designations themselves, such as 'Canadian,' rely on collective assumptions of a united identity – the term referring to all those nominated by it and belonging to it. This in turn raises questions about what kinds of things ground the designation in something beyond the sheer multiplicity of people living in a particular geographical space. Germans should rest assured that they have a 'crowd symbol' – the army; Canadians have had national symbols, such as 'The Mountie' (at least it's not an army). The perennial problem is, of course, that we as Canadians are searching for our crowd symbol, and this has prompted the CBC, for example, to engage in the various kinds of projects (as we identified in chapter 1) that seem vexed by, or that want to make clear to us, 'who we are.' If Canadians do reveal scepticism towards icons, myths, and so on, then certainly the CBC has contributed to this scepticism precisely by raising the question over and over.

In this chapter we entertain themes of Canadian humour as we witness them on the CBC. We acknowledge the diversity of comedy forms in Canada, and the issues and orientations grounded in regional sensibilities, but we would add that the notion of 'Canadian' humour must be seen to speak to or express Canadians *en masse;* regional particularities, then, must somehow get worked into this national framework. We will try to refrain from any essentializing of 'Canadian' humour – while a chapter in a book on a theme such as national identity, written by two academics, should demonstrate serious pedagogical intentions, the thought of playing with supposedly Canadian attributes and even 'crowd symbols' sounds too good to resist. Indeed, given such themes as lack of identity and the statist administration of culture addressed in earlier chapters, we hope you can understand the comedic desire to mock or render absurd any serious or official renderings of Canadianness.

Humour/comedy has both subversive and conservative uses and implications. Stott explains that humour is at some level always disruptive of some level of order. This in itself, does not, however, mean it is necessarily subversive:

Instances of joking, humour, or irony invoke a separation between 'authorized,' egocentric, or rational versions of the world and their revealed alternatives, commenting on established conventions as they go. This does not mean that joking opens up a path to 'truth,' or even that it has the ability to cut through untruths, as it generally does not provide coherent counter-arguments and its efficacy as a platform for change is questionable. (Stott 2005, 14)

Take for, example, this famous speech by Groucho Marx:

One morning I shot an elephant in my pajamas. How he got in my pajamas, I don't know. Then we tried to remove the tusks. The tusks. That's not so easy to say. Tusks. You try it some time. As I say, we tried to remove the tusks. But they were embedded so firmly we couldn't budge them. Of course, in Alabama the Tuscaloosa, but that is entirely ir-elephant to what I was talking about.

(Groucho Marx, *Animal Crackers* [film], 1930)

This joke is disruptive primarily of speech – it plays on the ambiguity of English syntax (which can place the pajamas on Marx or the elephant), the sound of words (tusks), punning on sound (tusks are looser / Tuscaloosa and irrelevant / ir-elephant). But some of his other humour is more 'serious' on this front. In a famous incident, Marx ran up against official authority when he clowned with a customs form while crossing an international border. As the story goes, he (variously) answered on the form: 'eyes – two'; 'hair – thinning'; 'sex – yes, please'; 'occupation – smuggler.' According to legend, pandemonium ensued. At least two levels of disruption to official authority were at work here. At one level, Marx was disrupting the taken-for-granted understanding of bureaucratic categorization. Everyone knows in that context that 'eyes' means 'what is your eye colour?' But Marx was also subverting the state's right to practise surveillance. Instead of learning that Marx was a male comedian with brown hair and eyes, it learned that he was aging, horny, and dangerous. Airports now warn passengers that any jokes about security will be treated as not funny. There is no cultural allowance for humour in this context.

Of course, comedy also has a long history of attacking the powerful:

In its earliest form, comedy engages with politics and the state. Aristophanic comedy, for example, frequently defames identifiable Athenian

public figures and derides their policies . . . Abuse that we would now consider libelous was a fundamental part of the comedy, with named officials,
military officers, and prominent citizens all insulted in considerable detail.
(Stott 2005, 106)

But, as Bakhtin argued, not all attacks on authority are subversive. He
explained that medieval carnival humour turned the world of established social relations upside down, but that this inversion did not have
the permanent effect of uncrowning the king or displacing authorities.
The carnival was a sanctioned period of festivities that reverted to the traditional order of power and social relations once it was over. Ultimately,
this ritualized reversal of roles worked to reaffirm them (Bakhtin 1984).

Jokes often sidestep logic and resist closure and meaning (thus being
subversive in their aesthetic or formal characteristics). But we still must
consider the contexts or frames within which the joking takes place. Subversion of authority occurs in particular contexts, and so does support of
authority. Frames and contexts inform the ways in which things are said,
including the constraints on what can be said, the foci and targets of the
jokes, and the objectives of the humour. This is not to say that humour
is a mere reflection of its frame or context. The subversive and indirect
qualities of certain types of humour are often directed at the frames and
contexts themselves, as was the case with Groucho Marx's jokes. As such,
the discursive aspects of the humour – the relations among style, foci
and objects, and frame or context – can be complex.

Diverse comedy forms can be found on the CBC, yet its comedy programs do not exhaust the range of comedy that is encountered in Canada's various regions and cities, nor its various forms. Nevertheless, we
can ask how the CBC funnels comedy and humour into a 'Canadian'
framework. While certain examples might share generic features with
comedy anywhere else (such as stand-up comedy at comedy festivals),
CBC comedy programming, like all CBC programming, fits within the
communications mandate of the broadcaster and the state-bureaucratic
requirements of the CRTC and Broadcasting Act. It is offered by the
state and must appeal to Canadians. CBC comedy is thus a perfect object
through which to further explore this book's themes: the role of the
state, the state's uses of pleasure, and – more broadly – state/culture dynamics. Yet as noted in chapter 1, the CBC's programming policies and
its very existence as state broadcaster have contributed significantly to
the constitution of particular Canadian cultural characteristics.

In this chapter we focus primarily on the comedy of Rick Mercer, since he is, according to the CBC advertisements, 'Canada's favourite funnyman.' While his continued popularity among viewers might support this claim, the claim itself is another example of CBC self-referentiality. In other words, perhaps it is true if 'Canada Lives Here,' that is, if the CBC is homologous with Canada. Mercer is an established presence on the CBC through the various programs on which he has participated or starred (*The Rick Mercer Report, This Hour Has 22 Minutes, Talking to Americans, Made in Canada*), and he inhabits an interesting cultural space: he is a seemingly populist comedian who nevertheless performs comedy on the CBC network as one of its core performers and 'stars'. In other words, his comedy is situated within the CBC broadcasting mandate: its frame is mass-mediated, state-sanctioned comedy. At a personal level, he has progressed in his career from being very peripheral to, and critical of, the federal state, to being central to it, all the while moving from disaffected Newfoundlander to the face of national comedy as broadcast from the CBC National Broadcasting Centre in downtown Toronto. (To be sure, this biographic reality is not lost on Mercer, who treats this very status with playful irreverence.) Specifically, we will look at how – in parallel with his state institutionalization – Mercer has come to use his body in particular comedic ways that suggest a sacrificial relationship to the state. In other words, the ways he juxtaposes his body with powerful state technologies (e.g., tanks) and agencies (e.g., the armed forces), and the ways he exerts himself physically (e.g., athletics) all suggest a certain relation between the citizen–body and the state that shows a willingness to support state interests.

Rick Mercer is famous for his support of Canada's military and its troops. Certainly, he is a favourite of the military, and in 2007 he was even made an honorary colonel in the 423rd Maritime Helicopter Squadron (CBC 2007d). With this title come particular formal ceremonial functions such as authorizing parades and changes of command. According to the commanding officer of this squadron, a comedian was an unlikely choice for this post, but Mercer had long been outstanding for his public support for the military and its image. This CO also explained that Mercer would lift troop morale (Ibid.). While Mercer's relationship to the military is important to our discussion, we will focus on his more general use of symbols of state and the military. Because Mercer also aligns himself with other symbols of the state, he cannot be said to be *only* supporting the troops – unless this support is understood from a much broader context in terms of a recommendation for how all citizens are to think of the state in general.

To 'get' Mercer and the objects of his TV humour, it is important to consider the social and cultural context of his programs. As mentioned earlier, that context has been shaped by government policies and by a cultural and national milieu that includes, in particular, the CBC as state broadcaster. Mercer's programs mediate 'Canadianness' – that is, they both constitute and reflect Canadianness and Canadian identity and provide discursive Canadian objects. As a simple example of the latter, not only have particular newscasters (e.g., Barbara Frum, Peter Mansbridge) come to have an iconic Canadian status, but the newscaster as 'type' is often an object of humourous identification in CBC shows such as *This Hour Has 22 Minutes, Royal Canadian Air Farce,* and *The Rick Mercer Report.*

Most academic work on Canadian comedy examines its parody and satire and concludes from its sustained popularity that 'many Canadians share a healthy sense of scepticism with regard to Canadian icons and myths' (Rukszto 2005, 77). While we agree with this declaration of Canadianness to some extent (since the object of humour in programs like *The Rick Mercer Report* is national icons and myths), we also think it is one-sided. How does the circulation of such a belief itself buttress certain forms of authority and myth? Are there certain myths that are in some ways central to Canadianness? This question relates to the mediated nature of 'Canadian identity.' How do certain cultural attributes, whatever they are, get circulated and reinforced as icons of Canadianness? In other words, how do various attributes get fed back into mythologies of identity produced by the interests of technological nationalism? As we will discuss, the subversive or conservative authority-supporting aspects of humour are framed in particular ways. So we explore how the framing lends itself to the message of statism, not just as legitimate authority but as an object of Canadian desire.

Satire, Parody, and Self-Parody on CBC

Born in Newfoundland in 1969, Rick Mercer has had a long and successful career in Canadian political satire. He began by touring his one-man shows ('Show Me the Button, I'll Push It,' 1990; 'I've Killed Before, I'll Kill Again,' 1992). His early political satires were told from a pointedly Newfoundlander point of view, attacking central Canada and federal politics (including the privileging of Quebec interests over those of Newfoundland). *Maclean's* journalist Brian Bergman describes 'I've Killed Before . . .':

> Based on the premise of mainland Canadians flocking to Newfoundland after a massive nuclear accident, Mercer cast himself as the province's hangman, working at $4.25 an hour. And because capital punishment has been decreed for such crimes as bad taste and the composition of boring kids songs, a host of cultural icons – from Farley Mowat to Sharon, Lois & Bram – faced the gallows. (Bergman 1998)

While literary distinctions between kinds of humour are complex, we classify Mercer's early work as 'satire' and much of his later work as 'parody' because the former is more clearly aimed at discrediting some individual or institution. Both forms play with imitation, but parody is a comedic form that does not necessarily seek to harm the reputation of what it imitates. As we will show, Canadian comedy often falls into the category of parody (or even self-parody) as it references well-known institutions and individuals in a gentle or even supportive way. The CBC's long history of self-reference makes it an unlikely place for satire. So much that is officially Canadian is inside (or managed inside) the CBC that it is not in a position to satirize; instead, it gently recirculates its own signifiers. The continuous movement of 'serious' celebrities (such as national news chief correspondent Peter Mansbridge) into positions of comedy, and of 'non-serious' celebrities (such as Mercer) into positions of serious political debate, with politicians especially taking advantage of the opportunity to be clowns rather than objects of satire, makes the CBC a cultural site of parody.

In 1992 Mercer joined fellow Newfoundlanders Cathy Jones and Mary Walsh, from the highly regional and edgy *CODCO* show, to create *This Hour Has 22 Minutes*. During his eight-year tenure on *22 Minutes*, Mercer became famous for his political 'rants' and for a gag called 'Talking to Americans.' The latter was spun off in 2000, and attracted an audience of 2.7 million viewers, which made it the highest-rated comedy special in CBC history, according to the network. In 2004 he began his own show, named after himself. At an institutional level, Mercer has been widely recognized for his comedic writing and performance: he has won twenty Gemini Awards and numerous Canadian Comic and Writers Guild Awards. Within the broader community, he is now well known for his support of international aid (e.g., his 'Spread the Net' campaign to buy mosquito netting for Africans) and for his trips to Afghanistan to meet and entertain the troops. Like the famous American USO shows that featured comedians like Bob Hope and Joey Heatherton, these visits and shows are broadcast in Canada, presumably to boost civilian morale as well as that of the troops. As we will discuss, because Mercer has become so influential and famous, some artists question the appropriateness of Mercer taking on this posture vis-à-vis the Canadian military and the war. Indeed, likening Mercer to Bob Hope is instructive – with the difference, however, that Mercer's stardom has been generated through the state broadcasting system.

In terms of the subversive or conservative uses of humour, it is interesting to consider troop visits by comedians, and the use of humour as reward and placation. On the surface, the troops simply deserve a reward for their privations and sacrifice, but the reward being discussed here is also a form of placation or a lining-in of the soldiers to ongoing commitment to the state's military objectives. In other words, the humour, although it may be aimed at incompetent authority figures, serves the state indirectly by shoring up the ideological and emotional commitment of the troops. Bob Hope did this as a 'free enterprise' comedian; Mercer, by contrast, while he supports the military personally, displays that support as a representative of the state broadcaster. Both comedians also poke fun at politicians. Hope's humour has been characterized as 'authority-supporting,' in that he often chose generic subjects that could provide a punch line with mass appeal, such as doing taxes:

> Well, like everybody else I've paid my income taxes and I'd like to congratulate our cameramen for their trick photography. You'd never know I'm not wearing a shirt; and the IRS took my pants too. (Paletz 1990, 488)

Paletz remarks on this:

> What is being asserted here is that a law-abiding citizen paid his taxes, followed by the highly optimistic claim that everybody else has done likewise. As to his avowal of penury, his audience knows that Hope is one of America's wealthiest men. On the same comedy special he can also be seen serving as the spokesman for Texaco in that company's commercials. (488)

This analysis suggests that Hope was a representative, and a very successful one, of the economic system – a shill, not just for Texaco, but for capitalism and the American Dream. During the Vietnam War, Hope's work became especially important to legitimizing U.S. involvement in that country. Other comedians, notably the Smothers Brothers, were taken off the air for their criticism of the war and the president. Bob Hope became – along with allegedly Mafia-connected comic Dean Martin – the object of much humour himself. Fictional comedians like *The Simpsons'* Krusty the Clown also seem to have shadowy and powerful friends. It seems that power when connected to comedy invites such attention and raises the question of how the two may be mutually supporting. Mercer, though, shills for a different type of organization: the CBC, a state institution. We would also point out that both Hope and Mercer, as comedians, have enjoyed significant budgetary support and resources to put on their comedy programs – very few comedians have their own specials or weekly programs. At the same time, the 'mass' positioning of these regular programs is a constraint on the style of humour and what can be said (Ibid.). Subversive comedy is more likely to be found in small comedy and night clubs with much smaller audiences.

Mercer's popular TV shows – *Made in Canada, This Hour Has 22 Minutes,* and *The Rick Mercer Report* – have all parodied TV news or TV production and have aired on the CBC. His work follows on a tradition of popular and long-running Canadian comedy built fully or in part around news parody, much of it aired on the CBC. Examples include *Royal Canadian Air Farce, CODCO,* and *SCTV* (in its later years). The satirical objects of Mercer's earlier shows have included typically anyone with authority and/or power – politicians, government bureaucrats, institutions and their representatives, rich entrepreneurs, corporations, celebrities. Perhaps Canada's most cynical TV satire was Mercer's own *Made in Canada,* which picked up on the political trend to produce generic, popular shows for export that were in no way particularly Canadian except for their willingness to use government grants and their inexpensive production values. A feature of Canadian TV comedy is not only the persistence of the news parody genre, but also, as Rukszto (2005) notes, the 'undisputed fact that much of successful Canadian comedy has recognizably Canadian institutions, personalities, political figures and specific Canadian audiences as its target' (77). The recognizably 'Canadian' things in these programs owe their existence to mass mediation. In particular, their familiarity as Canadian things is a feature of the desire and mandate of the CBC to nation-build and generate Canadianness. And since the Canadian state's cultural policy is one object of humour, the CBC becomes an obvious target, along with its institutionalized personalities ('stars').

The possibility of parodying Canadian objects on TV is itself an outcome of cultural development. Keohane (1997) reminds us of 'the Monty
Python Incident.' The CBC had begun broadcasting *Monty Python's Flying
Circus* in 1970. In early 1971, the broadcaster pulled the series off the air,
apparently in part due to complaints made by some Canadians about
the episode with the now famous 'Lumberjack Song' – where the manly
Canadian lumberjack (supported by a chorus of Mounties) sings about
his lumberjack work, but also reveals his penchant for wearing women's
clothing and hanging around in bars – 'I wish I'd been a girlie, just like
my Dear Papa . . .' Keohane (1997) suggests that the CBC's airing of the
series – with its mockery of all manner of British customs and characters –
was an effort to support Canadian nationalism, which

> necessitated the denigration of their counterparts in the fading symbolic
> order of the British empire . . . But the CBC could not find comic at all a
> ludicrous representation of figures which they were attempting to elevate
> to the status of sublime objects: the true Canadian man, the beauty of Ca-
> nadian womanhood, and the good law embodied in the Mountie. (150)

When discussing news parody on the CBC, it is important to note its
tightly self-referential nature. The CBC is ripe for such comedic treatment. It is mandated by law to present Canada to Canadians; thus, the
people and personalities presented on the CBC are in some way 'officially' sanctioned representatives of viewers and of the nation as a whole.
The social position of CBC celebrities is far more complex than that of
celebrities who appear on private broadcasters, for they are simultaneously celebrities, typical Canadians, individual personalities, and representatives of state cultural policy. Consequently, much of this comedy
depends on the viewers having watched the other CBC shows that are
being lampooned, as the shows and their stars are often imitated and
parodied directly.

Canadian parodic comedy shows of this type are not easily exported
to foreign markets because they depend so heavily on institutional
self-reference (unlike other popular comedies, like *Little Mosque on the
Prairie*, *The Red Green Show*, and *Corner Gas*, each of which nevertheless focuses on cultural or regional idiosyncrasies). But in offering Canadians
a chance to laugh at themselves – that is, to laugh at the representations
of national selfhood that they accept by watching and listening to CBC –
the CBC is also also legitimizing itself as an institution. The CBC, then,
is colonizing humour for nation-building purposes, including humour

that is potentially subversive of state interests. Besides that, the opportunity to be lampooned is invaluable to humanizing what would otherwise be a policy-driven political bureaucracy. Furthermore, when they watch the CBC, audience members can tell themselves that they, as Canadians, are self-deprecating and self-critical. As we will discuss, this is an important quality to which Canadians resort in order to establish moral superiority over Americans. In fact, some critics suggest that Canadian parody offers its audience only 'authorized laughter' rather than laughter at authority (Druick 2008). Comparing Canadian news parody to its British and American counterparts, Druick concludes that

> although intelligent and often highly amusing, these shows risk restricting political opposition to the double-voiced or intertextual discourse of parody, a parasitic relationship that ultimately reinforces the primacy and authority of news even while it brings authorized discourse into question. (123)

Druick's observation is important in the context of Canadian politics because generations of academics have argued that Canadians are highly ironic and hence critical of official discourses. For example, Hutcheon (1990) argues that Canadian 'self-deprecating irony . . . allows speakers to address and at the same time slyly confront an "official" discourse, that is, to work within a dominant tradition but also to challenge it – without being utterly co-opted by it' (9). A number of things are of note here. First, this insistence on a national ironic, self-deprecating, doubled-collective personality is long-standing. Second, it announces an irony and humility ('we are ironic,' 'we are self-deprecating,' etc.) that are not in themselves humble or apparently ironic; instead, these are earnest and prideful claims. Third, this received and repeated self-definition needs to be examined as an ideology in itself. Druick asks whether this insistence on our own ironic self-awareness is a cover for the opposite – the use of doubling, irony, and parody to generate closed circles of reference and hence reinscribe legitimacy.

Mercer himself is well aware of this quality of political parody, describing his relationship with Canadian politicians as 'mutually parasitic' (2007, 167). He explains: 'It amazes me when I look back at the number of politicians who have been on the show and what some . . . have agreed to do with the cameras rolling' (167). This relationship between Mercer and politicians emerged during his years on *This Hour Has 22 Minutes,* when politicians began to offer themselves up as willing participants in

Mercer's clowning, instead of waiting to be cornered randomly by aggressive characters such as Mary Walsh's Marg Delahunty / Princess Warrior or just to be objects of Mercer's rants. Druick notes that

> as the show became more and more well known throughout the 1990s, however, the ambushes diminished and politicians became cooperative participants on the show, goofing around with the cast in a variety of situations. Prime Minister Jean Chrétien shared a burger at Wendy's with Rick Mercer. (116)

Druick is right to point out this move away from the ambush towards the invited and planned 'date' with Mercer. Indeed this has become a regular feature of *The Rick Mercer Report*. These scenes have included skinny-dipping with politicians, having a slumber party with Prime Minister Stephen Harper, and 'helping' opposition party leader Michael Ignatieff move into his official residence. In all these gags, Mercer moves as far as he can into politicians' intimate and private spaces and situations, threatening what he calls their 'comfort zone' (Mercer 2007, 167). Certainly, from the point of view of the TV audience, Mercer is allowed to go places and do things to and with politicians that would be unthinkable to the average Canadian.

This does not necessarily mean that Mercer is less critical of politicians. That politicians feel compelled to appear on the show and clown with Mercer (even though they are also routinely victims of the 'Rant') speaks to Mercer's power as a jester who knows he has won the attention and admiration of the court audience. To refuse to appear on his show would risk showing both fear of Mercer's power and fear of being made the object of humour more generally. Indeed, Mercer has achieved a place on the Canadian cultural scene where politicians must seek out his playful attention in order to play at politics in Anglo-Canada. And by appearing on his show, they lend a wider legitimacy to Mercer as jester/critic, which in turn strengthens his authority when he turns to 'The Rant' segment of the show. 'The Rant' – a comment on current political events, policies, and decisions – is the most clearly editorial part of *The Rick Mercer Report*. During that segment, Mercer walks aggressively towards the camera/audience, stopping, starting, and turning such that a real interlocutor would have to back away from him as he advances. This regular segment is filmed out of doors (in Toronto's graffiti-filled alleys). Mercer generates laughs by exposing the ridiculous reasoning and behaviour of politicians, bureaucrats, business leaders, and organizations. Sometimes the target is more general – for example, how Torontonians can't drive in snow (he calls them 'Toron-tarded'). It is also, however, a serious editorial that allows Mercer to become physically agitated and confrontational about how the country is being run. While Mercer's rants can be pointed, aimed at political and bureaucratic incompetence, some of his banter in his interactions with Canadians (be they officials or regular Canadians) in other segments of the show can be very light.

In part, Mercer's shenanigans with politicians express larger cultural forces, precipitated by a media-saturated environment in which the public/private distinction is increasingly tenuous and in which politicians must adjust to the fact that their Goffmanian 'back stages' are getting harder to protect (Goffman 1959; Meyrowitz 1984). Certainly, information control and impression management are necessities for contemporary media-oriented politicians, who can also use the media's very ubiquity to their strategic advantage. It has become commonplace to see politicians on entertainment programs, where they chit-chat with the host and appear to be like regular folks. Indeed, in today's media environment, it seems to have become increasingly important for politicians to reveal their 'ordinary' sides so as to connect with the 'people' and thus conduct some strategic, if friendly, politicking. In this sense, political performance is being based more and more on the principles of celebrity. Mercer provides politicians with an opportunity to demonstrate that they have a sense of humour and that the broader political system *allows* humour. But if politicians are often the targets of Mercer's comedy, they are also *easy* targets. Democracies, after all, are structurally inclined to encourage humour directed at politicians:

> Democracies, by their nature, would seem to invite humor publicly directed at their ruler. After all, elected authority-holders are chosen from the people and can expect, eventually, to be returned to them either by electoral defeat or because of limits on the number of terms they may serve . . . In contrast to autocrats, whose vengeance can be swift and sure, rulers in democratic societies are usually unable summarily to punish the people who devise and direct humor at them. (Paletz 1990, 484)

Yet humour directed at politicians – even authority-critiquing forms of humour – need not have any real consequences for the political system itself:

Humor aimed at particular office-seekers and -holders tends to be directed
at their foibles and proclivities rather than at more damaging characteristics. (Ibid.)

By playing along with Mercer, Canadian politicians indicate not only that
they have a sense of humour but also that they respect democracy and
freedom of speech. But, as Paletz argues, if this may be risky business for
individual politicians, it does not necessarily follow that Mercer's political humour is a challenge to state authority.

The line between entertainment and news is an issue for all broadcasters. There is tension between appearing authoritative, accurate, and
truthful, on the one hand, and being interesting and engaging on the
other. For the CBC these issues have a particular history and shape tied
to the corporation's own institutional mandate. As Hogarth (2008) has
noted, CBC radio and television have from their beginnings embraced
social realist journalism in their efforts to present the typical or average Canadian to Canadians as a part of the nation-building agenda. In
other words, CBC journalism was always 'a full-fledged apparatus of desire designed to invoke new modes of attachment to the nation in all its
represented forms' (25). That journalism is about 'real' situations – just
as much as the composite Canadian constructed with the help of social scientists or the carefully chosen featured citizens are 'real' – only
enhances its power as an imaginative site of collective identity. Hence
for the CBC, institutional self-referencing has created a tight and mutually reinforcing circle of shows, celebrities, and jokes such that 'serious'
shows are parodied on comedy shows, news journalists become celebrities (and guests on comedy shows), and comedians are serious commentators on politics and news shows. The common background referent
and cultural site that holds this all together is the CBC (a general host)
itself. The CBC is, in other words, the ultimate referent of this circle of
meaning, without which (presumably) all of this entertainment and collective identity could not be generated. It is little wonder in this context
that politicians and their handlers have picked up on the fact that they
have to become active participants in this system of signification.

This circle of references works not only from the humorous to the
official and serious, but also in reverse. For example, during the 2008
federal election, the CBC included Mercer on its election-night expert
panel, where he was asked serious questions. Mercer's place on this
panel may speak to the insightful knowledge of federal politics that he
has demonstrated in his comedic work, but it also shows that the lines

between celebrity and expert, between official and comic, are particularly hard to distinguish on the CBC. Of course, expertise itself is also a product of news coverage. One of the most astute comic attacks on this notion is found on an episode of *The Simpsons* during which news anchor Kent Brockman asks the professor/expert if it is 'time to panic,' to which the latter replies 'yes.' Of course, the answer to this journalistic question is always 'no,' regardless of the real conditions being discussed, because experts are in a powerful position to generate panic. As critics have pointed out, Mercer has become closer and closer to authority and its legitimation as he has become a free-standing celebrity (and representative/conduit for Canadianness). He has little choice but to take seriously his role as mediator between citizens and their national institutions. Aside from his place on the CBC, he is on the board of directors of the Historica–Dominion Institute, 'the largest independent organization dedicated to Canadian history, identity and citizenship' (Dominion Institute 2010). During the 2011 federal election, one of Mercer's rants was directed at getting apathetic Canadian youth to vote: a number of 'vote mobs' coalesced, many on university campuses, to generate voting interest among students. That he is taken seriously is beyond doubt. One CBC radio host has characterized Mercer as 'Canada's premier political analyst.' His expertise apparently trumps that of any political scientists, legal scholars, parliamentary journalists, or experienced politicians who might have a claim on this title.

The Rick Mercer Report also features fake advertisements that lampoon government programs, banks, airlines (especially Air Canada), and all things that tend towards monopoly (of access or interpretation). For example, the long-running and earnest Heritage Minutes ads, which strongly emphasize technical inventions and heroism, are often sent up with silly and insignificant inventions and discoveries offered as culturally and historically important. In one such 'Great Moments in Canadian History,' two men work feverishly designing some unseen object. It turns out to be the B52 shooter cocktail (tested by the inventors in a bar until they can't feel their legs), which is then juxtaposed with 'insulin' and 'peacekeeping,' all important Canadian achievements. As noted earlier, CBC celebrities are also objects of jest, but they participate in the parodies. For example, Terry Milewski, *The National*'s investigative journalist, is offered up to investigate the most trivial, personal questions, such as why a friend has not returned a phone call. Clearly, one general object of this humour is the audience itself. It depends on viewers having seen – and perhaps been touched emotionally by – the Heritage ads, or on them having imagined that they have been informed by Milewski. If this recognition does not take place, the humour cannot work.

Finally, the show's website serves as a strong interactive component. Not only does it provide a weekly opportunity to play with photos of politicians, but famously it has also produced huge responses to campaigns such as the one asking Canadians to sign a petition to change politician Stockwell Day's name to Doris. This was in response to Day's extreme populist stance that the government should craft its policies directly from public opinion. According to the CBC, more than one million votes were cast during that campaign; according to the rules Day himself had proposed, this would have compelled him to change his name. If Stockwell Day thought he could shift the ground of political life away from Mercer to simple referenda, he had another thing coming.

The most successful segment of *This Hour Has 22 Minutes* was Mercer's 'Talking to Americans,' a play on the classic man-on-the-street interview. Of course, this aspect of news coverage verges on self-parody. As Neil Postman (1985) and Jean Baudrillard (1985) both argue, polling people about their opinions works to shore up the fiction that the news makes them informed in some meaningful way – in other words, that considered debate and complex reasoning still exist in this electronically mediated world. Interviews like these are structured so as to imply knowledge that may not exist – for example, they might ask 'Should Canada get out of Afghanistan?' but not 'Where is Afghanistan on a map?' or 'What is the official language of Afghanistan?' This journalistic rhetoric is heavy with comedic potential. For example, American comic Jay Leno has featured a similar segment called 'Jay Walking,' in which he seeks out the 'average' person, who turns out to know shockingly little about his or her own national history and geography. (In one segment of 'Jay Walking,' Leno repeatedly prompts his interviewee with the answer to the question, 'What is the state immediately west of Virginia? . . . west of Virginia, west of Virginia?' Even with help, the interviewee cannot come up with the answer – West Virginia.) Leno is both playing with the notion of the informed citizen and pointing to the ignorance Americans apparently have about themselves. In contrast, Mercer's 'Talking to Americans' involved asking Americans about Canada and duping them into believing stereotypes about Canada (it is all snow, it has pre-modern technologies, it has 'barbaric' Aboriginal laws). Interestingly, the Canadian audience is never put to the test of answering questions about their own country or the United States. So while the American viewers of 'Jay Walking' may be silently embarrassed that they too don't know what is west of Virginia, the Canadian audience can remain confident that they will not be similarly tested about their own civic knowledge.

The aiming of the humour in 'Talking to Americans' away from Canadians and towards Americans perhaps reveals, but also challenges, the notion of 'gentle,' 'friendly' Canadian humour (Keohane 1997). Insofar as Canadian humour has been characterized as non-aggressive towards its objects, Canadians are spared the laughter that would arise at the expense of their own ignorance. In other words, the gentle way avoids or is uncomfortable with comic aggression towards Canadians. This also suggests that American humour is more robust; in this regard, 'Jay Walking' demonstrates how Americans can be the object of humour (even if the participants come across as really stupid) and at the same time be good sports about it. A difference between the two approaches is the collectivist orientation of the Canadian program: the show is for Canadians collectively to laugh at Americans. If this notion of gentle humour characterizes a Canadian sensibility, it perhaps accounts for why Canada has not produced truly outspoken, critical, and subversive comedians like Lenny Bruce, George Carlin, and Richard Pryor. We could also say that these comedians were strong individualists. However, the laughter at Americans' expense in 'Talking to Americans' challenges, or points to a change in sensibility from, the idea that 'others are rarely the butt of Canadian jokes; we make fun of ourselves, or our alleged mediocrity vis-à-vis Others' (Ibid., 158). But this making fun of ourselves has not been the aggressive, hostile form of humour (often politicized and aimed squarely at the state and its institutions) of the American comedians mentioned.

What Canadian viewers learn in 'Talking to Americans' is that Americans are woefully ignorant about Canada – or perhaps just innocent and trusting. The CBC description of the popular 'Talking to Americans' spin-off special makes it clear how its audience it meant to interpret the show:

> Rick Mercer continues his quest to expose ridiculous degrees of American ignorance about Canadian issues in this hour-long comedy special. Mercer and his crew head south to trade quips and quiz unsuspecting Americans at the beach in Miami, the White House in Washington, the Golden Gate Bridge in San Francisco and the streets of New York City about Canadian politics, culture, current events and public figures. Featuring out-takes and

clips from behind-the-scenes, the special relishes in Americans' uncanny ability to go on at great lengths on subjects they know nothing about. (CBC 2009j)

This language establishes an interesting triad of positions: Mercer's 'quest' to 'expose'; the 'ignorant' and 'unsuspecting' American; and the Canadian audience that is to 'relish' this scene. Trumpeted by the CBC as its most popular comedy special to date, this show's popularity highlights for us how Canadians are invited by their public broadcaster to think about themselves – that is, as delighting in being misrecognized by powerful others. Broadly speaking, this gag can be classified as 'derisive' humour. As Farber (2007) explains, 'derisive humor, pitting our need for superiority against our sense of the apparent superiority of others, requires that someone go down' (73). As discussed in chapter 1, Canadian concern with Americans' inability to recognize Canada seems to be important cultural work, rooted in a degree of ressentiment (obsessional hatred of a powerful other). This version of identity, based in the failure of the other to reflect ourselves, is similar to the notion of self-referentiality that we will discuss here. Both involve a tight circle of in-house jokes whose humour is rooted in exclusivity. Of course, as is not the case with 'Jay Walking,' the targets of this humour are unlikely to view it. Nevertheless, Mercer has declined to make 'Talking to Americans' since the 9/11 attacks on the United States.

As a whole, *The Rick Mercer Report* is structured, like *This Hour Has 22 Minutes,* around the parody of news reportage. And while *This Hour* features (ridiculously) four anchors who share rapid and alternating headshots, *The Rick Mercer Report* opens and closes with Mercer alone in front of or behind a glass-topped news desk. Mercer appears in a dark suit on a very stark set; in this way his show makes reference to traditional TV news reportage, in which the authority rests with a single, white, male anchor. Only Mercer's now famous smirk and the over-the-top 'serious' music alert the viewer that the broadcast may not be in earnest. But before this interior shot of Mercer at his desk, the show begins with a clichéd reference to the news transmission technology – in this case a satellite in space, so often used to introduce news shows by announcing their power to collect and disseminate information. Of course, this trope of technological power guarantees the speed and reach of the broadcasting medium, while telling the viewers nothing about the quality or accuracy of its content. From this Archimedean position in 'space,' escorted by portentous music, the viewer quickly descends towards the night lights of Canada's largest city, Toronto, and finally to Mercer standing atop the CBC's national broadcasting centre, where he is holding up a cardboard sign with the day and date hand-lettered on it. This is another comedic moment: a flimsy sign held up by the show's host/anchor/ star announces the powers of technology, centralized authority, and the nation-state and makes him their spokesperson. From the outset of the show, Mercer is both small (only a speck in this vast world of technology, state, and cultural apparatus) and large (the comedic centre of this Anglo-Canadian universe).

As the show's name indicates, *The Rick Mercer Report* features Mercer himself. This stands in contrast to *This Hour Has 22 Minutes*, whose title references an old CBC news show, *This Hour Has Seven Days*. Because most of *The Rick Mercer Report* features Mercer on screen alone, the show must gain variety and texture by placing him in slightly different characters. Hence, he acts as anchor/host from behind a news desk at the opening and closing of the show, as an editorialist while walking in a graffiti-filled alley during his pointed and aggressive 'rants,' as an ironic educator while explaining public issues with the help of a TV screen and pointer, and as a journalist in the field. Since he plays all these roles, the line between parody and reportage becomes thin. Is Mercer sending up news reporting? Is he using this genre to turn himself into a comedic reporter? Or are both happening at once?

Certainly, his rants and commentaries are political critique, aimed at generating serious reflection and action on the part of viewers. As with *The Daily Show with Jon Stewart* and *The Colbert Report* – popular American productions – comedy, parody, and satire are mixed with criticism and analysis, making these shows themselves sources of news and debate. Since 'serious' news has become populated by dim-witted, good-looking anchor/stars, the door has been opened to intelligent and well-informed comedians like Mercer, Stewart, and Stephen Colbert to take over the serious work of politics. So while *The Rick Mercer Report* is a comedy show, Mercer himself carries a serious responsibility as a type of legitimate authority, known for 'telling it like it is' and for having access to powerful people and a large audience.

However, there is a difference in framing between the American programs and *The Rick Mercer Report*. While the latter leans toward parody, the former are more satirical and edgy in their approach. In a discussion of the historical significance of Wayne and Shuster for Canadian comedy, Rick Salutin notes that while the comedians were pioneers of sketch comedy (influencing the likes of *SCTV* and *Kids in the Hall*), they 'never did much political humour.' Further, he notes a difference in approaches to politics between Mercer and the American programs:

> The other interesting current is political humour. I used to think Canadians like (Lorne) Michaels who went to the U.S. had an edge politically since U.S. comics tended to be so outraged by what they felt was the betrayal of principles they'd learned in school that they lacked the distance to be funny about it. But *The Daily Show* and *The Colbert Report* have mastered that challenge. Meanwhile, as our own politics gets polarized along U.S. lines, comics here like Rick Mercer start to seem too mild to handle it. Look how politicians line up to go on his show. If they appear with Colbert or Jon Stewart, they do it with trepidation. (Salutin 2011)

From within this media and political context, Mercer's adventure segments begin to take on meaning. Like the broader show, these segments parody the news, particularly the journalist-on-assignment who has been sent into the field to make a spectacle of himself or herself. In these stories journalists are not distanced and objective but instead celebrate heroism, good fortune, and community, insinuating themselves in these emotional stories to humanize themselves and the news. So at this most obvious level, leaping out of planes, driving tanks, being chased by police dogs, and fighting fires makes Mercer into the ridiculous journalist who must risk life and limb for audience attention and approval (and who is ordered out into the field by someone who remains safely in the office). These segments again challenge the line between entertainment and news – a line that is both asserted and underlined in 'real' news journalism.

Body Gags and Tank Pranks

> Rick visits Canadian Forces Edmonton, where he drives a tank, and he visits the women's volleyball team at the University of Alberta.
> Rick goes to Washington to meet with Frank McKenna and gets to learn what it takes to be a Firefighter.
> Rick helps Michael Ignatieff move into Stornoway and flies with the Calgary Police Air Services Unit.
> Watch to see Rick get pushed out of an airplane, and Stephen Harper in a more natural state.
> Rick visits with the Peel Regional Police K-9 Unit and visits Ottawa, where he becomes Minister of Agriculture MP Chuck Strahl's driver for the day.
>
> TV.com (2009)

Above is a small sample of TV guide descriptions of *The Rick Mercer Report*. While this show is part of a long tradition of Canadian news parody, it is unique in its ritualized and regular employment of the host's body in physical adventures at various sites across Canada – driving tanks, being subdued by police dogs, jumping out of planes, flying helicopters, putting out forest fires. As these descriptions indicate, Mercer puts his body in dangerous situations as he participates in police, military, and civil defence exercises, making use of their high-tech equipment and obliging personnel. We suggest that Mercer's body takes on the position of clown but also invokes a sacrificial posture that demonstrates the citizen's patriotic relationship to the state – that is, the body as an extension of the state's legitimate use of force. Similarly, while Mercer has been criticized for his supportive relationship to the state (especially the military), there has been little analysis of how his humour works to establish and maintain this position.

There is more at work than simply Mercer's exploitation of his popularity. Mercer has established comedic connections between his body, the state, and his audience that are both recognizable and pleasing. As discussed, his success at making these connections must be understood in the context of his place as a celebrity and as a CBC TV comic. Much like Don Cherry (who, as we discussed in chapter 3, appears as an unofficial but nevertheless state-sanctioned 'spokesperson'), Mercer has attained the status of Canadian celebrity through the CBC's 'star-making' machinery. As celebrities, Cherry and Mercer do more than represent Canadians; as recognizably Canadian cultural objects, they also serve in particular ways in nation-building interests.

As noted in chapter 3, Max Weber ([1919]1946a) famously defined the modern state as 'a human community that (successfully) claims the *monopoly of the legitimate use of physical force* within a given territory' (78; emphasis in original). Weber's definition is particularly useful because he links together legitimacy, monopoly, and physical force, suggesting that the state needs to appear in symbolic and ritualized ways that fortify both its claim to absolute force over the citizen body and the exclusiveness of this force. His definition may strike readers as overly focused on the state's massive and unmitigated power over citizens (to imprison, conscript, even kill); but as he points out, it is essential that the state be 'successful' in its claims. In other words, in a liberal democracy like Canada, this undeniable force must be seen as legitimate, even (as we will argue) friendly and fun. Mercer's use of his body draws a sharp distinction between government (the politicians who hold power for defined periods of time) and the state (for Mercer, the unchanging structure of defence and stability). Part of Mercer's comedic work aims to reinscribe the line between these two political structures, treating the former as more ephemeral and inessential than the latter.

One particular incident stands out in recent Canadian political history that demonstrates Mercer's commitment to the government/state distinction. When in December 2008 the head of state (Queen Elizabeth II as represented by the Governor General) exercised her legal right to dissolve Parliament, Mercer spent a number of segments (one of them nine minutes long) explaining to his audience the legality of this move. He was particularly incensed that some politicians had implied to the populace that this practice was illegal and unconstitutional. Clearly it was important to Mercer to explain that the state controls the government and not the other way around. While generally an anti-monarchist, arguing that the Canadian state should become completely sovereign rather than a constitutional monarchy, he nevertheless trusts state mechanisms over politicians to guard the political sphere. Patriotic allegiance, then, is owed to the state, while critique and suspicion are owed to governments and individual politicians. This important distinction is played out in both the content and the structure of *The Rick Mercer Report.*

As we will show, Mercer's state protects its citizens from disorder and danger, including the dangers of nature and foreign incursion, and is not in itself disorderly or dangerous. Nothing could better demonstrate this faith than his playful and regular sacrifice of his body to state agencies and projects. Mercer's comedy, which in no small respect offers a pedagogy of state institutions, points to the ways in which humour's subversive possibilities are contextualized. Put differently, Mercer's clowning is situated within a state-friendly frame, and while this may not be its explicit intent, it lends itself to conservative messages. While there is a gentle parody of the CBC's mandate to explore all regions and small communities in Canada – most overt in his closing: 'If you're in [some small town] this weekend be sure to check our their [name of some quaint and somewhat silly] festival' – he is actually performing the mandate to make the rural and the outpost a part of the Canadian identity. Much like the exposure that the *Hockey Day* program and the *Hockeyville* contest give to communities across Canada, Mercer's visits allow small communities to appear on the national stage, and allow the members of those communities to perform their activities for the rest of the nation. Indeed, we might contrast the pedagogical features of *The Rick Mercer Report* with the anti-utilitarian pleasure of jokes: laughter as an end in itself, whose effects are less obviously directed at instruction.

Mercer's ongoing homage to 'those brave men and women' in the military, the police, and the like, helps separate them from the ambitions and machinations of politicians, while aligning them with faithful service to Canada and the world. This idea is particularly important in the context of Canadian military history, which has shifted from heroic peacekeeping during the Cold War towards more recent active war engagement (fighting the Taliban in Afghanistan), horrific military scandals (prisoner torture in Somalia, allegations of torture of Afghan detainees, the arrest of a high-ranking officer for predatory serial murder), and heartbreaking attempts at keeping international order (genocide in Rwanda). Meanwhile, at the level of territorial sovereignty, foreign vessels have brazenly violated Canadian space without compunction. Domestically, the national police have faced similar challenges to their legitimacy. Most notoriously, they pepper-sprayed protesters in 1997 at an APEC meeting in Vancouver, and in 2007 fatally tasered an immigrant arriving at the Vancouver airport. Now that domestic forces (especially the RCMP) and military forces (especially UN Blue Helmet peacekeepers) have become core to Anglo-Canadian identity, any threat to their image as state agencies also challenges the broader sense of nation. Here is where Mercer's humour can begin its work.

As we have suggested, it is important to consider Mercer's use of his body to generate humour in these segments in the context of Canadian bodies and the state. At least one segment of each show involves Mercer going on-site to a place were he displays his body in the context of an athletic or occupational challenge (usually involving risk of injury); of a rural setting (doing something odd or ritualized, such as participating in a traditional festival); of nature (in the elements, especially in the cold and snow or with wild animals); of a technology (often related to law enforcement or the military); or of a state agency (such as the military, where the state is about peacekeeping, legitimate defence of territory, and search and rescue). Within the show, however, the bodies of politicians are used quite differently. At the end of each show, Mercer displays photographs of politicians that have been manipulated by viewers, at Mercer's invitation: the 'Photo Challenge.' Usually the politician's head has been 'cut off' (the ritual decapitation of the head of the leader) and placed on a ridiculous body (a young woman in a bikini, a male bodybuilder, or an animal, often a monkey or ape). As these photographic humiliations are executed by the audience, Mercer is somewhat distanced from this action. This reflects a classic reversal of power between the governed and the governors.

The body has long been a performer and prop in humour – primarily in slapstick, but also in vaudeville and in forms of the carnivalesque. In early film comedy and continuing into early TV, the body was shown confronting modern industry, the city, and the effects of industrialization. Memorable examples include Harold Lloyd hanging from a clock and dangling from a tall building; Charlie Chaplin getting sucked into the massive machinery at a factory and later suffering imprisonment and starvation; and Lucille Ball on *I Love Lucy* losing control of the assembly line where she is wrapping chocolates. The body in military life is often shown in terms of absurd abuse at the hands of sadistic/corrupt/insane drill sergeants and a generally irrational military system (e.g., *MASH*, or Monty Python's various military spoofs, including its 'marching up and down the square' skit, and the character of the stern sergeant who, roving in and out of various skits, declares 'This Is Silly'). Rarely is humour and the body used to *support* the military. There have been comedies about the military, but these cannot be said to be explicitly supportive (e.g., *Hogan's Heroes* made fun of the German military while showing the Americans to be congenial slackers; and *The Phil Silvers Show* depicted American military personnel in their comedic attempts to subvert the disciplinary demands of the institution and the authority of its supervisors).

But Mercer's humour invokes the willing sacrifice of the body to various values – such as those inherent in sport, military service, and the preservation of nature. As in slapstick, Mercer's body is always in danger of falling or losing control and getting hurt; the difference is that he *himself* places it in danger. What is the rhetoric here? How is Mercer's body given over to various values and institutions? What version of these state institutions is being offered?

It is worthwhile here to consider formulations of the body in relation to conceptions of the individual's relationship to the collective. Anthropologists would have us recognize the ways in which the pre-modern collective ritualistically inscribes itself onto the body of the member (e.g., tribal scarring and piercing, circumcision). In modern societies, though, the body is claimed by the individual as his or her own (in such a way that bodily inscription is an expression of personal desire or medical necessity). The body can become the locus of modern values (an individual project of beauty, pleasure, fitness, obsession) or the locus of sacrifice to the collective good. In other words, in modern societies the body is central to the production of the self as individual or individuated, as 'an entity which is in the process of becoming; a project which should

be worked at and accomplished as part of an individual's self-identity'
(Shilling 1993, 4, 5). The collective's capacity to overtly inscribe itself on
the body has diminished. Only temporary postures (standing for the National Anthem) and collective administrations of health (inoculations)
prevail. The body is highly regulated (through seat belt laws, the control
and/or illegalization of intoxicants, the promotion of rationalized regimes of birth control and weight control, and so on), but this has little
to do with *sacrificing* the body. In fact, the ideal citizen's body works to
regulate and control risk, making its management and prediction eas-
ier. As we will discuss, this involves rituals of fitness and health that are
strongly connected to the modern notion of the good citizen. Hence,
the public and ritual offering up of the body can still be reproduced in
contemporary societies like Canada.

We turn now to examine Mercer's use of his own body as an object
of and for the state, especially in its most obviously powerful forms –
the military and the police – and in the forms that practise and defend
public safety, such as fire fighting. At the most obvious level these segments celebrate the 'brave men and women,' as Mercer puts it, who work
in these jobs. In other words, Mercer is working to remind Canadians
that public service and selfless bravery still exist in a modern world of
'possessive individualism.' This is a clearly political stance that seeks to
reassert the apparent Canadian value of collectivism and self-sacrifice.
Hence, it is important that he offer up his own body to the risky situations faced by these soldiers, police officers, and firefighters. And while
these scenes are orchestrated to maximize Mercer's safety, nevertheless
he *has* jumped out of planes, put out forest fires, and been attacked by
police dogs. Mercer faces these risks as a part of a rhetoric about the
place of the body vis-à-vis the collective good, asserting the necessity (and
joy) of making oneself the sacrificial body to the collective. It is important to note that Mercer's sacrifice to community and the common good
is very much tied to symbols of the state and its agents. Mercer makes
it clear in these scenes that when he is introducing us to particular soldiers, police officers, and firefighters, they are representative of a named
and celebrated military detachment, police force, or fire department. In
other words, these particular people are meant to stand for their whole
group, and more broadly for all Canadian soldiers, police, and firefighters taken together as well as their organizations.

All of Mercer's bodily adventures with state institutions share a similar structure. Each segment begins with the same excited action music.
Mercer welcomes the audience and introduces the place and institution,

often informing the audience of its normal status as off limits to civilians. He is first seen standing outside the institution's entrance – this may include shots of signs that identify the place and organization as well as any Danger or No Trespassing signs. Mercer meets, shakes hands with, and introduces the officer (professor, scientist) who will host Mercer during his adventure. Because these representatives are not actors, they are often awkward on camera. They may also be somewhat nervous because they know that Mercer will gently make fun of them and will try to get away with as much mischief as possible. These officers are responsible for making Mercer welcome (as he is a great publicist for their agency), but also for making sure he comes to no harm while he is risking his body. In some situations, Mercer directly offers himself up to be subject to their authority. For example, when he visits the K-9 police dog unit, he plays the criminal who is escaping the police. A dog chases and takes down Mercer. Mercer follows the police instruction as to how to be best subdued by the dogs, but ultimately it is the dog's training that makes for a safe takedown. Apparently, one lesson here is that if you are being chased by a police dog, do not resist. Any injury will be considered a product of your lack of deference to the dog. As is the case in most such adventures, Mercer shows real fear; but he puts himself in the hands of the authorities, trusting their competence. When, for example, he helps fight a forest fire, he comments on the extraordinary heat and the proximity of the flames. This scene is not simulated; he is getting as close to the real action as possible.

As is true of any body, Mercer's cannot be understood without the context of biography. While Mercer's clowning with authority and technologies is funny, it is enriched by his own body's particularities. As he is such a popular figure in his own right, many viewers understand that his mild homoerotic references, quips about education, and thrill with machinery are linked to his own status as a gay, 'Newfie,' high school dropout. These pieces of knowledge about Mercer are extras in that they are only subtly referenced – Mercer 'passes' as straight, has no stereotypical Newfoundland accent, and is highly informed and articulate. In other words, these gaps between his 'real' self and his apparent self allow Mercer to add tension to these scenes by giggling at homoerotic references, asking about education requirements for the dangerous task at hand, and playing on the notion of the backward 'Newfie' exposed to the thrills and wonders of modern technology. He plays at the suggestion that he is getting away with something – that the authorities don't quite realize whom they have let into their midst. (At a political level it may be argued that Mercer is also moving these three minority statuses closer to the mainstream of citizenship.) This personal information allows the viewer to identify with Mercer and vicariously experience the thrill he is enjoying by way of these breaches.

Symbolically, Mercer achieves verisimilitude by donning the uniform of the agency he is visiting. Like a child, he gets to dress up as a fire-fighter, police officer, soldier, and so on. In one such episode, 'What It's Like to Be a Chopper Cop,' Mercer gets to fly a police helicopter and capture a fake criminal. That Mercer is suiting up helps establish the viewers' vicarious relationship to the authorities and to the action. He says to the officer that they 'get the bad guys' and are the 'coolest look-ing cops in Canada.' Mercer wears (and asks to keep) their uniform, par-ticipates in a simulated arrest, and gets to fly and to track the 'bad guy.' Looking at the suspect through a screen from the air, he says, 'I gottcha you bugger, I gottcha.' Finally he pretends to try to keep the uniform. He is then chased by the chopper cops, who leave him alone, stripped to his underwear on a dark street. This scene plays both on the thrill of wear-ing the uniform and on the agency's authority to exclude others from wearing it (other than Mercer for a short time).

Many of Mercer's body gags bring together state agencies and their impressive technologies, which would normally be beyond the access of ordinary civilians. In 'Coast Guard Ice Breaker,' for example, Mercer in-troduces the scene as the St Lawrence Seaway, describing its importance and size and Canada's role in keeping it open in winter: 'Canadians have been busting ice for over a century.' From here he lands in a helicopter on the frozen seaway – 'Are you sure this is okay?' – and gets on a Cana-dian Coast Guard icebreaker – 'I'm very excited I'm on an icebreaker. This is part of Canada's job.' He plays with the authority of his hosting officer ('Can I call you "captain"? You like that, don't you?') and gets to drive the huge machine. Breaking ice, he says 'boom' and 'look at this go.' 'You've got quite an arsenal . . . Can I drive the hovercraft?' – 'that's huge,' 'unbelievable.' 'We're doing donuts in the St Lawrence. Ha, ha, ha . . .' At the end of the segment, Mercer says, 'Thank you Dave and thank you to the Canadian Coast Guard for a smashing good time.' The pleasure that this segment brings is not so much that of Mercer's ice-breaking puns and plays with authority, as with the incredible vicarious thrill the viewer gets from joining Mercer on this powerful machine. But this is not just about technology. It is about the legitimate and heroic use of technologies by the state for the sake of sustaining the Canadian way of life.

Mercer's bodily humour plays with the classic comedic devices of inversion and juxtaposition. At the most obvious level, the civilian is not supposed to cross into, never mind play with, these official spaces and their machinery. This inversion of order provides forbidden excitement for the viewer as civilian (Who wouldn't want to drive an icebreaker?) and as citizen (Who let Mercer drive an icebreaker?). The juxtaposition of the individual (the 'average' citizen) with the state and its machinery confirms and reinforces the legitimacy of the gap between individual and state. It also provides the humorous frame: the ridiculousness of Mercer driving an icebreaker (untrained) simultaneously with a display of his willingness to 'serve.' Because a civilian has been allowed to take charge momentarily, a tension has been created that ultimately reinforces the notion of expertise. Mercer having been permitted momentarily to take control of state technologies, there is the potential for disaster. Mercer himself is careful to reiterate that while he is operating these machines and using various technologies, he really has no expertise. His incompetence underscores the training and skill of the official characters in the scene. Arguably, the most basic comic juxtaposition is the official (serious, accountable, orderly) with the clown (playful, spontaneous, disorderly).

Perhaps the most impressive of Mercer's body gags has him driving a Canadian Forces tank. Mercer must work to make sure this machine is understood in a particular way. Certainly, the modern tank has become a central symbol of military force since the First World War. For Lewis Mumford (1934), the advent of such weapons amounted to no less than the complete reinvention of war so as to render it as anonymous, deskilled, and relentless as the new technologies themselves: 'The difference between the Athenians with their swords and shields fighting on the fields of Marathon, and the soldier who faced each other with tanks, guns, flame-throwers, poison gases, and hand-grenades on the Western Front, is the difference between the ritual of the dance and the routine of the slaughter house' (Ibid., 210).

In other words, tanks are not extensions of our human powers; rather, they are an extension of their own limitless and inhuman logic as machines. Tanks also bring to mind one of the most famous photographic images of the 20th century – China's anonymous 'Tank Man,' who blocked a procession of government tanks leaving Beijing in 1989. Indeed, this image of the tank/man standoff has become an icon of the Tiananmen Square student rebellion, which had been ruthlessly crushed the day before the photo was taken. Nothing could better capture the situation than this man (dressed in a white dress shirt and dark trousers and holding his jacket in one hand and a shopping bag in another) stopping a procession of tanks. Indeed, his apparently casual attitude and reassertion of ordinary life has a comic-tragic effect: the juxtaposition of size and power (individual vs state; human body vs tank) borders on the ridiculous. This photograph became iconic of the whole event and of the state's willingness to treat its own citizens as the faceless enemy.

Tanks have a history of being used for comedic purposes. In Chaplin's *The Great Dictator*, a parade of military technology becomes a point of competition between fascist dictators, with the Mussolini character claiming to the Germans that his tanks can fly. Often, the basis of tank comedy is the tank falling into incompetent/civilian hands, as with Mercer, who also picks up on the phallic competition between men that is suggested by Chaplin. In another comic movie, *Tank,* the hero uses his vintage tank to escape and ultimately thwart corrupt officials; here, the tank becomes a symbol of grassroots democracy as it is reappropriated by the citizens. In Mercer's humour, however, the right of the state and its officials to control this weapon is not undermined.

Given this broad social and historical context, it is indeed impressive that a tank can be domesticated towards humour. At the beginning of his tank-driving segment, Mercer need only smile at the camera as the officer explains that the seats are 'holes' and that a tank should be 'mounted from the front.' While this is sexually funny in itself, for those many viewers who know that Mercer is a gay man, there is an added layer of silliness in the latent homoeroticism of the closely juxtaposed (apparently heterosexual) male bodies of the four male soldiers who are pressed together in the tank. Mercer employs the techniques he uses in his other, similar segments – enthusiasm, awe, and deference mixed with mild ribbing of personnel and exhilaration while operating such a powerful piece of technology. At the end, he is allowed to completely crush an old car, thus bringing the fun to a climax in harmless destruction. Mercer momentarily renders the tank into a personal toy, symbolically harmless and far from the anonymous, terrifying state machine found in other historical and comic contexts.

And indeed, Mercer's own body must be readied for these adventures through his own disciplined exercise regimes, which provide the level of fitness and agility necessary to participate in a meaningful way. Mercer is able to jump, run, climb, lift, and carry in a way that reveals his commitment to fitness. He is the embodiment of a particular, exemplary type of citizen. The idea that exercise requires discipline (a commitment to spend the time, the creation of a regime and a schedule, and the actual work performed upon one's own body, among other things) assumes a social actor for whom discipline can be understood, not only as a means to an end, but also as a possible mode or part of life or as a version of citizenship. Both Michel Foucault (1977) and Norbert Elias (1978) have argued that the regulation and control of the body's behaviour and movement is highly entwined with the development of the modern state and its 'disciplined' or 'civilized' citizen. And while the fit body is often treated as the hallmark of the privatized, self-consumed, even narcissistic personality, Mercer recovers this interpretation by his ritualized gesture of offering his fit body into sacrificial danger. Mercer is ready and able to serve.

Hence we find *The Rick Mercer Report*'s other celebrated version of the citizen/body – the athlete, especially the Olympic athlete who in international competition represents not so much herself or himself but the nation-state. Mercer, then, also offers his body to athletic adventure. A regular feature that most closely resembles those already discussed is Mercer's participation in athletic rituals. Typically, Mercer avoids playing with professional teams or groups (which represent particular regions and are privately owned, profit-making operations). He prefers local community or university teams or Olympic teams and athletes. He also highlights women's teams (donning their ringette gear to hit the ice with the women) or disabled athletes (taking on whatever technologies and conditions they experience, such as wearing darkened goggles to ski with a blind athlete). Again, these athletes represent the nation-state, in contrast to professional athletes, who are easily traded and who play across the Canada–U.S. border in a common league. By playing alongside minorities – bodies that historically have been marginalized in sports – Mercer is able to generate a personally heroic figure who represents Canada. By embodying the contemporary Canadian citizen, he is able to align historical progress away from the professional/male/able-bodied athlete. In this way, more and more types of Canadians are invited to identify with the athlete, and more broadly progressive values of inclusion and multiplicity are celebrated. Now it is the non-athletic body in general that is on the outside and that sets up the necessary dichotomy between legitimate bodies and non-legitimate embodiment. As Butler (1993) puts it, 'bodies which fail to materialize provide the necessary "outside," if not the necessary support, for the bodies which, in materializing the norm, qualify as bodies that matter' (16). Now the female and disabled bodies are asserted as mattering, but only in their athletic, fit manifestation (evidenced by the increased media attention paid to Canada's female Olympic athletes and Paralympians in 2010).

Elliott (2007) notes the historical linkage of citizenship and the body in modern democracies. In Canada, during the Second World War, Official Food Rules were introduced to govern food consumption. This was directed towards both the conservation of rationed food and the development of the fit soldier or worker body. After the war the food guide was maintained, along with the association of the large body with the failed citizen. As Elliott explains, this discourse is now usually framed in terms of this body's excessive draw on Canada's socialized medical resources. She also notes that politicians' bodies are under constant media surveillance for such embodied bad citizenship that news stories about important social, economic, and political events are often eclipsed by the themes of weight gain. Interestingly, in the context of our discussion, Elliot reports that Prime Minister Stephen Harper's visit to Canadian troops in Afghanistan provoked media attention about his weight, sidelining discussion of Canada's military policies and actions. As Mercer says in one segment, 'You gotta look good in the uniform.'

Conclusion

The dynamics of comedy that we find in Rick Mercer's work do not just incorporate generic comedic structures or established comedic forms (parody, satire, slapstick, clowning); they also point to a particular humour/state dynamic. Among these, and most pertinent for our discussion, has been the political framing of humour, as Mercer attacks and lampoons politicians, authority figures, and governments, while also placing his clowning and bodily antics largely in the recognition or service of the state and its various institutions. Again, we note the material and communicative context in which the humour takes place: the state-owned broadcasting system in which a complex practice of self-reference occurs across the lines of official/non-official, serious/comic, and past/present.

Mercer reproduces a type of nationalist humour in that it reaffirms how Canadian identity is to find itself by way of parody, self-referencing, and celebration of state. So it is not incidental that he finds his status by way of working on and through the CBC. He extends its mandate to generate identity by working to keep Canadian humour within a particular set of parameters. Mercer himself becomes a symbol within the state. He recommends a non-exportable, in-house humour that educates its audience about Canadian institutions and how to think about them. (In a general ad for the CBC, Mercer is seen surreptitiously changing all the television channels in an electronics store to the CBC. As a star performer and symbol of the CBC, he is reminding the viewer that this is where their desire should lead them.) He recommends himself as a person committed to a tradition of self-referential CBC comedy that circulates its personalities within its field, making official and non-official indistinguishable.

As we have discussed, how Mercer comically places politics and politicians is important in terms of how they are distinguished from the state. From his rants to his playful clowning with politicians, Mercer makes it clear that politicians are not all that trustworthy. After all, they willingly lend themselves to almost any situation with him and seek out this publicity. While politicians have little choice but to make themselves available to Mercer, that they do so allows the viewer to question their limits and judgment. Is there any limit to their clowning, when we find them naked and frolicking with Mercer? Does Mercer now take over the role of authority, as our only trustworthy source of political truth?

And while politicians risk their credibility and authority by playing with Mercer, they have little choice but to take Mercer seriously as an important popular conduit to the kind of publicity they want – that is, publicity that frames them as down-to-earth and accessible. As such, as a popular TV commentator – in the context of appearing on the CBC, but also in the broader context where celebrity and politics are increasingly mixed – Mercer is a powerful interpreter of politics. As discussed, politicians' access to the show is limited to these clowning scenes. Otherwise, they appear in the context of criticism, as in Mercer's editorial rants. To have politicians participate in Mercer's bodily state adventures would be to muddy the distinction between politics and state that this humour defends.

Taken broadly, Mercer's show involves more than just clowning. By blurring the clear line between the 'official' journalist and himself, he has placed himself in the role of the legitimate public critic who apparently has nothing to lose from 'telling it like it is.' On going out with the press to follow the politicians as *Maclean's* correspondent for the 2011 federal election, he said, 'While I admit I am not a journalist, I do play one on TV, so the thought of sitting on an actual campaign plane hobnobbing with Craig Oliver has me very excited' (Mercer 2011). In his role as CBC comedian, he appears as the court jester who has some licence to criticize the powerful.

Athough Mercer is careful to acknowledge the sacrifices, courage, and expertise of the state personnel with whom he cavorts, his adventures of state involve more than state personnel. The centrepieces of these adventures are the technologies of state that allow the citizen body to be extended into highly dangerous situations. They offer the best opportunity to display a civic willingness to sacrifice oneself, as technologies require the body to submit to their design and intent. As technologies develop, they extend the body into situations that are articulations of the power of the technologies themselves to go farther, faster, and harder. By using technologies themselves as symbols of state, Mercer's humour further distances the state from any particular policies or personnel who may diminish its status. His humour allows a stark distinction between the (possibly wrongheaded and bloody) employment of these technologies towards particular ends and their purely symbolic nature as agents of Canada. So while almost all objects and people of any official status are potential targets of Mercer's humour, the Canadian state and its agents become reified into things beyond politics, especially as embodied in technologies and their agents. After all, the state, as an abstract force, needs to appear in concrete ways, and its power must be materialized. In Mercer's comedic hands, the concrete objects of state are given a fresh appearance and a renewed meaning.

Mercer's humour plays off the notions of 'technological nationalism' discussed in chapter 1, with transport, communication, and military technologies all working together to represent Canada. But if, as Charland (1986) argued, Canada is the nation-state analogue or McLuhanesque message of these technologies, they call for something to fill them. Mercer, we can say, populates these technologies with his sacrificial and comedic body. Working from within the CBC (as primary signifier of state) he then 'stacks' himself further into such locations. These symbols appear simultaneously – Mercer, the CBC, and concrete technologies. In a sense, these are all technologies or machines of state, working together and depending on one another. This could only be achieved by humour's capacity to mix, collapse, attack, and reaffirm ideas and materials at the same time. From this point of view, it is perhaps literally true that no one mounts a tank like 'Canada's favourite funnyman.'

Conclusion: 'Minding the Gap'

This discussion of Canadian identity, pleasure, and the state began with the famous assertion by Pierre Trudeau that the modern, democratic state must have a limited relation to the pleasures of its citizens. The state must mind its own business, as he put it. Undoubtedly, the Trudeau era was in many ways a turning point in the liberalization of Canada. It also marked the point at which the state and its agents began to take seriously the cultivation and management of pleasures in aid of national identity and the enactment of citizenship. By the late 1960s, this national identification could not be taken for granted by way of older notions of citizenship, such as the subordination of the individual to the group. Hence, the state has only *appeared to disappear* from the interest in citizen's pleasures. And when it does regulate us, it now does so by resorting to the language of enhancing our health or safety – that is, the language of pleasure rather than the older language of vice, sin, or duty.

This new relationship has significant implications for thinking about contemporary Canada. How do Canadians now come to desire Canada? How is desire shaped towards particular versions of citizenship and nation? In answering these questions we looked at five intersections of state and everyday pleasure and asked about the form of citizen being encouraged in each. Like any nation-state, Canada is an 'imagined community' that must be induced in and by its citizens. However, it is part of Canadian identity to celebrate and perpetuate the incompleteness of the national project. Canadian identity, we have argued, is one of desire, and desire is by definition always incomplete. To desire something (even the wholeness of identity) means that new objects or modes of desire must arise such that there is always something to be wanted. The objects of desire could be new or they could be old objects that have taken on a renewed value. But there is always a gap. This book has explored how Canadian identity is generated through this gap – and its pleasures.

In chapter 1, seemingly light CBC contests turned out to be heavily managed projects, illustrating that the desire to be Canadian and represent Canada is rarely simple or unmediated. Our examination of the Seven Wonders of Canada and Obama Playlist contests revealed some odd and interesting notions of the gap in Canadian desire. For CBC producers it was important to control the process and outcome of these contests so that particular themes and ideas were rearticulated. This was discussed in the historical context of cultural nationalism, which serves as the foundation of the CBC's mandate and which has been articulated by agents such as the CRTC and by regulations such as CanCon. We found that the CBC audiences both supported and reproduced protectionist ideas of nation and culture – and also challenged them. In the Obama Playlist contest, high-cultural notions of music, for example, tended to threaten protectionism because of the universal claims made to art over nation as the central criterion for inclusion. On the other hand, both the lyrical content and the choices of popular musical artists repeated themes of nation that had been taught to the audience by regulative, protectionist bodies. Hence we found themes such as 'Canada is unrecognizable to others,' and 'this country is an ahistorical and empty space,' as well as the recirculation of CRTC-generated stars. These contests were about far more than the recirculation of Canadian signifiers – places and songs. These contests were about the reassertion of a set of Canadian values.

We recognize the presumed good of the contests: Canadians were being solicited to participate democratically in representing Canada and to involve themselves in its ongoing collective life. Ultimately, though, the CBC's authority to administer and shape Canadian pleasure and identity was the underlying point of these contests. In short, while play was apparently solicited, it served as an alibi for administration. The resistance shown by these contests' audiences indicates the limits of enacting Canadian identity in CBC pleasures. This resistance to CBC management raises interesting questions. What would have been lost in letting the popular vote determine the Seven Wonders, even if, for example, Newfoundland had captured all the wonders? Would this have meant that in the following contests that were promised by the CBC, other regions could have playfully captured the wonders for themselves? We could ask, for example, what would have been at risk if the Seven Wonders contest had become a game of capture-the-flag among groups, regions, and provinces. What kind of playful debate could this more open play have induced?

The earnest and heavy regulation of these contests also seemed to speak to a fear among CBC producers that its audience would forget to mind and celebrate the gap of diversity – that minorities would be crushed by the tyranny of majority opinion. This is a strange contradiction. On the one hand, Canadians are said to constitute themselves by way of diversity and its celebration. On the other, cultural managers constantly defer the moment when diversity will be allowed to manifest itself directly in the diversity of taste. In other words, if cultural nationalism were to cultivate a taste or desire for Canadian things – including particular values – then a point in time would be reached when this would have to be fulfilled. If not, this particular gap of mistrust and the citizen's apparent moral arrested development would have to be explained. For the CBC, the paternalistic management of desire has become part of its *raison d'être;* perpetuating this version of the gap has become part of its ongoing work.

In the Seven Wonders contest, problematic and historically disturbing aspects of Canada were suppressed. This included the marginalization and vilification of francophone Quebec – a theme found in several of this book's chapters. Nevertheless, broad ideals like diversity were enacted by way of the even geographic placement of the wonders on the Canadian map. Some audience members defended the CBC's right and obligation to manage the contests in the name of protecting diversity. Certainly, this meant more than protecting the diversity of winning objects in the contest – that is, being 'fair' in some milquetoast version of inclusion. It meant protecting and celebrating the broad ideal of diversity itself as a signal Canadian value. Canadians have been encouraged by agents such as governments and public schools to prize ethnic, cultural, and linguistic diversity as a central value and symbol of Canada. Indeed, this is part of the gap of Canadian desire, in that the value of diversity means that Canadians must constantly defer knowing who they are. The immigrant, especially, comes to represent the constantly changing enactment of diversity – although, as discussed, multiculturalism also requires the new Canadian to become a frozen figure in the mosaic ideal, a figure that does not inject a real disruption of Canadian values. As we saw, the Tim Hortons immigration ads were able to capture these romantic themes more easily than the CBC contests because they were not hampered by their own cultural protectionist mandate and bureaucratic infrastructure.

The overregulation found on the CBC opens up a cultural space for private enterprise, especially Tim Hortons, to offer a seemingly more organic and natural way of constituting identity and pleasure. In fact, by taking over responsibility for Canadian history, war commemoration, sports, and the like, Tim Hortons has offered itself as a type of public sphere into which politics and state can move in order to gain legitimacy and visibility. Tim Hortons has been able to articulate community in images of family, sacrifice, belonging, and tradition. This friendly relationship to identity allows politicians and agents of state to find a seemingly natural cultural space in which to appear. Here we find a version of pleasure and identity that seems far less mediated by official bodies and that invites an immediate consumer pleasure to constitute the public sphere where the debate about the common good is at stake. But Tim Hortons ads also generate a gap in official discourses – such as the one that refers to the seamless good of multiculturalism – by introducing ambiguity and doubt. Nevertheless, advertising functions on the level of feeling and sentiment, that is, in an unmediated relation to our identity. Promoters of national sentiment and education (such as the Historica–Dominion Institute) have now taken up advertising as their model to promote national historical awareness and a civic consciousness in audiences. The CBC too is now held to market models of success such that audience share and profit have become the measures of its value over its capacity to generate deep public debate about important issues. Finally, politics and governance themselves have moved towards market models of communication and persuasion.

This raises the issue of what kind of citizenship is evolving in the conflation of citizen and consumer. If the ideal of the public sphere depends on the capacity of citizens to reflect, debate, and reason rather than just feel an identity, then what does it mean for a politician to appear at Tim Hortons rather than the CBC? After all, playful contests aside, the CBC is a public sphere organized by the values of journalistic freedom and responsibility. Tim Hortons is not. Tim Hortons introduces the very real issue of citizenship as sheer emotion, a theme also discussed in chapter 3.

Considering the ritualized Canadian pleasure of hockey, we found an inversion of the dynamics evident in the first chapter. Although it is broadcast in the context of CBC programming, rather than in the top-down administration of symbols and signifiers of Canada, *Hockey Night In Canada* offered the strongest example of an apparent organic Canadianness. Hockey is a bodily, physical spectacle that generates visceral identification with players and teams. As discussed, TV has turned hockey into 'our game,' a national symbol. If nation – the feeling of organic community – cannot be produced by the CBC contests, it is produced in hockey. Even the opening moments of *HNIC* highlight violent physical contact as the attraction. Here the state attaches itself to the nation in order to generate allegiance and to find members willing to sacrifice themselves. From this emotional identification with the group, the individual member is secondary to the collective, willing to sacrifice self and body. The violence on the ice is the enactment of the sacrifice of the warrior-player to the group.

The modern state faces the problem of how to manifest itself to its citizens. It is incomplete and unsatisfying to appear as just the negative regulation of pleasure. The state requires real bodies and emotions to help represent it. The problem, however, is that the state is the agent of non-negotiable force functioning within the culture of democracy. It holds the power to imprison, deport, and conscript the citizen into war. How does this aspect of state power show itself in a pleasing and legitimate way? How does it represent its own power and authority in a way that allows citizens to identify with it? Athletes and the physical, often rough nature of team sport – one cultural move from the warrior and war – provide a convenient cultural site.

For Canadians, this symbolic and real violence is both a pleasure and a contradiction in the enactment of identity, nation, and state. It may be that the hockey fight is part of the entertainment product provided by the National Hockey League and that the league has been able to maintain a definitional space that allows and defends fighting and other violent actions. It has been able to police itself. That said, the acceptance and persistence of fighting, the injuries of players, and the spectacle of violence in general indicate that there is more at work here than the most developed manifestation of sport-entertainment bodies in collision. The state's refusal to stop hockey violence indicates that the state depends on it. Sacred spaces – the ice surface, the hockey 'code,' the CBC, *Hockey Night In Canada,* and Coaches' Corner – have been stacked into one another, and as a result, a protected cultural space has arisen to symbolize the state's coercive power over citizens and their bodies. This stacking of sites into one another both mutually reinforces them and allows a relatively indirect representation of the state and its agents. Don Cherry, with his constant celebration of the military, is at the heart of this structure and helps the state appear indirectly. Cherry is both unofficially official – a hockey commentator who in speaking to the people also gives voice to the state – and officially unofficial, in that he occupies a special space in CBC culture where he can say things that would not be allowed in most other CBC contexts. The violence in 'our game' is a controlled and highly ritualized enactment, such that it is not to recommend itself beyond this special arena. It is, nevertheless, our particular brand of violence, nestled within a nation that is encouraged to think of itself as peaceful.

From within this visceral manifestation of pleasure there arises the question of whether the state has merged too strongly with the nation. As a rational-legal entity and legitimate authority, it is required in Canada to limit sentiments such as ethnic and regional nationalism, especially when these become essentialized ideas in the minds of citizens. Hence, it cannot take its cue too strongly from the nation, even while it depends on it. Here agents of the state themselves must mind the gap in the Canadian imaginary, reminding citizens that they are not an organic thing, but arbitrary and unfinished. Our willingness to be limited in our pleasures is historically also part of being Canadian. This amounts to more than being oversocialized or overly obedient to authority. It is the value of temperance of passion and the value of incomplete identity. When we compare direct national contestation – take, for example, the Olympics with all its jingoism – with ideas such as multiculturalism, a stark difference becomes visible. The first offers prejudicial emotion, while the second offers constant mediation. In terms of the Tim Hortons advertisements that make use of hockey, they cleverly privilege the values of mediation and tempered behaviour on the ice, recommending to hockey the lessons of multiculturalism.

In our fourth chapter we took up the question of the state's direct management of pleasure. With gambling, the citizen is recast in a neoliberal mould whereby the state is the main provider of gambling pleasure. However, inasmuch as the state appears to disappear by providing access to pleasure that was previously policed, the state *appears* in a strong way as monopolist – that is, as a provider, solicitor, risk manager, and beneficiary of gambling. Here we find a strange conglomeration of paternalism, neoliberalism, and utilitarianism that not only produces an incoherent concept of the citizen but also, again, transforms the citizen into a consumer. Whereas in chapter 2 we saw the state take advantage of the public sphere provided by a commercial enterprise, in this instance the state has become a market actor itself. The state has become a commercial enterprise producing consumerism and responding to markets. Furthermore, while hockey still assumes a collectivity, gambling threatens it through its utilitarianism. So in lottery ads, for example, the fantasy of escaping collective responsibilities and community is offered, while the proceeds of gambling are said to be for the common good. The common good now follows on and flows from our individual pleasure seeking. No sacrifice is necessary – it is all 'good.' The risks attendant to gambling – which are designed right into the casinos and electronic gaming machines themselves as psychological environments – are discursively offloaded onto the individual as a personal pathology. No one 'forces' the citizen, as a neoliberal agent, to gamble. This risky cultural site is entered into freely, and any injury incurred there is understood as a product of this personal choice.

Of all the pleasures discussed in this book, in this one more than any other we find the fragmentation of citizen into disconnected and contradictory moments. Various arms of the state are doing completely contradictory things and invoking contradictory versions of the citizen. The state is operating from an incoherent version of the citizen, and hence, the citizen has a harder time locating both self and state. The gap thus far formulated – as the place where national identity and pleasure can reflect on itself – now becomes fragmentary and disarticulated. When the citizen is fragmented, this unleashes the potential for administration by way of any and all discourses. The citizen cannot catch up with these contradictions as they are articulated and administered through discrete agencies and discourses. Or, put another way, if this is the new version of the citizen, then Canadians must find a way to mind this gap too – the gap and challenge of incoherence.

The final chapter comes full circle back to the playful pursuits of the CBC. Whereas in chapter 1 the state mandate threatened pleasure and identity by turning them into sheer administration, comedy programs such as *The Rick Mercer Report* show the state's 'sense of humour.' The CBC provides humorous content for Canadians, as well as a forum for them to laugh at themselves. Here, the state is in the business of pleasure as a way of soliciting the citizen's identification. But the state does not fully disappear; indeed, the subversive possibilities of comedy are put into question. The friendly and personable character of Rick Mercer represents the citizen's docile relationship to the state. Rick Mercer repeats – in a non-violent way – the sacrificial citizen. But the violence of the state reappears in the machinery and personnel with which he plays. Mercer rehearses traditional patriotic understandings of citizenship – his unwavering, although comedic, willingness to serve the commands of state. Within the highly self-referential CBC celebrity system, Mercer is an exemplary product. He is simultaneously a celebrity and an ordinary citizen, a serious political commentator and journalist as well as a comic who plays at commentary and journalism. Like Don Cherry, he has an identifiable presence in the Canadian imagination. Significantly, both Mercer and Cherry do important work in terms of the state and nation building. Both are examples of how pleasure and identity are offered to Canadians – of how Canadiannness is filled in with particular contents.

The role of mass mediation has been a dominant theme in this discussion, and the CBC has appeared as a central actor throughout. Those topics – Tim Hortons and gambling – not directly related to the CBC nevertheless would not have the presence they have in the everyday life of Canadians without their mediated representations, be it on television, on radio, or in print. Our discussion thus follows in the tradition of Canadian media theorizing found in the classic works of Innis and McLuhan and in the contemporary works of Vipond, Rutherford, Charland, Edwardson, and others. More particularly, we have sought to engage the difficulties of discussing identity – national identity – in relation to its mediated representations. We have examined some of the ways in which particular contents have been presented to Canadians as evidence of, and solutions to, their desire for identity. But these mediated solutions include far more than broadcast messages. In keeping with the Canadian intellectual tradition to which we are in debt, mediation must be understood as a far more complex practice than that of sending and receiving messages. We have also found Canadians offered discourses, ideologies, administrative techniques, complex symbolic representations, and sheer technological mediation itself.

Taken together we have located many articulations of Canada as a gap or endless desire – deferment, fragmentation, multiplicity, nostalgic longing, containment of passions, and so on. In some cases the principle of incompleteness supports democratic ideas of inclusion, change, diversity, and temperance. In other cases, the longing for completion has supported statism, neoliberalism, ressentiment, and consumerism. The longing for completion and identity is understandable. It is hard to love the gap as the basis of identity. The highly diverse manifestations of Canadian desire, identity, and pleasure in everyday life show the complexity and promise of minding the gap in an imaginative way. The ability to continue to observe how citizenship and identity are induced and organized by way of our pleasures – and relationship to state – is at the same time the ability to identify and understand the increasingly complex and subtle phenomena that are at work in the cultural and political fields of the everyday. If the gap between conceptions of identity and their reception is a source of pleasure for Canadians, then we must learn to understand the significance of this gap, not as a form of collective repetition compulsion, but in terms of a question that orients to the good. Desiring Canada is the practice of minding the gap – as a pleasure and as an identity.

Notes

Introduction

1 For example, Valverde (1991) has examined the efforts of early-twentieth-century moral reformers to influence the state and shape the moral fabric of Canada. Illegal drugs in Canada have been examined by Carstairs (2006a), who focuses on regulation between 1920 and 1961, and by Martel (2006), who focuses on drug policy between 1961 and 1975. Grayson (2008) has examined the state's construction of certain drugs as illicit and the ways in which state conceptions of security interact with representations of Canadian identity. Heron (2003) provides a social history and discussion of the moral career of alcohol use in Canada. Thompson and Genosko (2009) discuss the surveillance and prohibition of drinkers from 1927 to 1975 in Ontario. Morton (2003) examines gambling in Canada between 1919 and 1969 – years when that activity that was illegal but also culturally (albeit covertly) popular, and thus morally ambiguous in terms of the state's regulatory approach to it. The regulation of sexual desire in Canada has been the focus of work by Kinsman (1996). Kinsman and Gentile (2010) argue that whatever Trudeau declared, the state did not withdraw from Canadians' bedrooms – rather, it conceived gays and lesbians as a threat to security and thus subject to RCMP surveillance and harassment. As this list suggests, Canadians' desires for drugs, alcohol, gambling, and sex have been subject to particular moral and political framings and state regulation.
2 We thank Dr Lynda Harling Stalker of the Department of Sociology, St Francis Xavier University, for this point.

1. Contesting Canada at the CBC

1 This gesture at highbrow erudition falls short when held up to Augustinian scholarship. Augustine intentionally contrasted *populus* with *res publica* – public thing or commonwealth – and with *civitas* – organized collectivity. These latter two words would have been more reasonably translated as 'nation' in Augustine's text than *populus*. We thank Robert Kennedy of St Francis Xavier University for this Latin translation and contextual explanation of *The City of God*.

2 According to Statistics Canada, more than 13 million ballots were cast in the 2004 federal election.

3 'Hoser' is an English-Canadian slang term, referring typically to a working-class, white Canadian male from the suburbs or the countryside, who likes to drink large quantities of beer and listen to hard-rock music (bands such as Rush or Triumph). They are ineloquent and are often identifiable by their winter coats, flannel shirts, and tuques. They have been famously celebrated by Canadian comedians Dave Thomas and Rick Moranis, who play Bob and Doug McKenzie, 'The McKenzie Brothers,' in *SCTV* television skits. The characters 'Garth' and 'Wayne' of the film *Wayne's World* are also based on the hoser.

2. Tim Hortons and the Consumer-Citizen

1 Indeed, earlier published work on this topic by Cormack garnered much media attention, especially from the CBC.

2 Cormack gratefully received a second-hand commemorative 40th Anniversary Tim Hortons mug after its initial recipient rejected it.

3. Hockey, Civilizing Projects, and Domestic Violence

1 A.C. Holman's edited collection (2009) *Canada's Game: Hockey and Identity* (Montreal and Kingston: McGill–Queen's University Press, 2009), offers several essays examining hockey themes in Canadian fiction. Skinazi's essay 'The Mystery of a Canadian Father of Hockey Stories: Leslie McFarlane's Break Away from the Hardy Boys' (2009), includes a useful list of hockey fiction published in Canada between 1950 and 2007.

2 On top of those deaths, a Russian plane carrying Kontinental Hockey League team Lokomitiv Yaroslavl crashed near Moscow in early September. Forty-four of the forty-five people on the plane died. Several of the passengers had played in the NHL, including the Lokomotiv coach Brad MacCrimmon (who

had just left the NHL as an assistant coach with the Detroit Red Wings), as well as players Pavol Demitra, Josef Vasicek, Karlis Skrastins, Igor Korolev, and Ruslan Salei. www.cbc.ca/news/world/story/2011/09/07/russia-plane-crash.html.

3 For a discussion of violence in Canadian hockey fiction, see Jason Blake, ' "Just part of the game": Depictions of Violence in Hockey Prose,' in Holman, *Canada's Game,* 65–80.

4 The CBC broadcasts *Hockey Night in Canada in Punjabi,* which has a large following. It would appear that the desire to play and watch hockey among young Canadians is declining. While minor and professional hockey leagues are trying to draw ethnic communities into the game, 'visible-minority teenagers play the sport at about half the rate of their white peers, according to Statistics Canada data. A study this summer (2009) found that only about one-third of Canadian teens regularly watched NHL games on TV in 2008, down 10 points since 1992.' See E. Anderssen, 'Nazem Kadri: Canada's New Game Face,' *Globe and Mail,* 16 October 2009.

5 This has been written about, for example, in Ross Benstein, *The Code: The Unwritten Rules of Fighting and Retaliation in the NHL* (Chicago: Triumph, 2006).

6 Cherry was also critical of the NHL's move to penalize headshots. The CBC's support of Cherry has come under severe criticism from journalists such as Bruce Dowbiggin (2011c). It would appear, though, that the NHL is moving away from the position of Cherry and *HNIC.*

7 Burke's life and accomplishments were presented in a CBC *5th Estate* documentary, *The Legacy of Brendan Burke.*

8 The military representations in Canadian hockey broadcasts pale compared to the explicit nationalist-militarist representations found in American broadcasts of the Super Bowl, a consequence of the events of 9/11 and of the ongoing 'War on Terror.' See Michael Butterworth, 'Fox Sports, Super Bowl XLII, and the Affirmation of American Civil Religion,' *Journal of Sport and Social Issues* 32, no. 3 (2008): 318–23.

4. Peace, Order and Good Gambling

1 Prostitution laws are currently being challenged in Canada on this basis.

2 This defining and organizing of gambling is an example of what French sociologist Pierre Bourdieu refers to as symbolic violence: the ability of institutions to impose categories of thought and perception on dominated subjects, who come to take these modes as right. In this way, power and legitimacy are naturalized.

3 Lottery corporations have preferred to settle cases out of court so as to not
find themselves liable for 'duty of care' to casino patrons who develop gambling problems. The judge in the OLG class action suit ruled against the suit
proceeding. Justice Maurice Cullity 'didn't dismiss the merits of [the] claims
against OLG, but said the gamblers' claims were based on their own unique
personal circumstances – so they'd have to file individual lawsuits.' Andrew
Chung, 'Gamblers $3.5B suit against OLG rejected,' 21 March 2010, http://
www.cbc.ca/canada/toronto/story/2010/03/21/on-olg-lawsuit.html.
4 The Canada Safety Council has estimated there to be about 360 gambling-
related suicides per year. Canada Safety Council, *Newsletter*, 17 December
2004.
5 The rates of problem and pathological gambling typically range from 1 to
5 per cent of the population, with the number of pathological gamblers
comprising a smaller portion of the total percentage than the problem gamblers. However, these figures may represent tens or hundreds of thousands
of actual people in a jurisdiction with gambling problems. Also, this 'small'
number of individuals is perceived to be different from the rest of the population, who – we are told – can treat gambling responsibly and relate to it as
entertainment.

5. The Funny State Apparatus

1 Laurel Halladay's research argues that the Massey Commission has been
given too much credit for reshaping postwar Canada. She suggests that
entertainers Wayne and Shuster and others became popular through their
wartime troop entertainment. These performers retained and honed their
entertainment skills on returning to Canada, thus contributing greatly to the
Canadian arts and entertainment scene. Harris, 'Canada's Military Planted
Seeds for Flourishing Arts Scene.' http://www.ucalgary.ca/mp2003/news/
nov04/wartime-shows/index.html.

References

Abt, V. 1996. 'The Role of the State in the Expansion and Growth of Commercial Gambling in the United States.' In *Gambling Cultures: Studies in History and Interpretation*, ed. Jan McMillen. London: Routledge. 179–98.

Adams, M. 2003. *Fire and Ice: The United States, Canada, and the Myth of Converging Values*. Toronto: Penguin.

– . 1998. *Sex in the Snow: Canadian Social Values at the End of the Millennium*. Toronto: Penguin.

Adams, P. 2007. *Gambling, Freedom, and Democracy*. New York: Routledge.

Advertising Age. 2010. 'A World of Inspirational Problem-Solving, Savvy Brands, and Smart Marketing.' http://www.adage.com/globaclnews/article_id = 144404, accessed 29 June 2010.

Allain, K.A. 2010. 'Kid Crosby or Golden Boy: Sidney Crosby, Canadian National Identity, and the Policing of Hockey Masculinity.' *International Review for the Sociology of Sport* 46, no. 1: 3–22.

Anderson, B. 1983. *Imagined Communities: Reflections on the Origin and Spread of Nationalism*. London and New York: Verso.

Anderssen, E. 2009. 'Nazem Kadri: Canada's New Game Face.' *Globe and Mail*. 16 October.

Ang, I., and J. Stratton. 1998. 'Multiculturalism in Crisis: The New Politics of Race and National Identity in Australia.' *Topia* 2 (Spring).

Arendt, H. 1968. 'Introduction.' In *Illuminations*, by Walter Benjamin. New York: Schocken.

– . 1961. 'The Crisis in Culture: Its Social and Political Significance.' In *Between Past and Future*. New York: Viking. 197–202.

– . 1958. *The Human Condition*. Chicago: University of Chicago Press.

Azmier, J. 2001. *Gambling in Canada: An Overview*. Gambling in Canada Research Report no. 13 (August) Calgary: Canada West Foundation. CWF Publication no. 200107.

Bakhtin, Mikhail. [1941]1984. *Rabelais and His World*, trans. Hélène Iswolsky. Bloomington: Indiana University Press.

Baudrillard, J. 1990. *Fatal Strategies*. New York: Semiotext(e).

– . 1985. 'The Masses: The Implosion of the Social in the Media.' *New Literary History* 16, no. 3: 577–89.

– . 1983. *In the Shadow of the Silent Majorities*, trans. Paul Foss, John Johnson, Paul Patton, and Andrew Berardini. New York: Semiotext(e).

Becker, H. 1953. 'Becoming a Marihuana User.' *American Journal of Sociology* 59: 235–42.

Benjamin, W. 1968. *Illuminations*, trans. Harry Zohn, ed. Hannah Arendt. New York: Schocken.

Bennett, A. 2000. 'Theorizing Music and the Social: New Approaches to Understanding Musical Meaning in Everyday Life,' *Theory, Culture, and Society* 17, no. 3: 181–4.

Benstein, R. 2006. *The Code: The Unwritten Rules of Fighting and Retaliation in the NHL*. Chicago: Triumph.

Bergman, B. 1998. 'Show No Mercy Mercer.' *Maclean's*, 12 October. http://www.angelfire.com/celeb/rickmercer/shownomercy.html, accessed 10 May 2010.

Bhamra, A.S. 2009. 'B.C. Lottery Corp. Raises Weekly Play Limit to $10,000.' http://www.theglobeandmail.com/news/national/bc-lottery-corp-raises-weekly-play-limit-to-10000/article1258091, accessed 20 August 2009.

Billig, Michael. 1995. *Banal Nationalism*. London: Sage.

Bissoondath, N. 1994. *Selling Illusions: The Cult of Multiculturalism in Canada*. Toronto: Penguin.

Blake, Jason. 2009. ' "Just part of the game": Depictions of Violence in Hockey Prose.' In *Canada's Game: Hockey and Identity*, ed. Andrew C. Holman. Montreal and Kingston: McGill–Queen's University Press. 65–80.

Bourdieu, P. 1999. 'Rethinking the State: Genesis and Structure of the Bureaucratic Field.' In *State/Culture: State Formation after the Cultural Turn*, ed. George Steinmetz. Ithaca: Cornell University Press. 53–75.

– . 1993. *The Field of Cultural Production*, trans. Randal Johnson. New York: Columbia University Press.

– . 1984. *Distinction: A Social Critique of the Judgement of Taste*. Cambridge, MA: Harvard University Press.

Brady, R., and S. Gordon. 2011. 'The Mystery of Violence: Why Despite the League's Claims, Fighting in Hockey Is Not Worth Fighting For.' *Globe and Mail*, 14 February, A16.

Brunt, S. 2009. 'Roy Ruling: Court Balks at Setting Precedent.' http://www.theglobeandmail.com/sports/roy-ruling-court-balks-at-setting-precedent/article1316146, accessed 9 October 2009.

Buist, R. 2003. *Tales from under the Rim: The Marketing of Tim Hortons.* Fredericton: Goose Lane.

Butler, J. 1993. *Bodies That Matter.* London: Routledge.

Butterworth, M. 2008. 'Fox Sports, Super Bowl XLII, and the Affirmation of American Civil Religion.' *Journal of Sport and Social Issues* 32, no. 3: 318–23.

Campbell, C.S. 2009. 'Canadian Gambling Policies.' In *Casino State: Legalized Gambling in Canada,* ed. James F. Cosgrave and Thomas R. Klassen. Toronto: University of Toronto Press. 69–90.

Canada. 2010a. 'Discover Canada: The Rights and Responsibilities of Citizenship.' http://www.cic.gc.ca/english/resources/publications/discover/section-11.asp, accessed 8 June 2010.

– . Citizenship and Immigration Canada. 2010b. 'Multiculturalism.' http://www.cic.gc.ca/multi/multi-eng.asp, accessed 6 June 2010.

– . Office of the Prime Minister. 2008. 'Prime Minister Harper Announces the John G. Diefenbaker Icebreaker Project.' 28 August. http://pm.gc.ca/eng/media.asp?id = 2258, accessed September 2008.

– . 1991. Broadcasting Act. http://laws.justice.gc.ca/eng/B-9.01/page-2.html#anchorbo-ga:l_III, accessed 20 January 2010.

– . 1951. *Report of the Royal Commission of National Development in the Arts, Letters, and Sciences* (Massey Commission).

Canadian Encyclopedia of Music. http://www.thecanadianencyclopedia.com/index.cfm?PgNm = TCE&Params = U1ARTU0003223, accessed 15 January 2012.

Canadian Press. 2010. 'Criminal Charges for On-Ice Hit by Former World Junior Captain Cormier.' *Globe and Mail.* http://www.theglobeandmail.com/sports/criminal-charges-for-on-ice-hit-by-former-world-junior-captain-cormier/article1564473, accessed 18 July 2010.

Canadian Safety Council. 2004. Newsletter, 17 December.

Canetti, E. 1984. *Crowds and Power.* London: Penguin.

Carrier, R. 1979. *The Hockey Sweater and Other Stories,* trans. Sheila Fischman. Toronto: House of Anansi.

Carstairs, C. 2006a. *Jailed for Possession: Illegal Drug Use, Regulation, and Power in Canada, 1920–1961.* Toronto: University of Toronto Press.

– . 2006b. 'Roots Nationalism: Branding English Canada Cool in the 1980s and 1990s.' *Histoire Sociale / Social History* 39, no. 77: 235–55.

CBC. 2011. 'Air Canada Threatens to Halt NHL Sponsorship: Other League Sponsors Express Concern over Rash of Head Hits.' http://www.cbc.ca/news/business/story/2011/03/10/nhl-air-canada-sponsor.html, accessed 29 August, 2011.

– . 2010a. 'Hockey Day Magic.' http://www.cbc.ca/sports/hockey/story/2010/01/01/sp-hockey-day.html, accessed 30 January 2010.

– . 2010b. 'The Don Cherry Lexicon.' http://www.cbc.ca/sports/indepth/doncherry/stories/lexicon.html, accessed 13 May 2010.

– . 2009a. 'Obama Playlist.' http://www.cbc.ca/obamasplaylist, accessed 5 January 2009.

– . 2009b. http://www.cbc.ca/radio2/blog/2008/12/29/49_songs.html, accessed 9 January 2009.

– . 2009c. 'Obama Playlist Rules.' http://www.cbc.ca/radio2/obamasplaylist/rules, accessed 5 January 2009.

– . 2009d. 'Calling Classical Listeners.' http://www.cbc.ca/radio2/tempo/2009/01/calling_classical_listeners.html, accessed 10 January 2009.

– . 2009e. 'Obama Playlist: The Playlist.' http://www.cbc.ca/radio2/obamasplaylist/theplaylist.html, accessed 12 January 2009.

– . 2009f. 'Obama's Playlist.' http://www.cbc.ca/radio2/blog/2009/01/20/obamas_playlist_reve.html, accessed 20 January 2009.

– . 2009g. http://www.cbc.archives.ca/arts, accessed 20 February 2009.

– . 2009h. 'Stanley Cup Birthday Bash for Crosby.' http://www.cbc.ca/canada/nova-scotia/story/2009/08/07/sp-crosby-cup.html, accessed 12 January 2010.

– . 2009i. 'Court to Rule in Goalie Roy's Court Case.' http://www.cbc.ca/sports/story/2009/09/08/quebec-roy-hockey-fight-remparts.html, accessed 12 January 2010.

– . 2009j. 'Program Guide: Talking to Americans.' http://www.cbc.ca/programguide/program/talking_to_americans, accessed 7 April 2009.

– . 2008a. 'Seven Wonders: Sounds Like Canada.' http://www.cbc.ca/sevenwonders/sounds_like_canada, accessed 25 February 2008.

– . 2008b. 'Niagara Falls, Prairie Skies.' http://www.cbc.ca/news/yourview/2007/06/niagara_falls_prairie_skies_th.htm, accessed 4 June 2008.

– . 2008c. 'More on the Seven Wonders.' http://www.cbc.ca/national/blog/content/editors_blog/more_on_the_seven_wonders_of_c_2.html, accessed 25 February 2008.

– . 2007a. 'Seven Wonders: Criteria.' http://www.cbc.ca/sevenwonders/criteria, accessed 5 October 2007.

– . 2007b. 'Seven Wonders: The Judges.' http://www.cbc.ca/sevenwonders/
the_judges, accessed 5 October 2007.

– . 2007c. 'Seven Wonders: More Wonders.' http://www.cbc.ca/sevenwonders/
more_wonders, accessed 5 October 2007).

– . 2007d. 'That's Col. Rick to You: Mercer Gets a Military Gig.' http://www.cbc.
ca/arts/story/2007/01/24/mercer-colonel.html, accessed 4 May 2010.

– . 2004a. '"Double-double"? Now You Can Look it Up.' http://www.cbc.ca/
arts/story/2004/06/30/doubledouble040630.html, accessed 26 January
2010.

– . 2004b. 'Brimming with Caffeine and Nicotine?' (17 February 2004). http://
archives.cbc.ca/programs/209, accessed 24 April 2011.

Charland, M. 1986. 'Technological Nationalism.' *Canadian Journal of Political
and Social Theory* 10, nos. 1–2: 196–220.

Cherry, D. 2009a. *Hockey Night in Canada* telecast. 8 September.

– 2009b. *The Hour* telecast. 28 January.

Chung, A. 2010. 'Gamblers $3.5B Suit Against OLG Rejected.' http://www.cbc.
ca/canada/toronto/story/2010/03/21/on-olg-lawsuit.html.

Coakley, J., and P. Donnelly. 2004. *Sports in Society: Issues and Controversies.* 1st ed.
Toronto: McGraw-Hill Ryerson.

Cohen, A. 2007. *The Unfinished Canadian: The People We Are.* Toronto: McClelland and Stewart.

– . 2003. *While Canada Slept: How We Lost Our Place in the World.* Toronto: McClelland and Stewart.

Cohen, L. 2003. *A Consumers' Republic: The Politics of Mass Consumption in Postwar
America.* New York: Vintage.

Cole, C. 2011. 'Even in the Throes of an Epidemic of Concussions, the NHL
Seems Unlikely to Change Its Punishing Culture Anytime Soon.' *National
Post,* 4 March, S1, S3.

Cook, R. 1971. *The Maple Leaf Forever: Essays on Nationalism and Politics in Canada.* Toronto: Macmillan of Canada.

Cooper, B. 2007. 'The Unfounded Country.' In *Great Questions of Canada,* ed.
Rudyard Griffiths. Toronto: Key Porter.

Cosgrave, J.F. 2010. 'Embedded Addiction: The Social Production of Gambling
Knowledge and the Development of Gambling Markets.' *Canadian Journal of
Sociology* 35, no. 1: 113–34.

– . 2009. 'Governing the Gambling Citizen: The State, Consumption, and
Risk.' In *Casino State: Legalized Gambling in Canada,* ed. James F. Cosgrave and
Thomas R. Klassen. Toronto: University of Toronto Press. 46–66.

Cosgrave, J., and T.R. Klassen. 2001. 'Gambling against the State: The State and
the Legitimation of Gambling.' *Current Sociology* 49, no. 5: 1–22.

Crossland, D. 2006. '60 Years on, It's Safe to Tell Nazi Jokes.' *The Times*, 31 August. http://www.timesonline.co.uk/tol/news/world/europe/article623349. ece, accessed 30 April 2010.

Day, R. 1998. 'Constructing the Official Canadian: A Genealogy of the Mosaic Metaphor in State Policy Discourse.' *Topia: Canadian Journal of Cultural Studies* 2: 42–66.

Debord, G. 1983. *Society of the Spectacle*. Detroit: Black and Red.

Delacourt, S., and A. Marland. 2009. 'From Sales to Marketing: The Evolution of the Party Pitch.' *Policy Options* (September): 6–10.

Delaney, G. 2005. 'Cree Visitors Get Southern Exposure.' *Halifax Chronicle Herald*, 19 July, B1.

Dennis, R. 2009. 'Forever Proud? The Montreal Canadiens' Transition from the Forum to the Molson Centre.' In *Canada's Game: Hockey and Identity*, ed. Andrew C. Holman. Montreal and Kingston: McGill–Queens University Press. 161–79.

Dixon, G., and J. Bradshaw. 2009. 'The CNN-ificiation of CBC.' *Globe and Mail*, 31 October, R1, R7.

Dominion Institute. 2010. 'Canada's Largest History and Citizenship Organization.' http://www.dominion.ca/release08092009.pdf, accessed May 2010.

– . 2009a. 'Dominion Institute's new Canadian Icons Survey Reveals Some Not-So-Familiar Faces.' 29 June. http://www.dominion.ca/release08092009.pdf, accessed May 2010.

– . 2009b. 'Landmark Merger Creates the Historica-Dominion Institute.' 8 September. http://www.dominion.ca/release08092009.pdf, accessed 15 July 2010.

– . 2008. 'In the Lead-up to the 90th Anniversary of the End of the First World War, a Dominion Institute–Ipsos Reid National Poll Gauges Canadians' Knowledge of The Great War.' 7 November. http://www.dominion.ca/release08092009.pdf, accessed May 2010.

Dorland, M. 1996–7. 'Review of T. Madber, *Canada's Hollywood: The Canadian State and Feature Films*.' *Journal of Canadian Studies* 31, no. 4: 178.

– . 1988. 'A Thoroughly Hidden Country: Ressentiment, Canadian Nationalism, Canadian Culture.' *Canadian Journal of Political and Social Theory* 12, nos. 1–2: 130–64.

– , ed. 1996. *The Cultural Industries in Canada: Problems, Policies, and Prospects*. Toronto: James Lorimer.

Douglas, M. 1966. *Purity and Danger: An Analysis of Concepts of Pollution and Taboo*. London: Routledge and Kegan Paul.

Dowbiggin, B. 2011a. 'CBC Gives Short Shrift to Boogaard Story." *Globe and Mail*, 16 May, S10.

– . 2011b. "Hockey as Secular as the Nation That Worships It."
http://www.theglobeandmail.com/sports/bruce-dowbiggin/
hockey-as-secular-as-the-nation-that-worships-the-sport/article2018255.

– . 2011c. 'CBC Rides Shotgun on Cherry's Stagecoach.' *Globe and Mail,* 8
October, S1, S5.

– . 2008. *The Meaning of Puck: How Hockey Explains Modern Canada.* Toronto: Key
Porter.

Dowler, K. 1996. 'The Cultural Industries Policy Apparatus.' In *The Cultural
Industries in Canada: Problems, Policies and Prospects,* ed. Michael Dorland. Toronto: James Lorimer. 328–446.

Druick, Z. 2008. 'Laughing at Authority or Authorized Laughter?' In *Programming Reality,* ed. Z. Druick and A. Kotsopoulos. Waterloo: Wilfrid Laurier
University Press.

Dryden, K. 2011a. 'This Is a Difficult Time for the NHL, for Its Commissioner,
Gary Bettman, and for Hockey.' *Globe and Mail,* 1 October, F7.

– . 2011b. "What Will They Think of Us: Head Shots Should Be History." *Globe
and Mail,* 12 March, 1, 5–7.

– . 1983. *The Game: A Reflective and Thought-Provoking Look at a Life in Hockey.*
Toronto: MacMillan of Canada.

Durkheim, É. [1895]1982. *The Rules of Sociological Method,* trans. W.D. Halls, ed.
S. Lukes. New York: Free Press.

– . [1912]1965. *The Elementary Forms of the Religious Life,* trans. J.W. Swain. New
York: Free Press.

Edwardson, R. 2008. *Canadian Content: Culture and the Quest for Nationhood.* Toronto: University of Toronto Press, 2008.

– . 2003. 'Of War Machines and Ghetto Scenes: English-Canadian Nationalism
and the Guess Who's "American Woman." ' *American Review of Canadian Studies* 33, no. 3: 339–56.

Elias, N. 1986. 'Introduction.' In N. Elias and E. Dunning, *Quest for Excitement:
Sport and Leisure in the Civilizing Process.* Oxford: Basil Blackwell.

– . 1978. *The History of Manners: The Civilizing Process,* vol. 1, trans. E. Jephcott.
New York: Pantheon.

Elliott, C. 2007. 'Big Persons, Small Voices: On Governance, Obesity, and the
Narrative of the Failed Citizen.' *Journal of Canadian Studies* 41, no. 3:
134–51.

– . 2002. 'Sipping Starbucks: (Re)Considering Communicative Media.' In *Mediascapes: New Patterns in Canadian Communication,* ed. P. Attallah and
L.R. Shadeeds. Toronto: Nelson Canada. 107–19.

Encyclopedia of Music in Canada. 1992, 2nd ed. Toronto: University of Toronto
Press.

Farber, J. 2007. 'Toward a Theoretical Framework for the Study of Humor in Literature and the Other Arts.' *Journal of Aesthetic Education* 41, no. 4: 67–86.

Fletcher, T. 2010. 'Patron Makes a Double-Double Take Over Ban.' *Vancouver Sun*, 8 February.

Foucault, M. 1977. *Discipline and Punish: The Birth of the Prison.* New York: Vintage.

Freud, S. 1938. 'Wit and Its Relation to the Unconscious.' In *The Basic Writings of Sigmund Freud*, trans. A.A. Brill. New York: Random House. 633–803.

Friedenberg, E.Z. 1980. *Deference to Authority: The Case of Canada.* New York: M.E. Sharpe.

Friesen, J., and L. Perreaux. 2010. 'The Great Melting Rink.' *Globe and Mail*, 21 May.

Frye, N. 1982. 'Sharing the Contintent.' In *Divisions on a Ground: Essays on Canadian Culture,* ed. James Polk. Toronto: Anansi Press. 52–70.

Fuller, D., and D.R. Sedo. 2006. 'A Reading Spectacle for the Nation: The CBC and "Canada Reads."' *Journal of Canadian Studies* 40, no. 1: 5–36.

Gadamer, H.-G. 1986. *Truth and Method.* New York: Crossroad.

Gephart, Jr, R.B. 2001. 'Safe Risk in Las Vegas.' *M@n@gement* 4, no. 3: 141–58.

Giasson, T., J. Lees-Marshment, and A. Marland. 2012. 'Political Marketing in a Canadian Context.' In *Political Marketing in Canada,* ed. A. Marland, T. Giasson, and J. Lees-Marshment. Vancouver: UBC Press.

Gillis, W. 2010. 'Most Think G20 Police Actions Justified, Polls Find.' 30 June. http://www.thestar.com/news/gta/article/830832-most-think-g20-police-actions-justified-poll-finds, accessed 13 July 2010.

Globe and Mail. 2012. 'Ontario Bets Big on Online Gambling.' http:// m.theglobeandmail.com/news/national/ontario-bets-big-on-online-gambling/article1358307/?service = mobile, accessed January 13, 2012.

– . 2009a. 'Tim Hortons Rehires Fired Woman.' http://www.theglobeandmail. com/news/national/article684498.ece, accessed 6 June 2010.

– . 2009b. 'B.C. Lottery Corp. Raises Weekly Play Limit to $10,000' http://www. theglobeandmail.com/news/national/bc-lottery-corp-raises-weekly-play-limit-to 10000/article1258091, accessed 20 August 2009.

– . 2009c. 'Loto-Quebec to Compensate Thousands of Addicted Gamblers.' http://www.theglobeandmail.com/news/national/loto-quebec-to-compensate-thousands-of-addicted-gamblers/article1422703, accessed 6 June 2010.

Goffman, E. 1959. *The Presentation of Self in Everyday Life.* New York: Anchor.

– . 1952. 'On Cooling the Mark Out: Some Aspects of Adaptation to Failure.' In *The Goffman Reader* (1998), ed. C. Lemert and A. Branaman. Oxford: Blackwell. 3–20.

Gordon, S. and A. Maki. 2011. 'Hockey's Hooked.' *Globe and Mail*, 3 September, S1.

Gray, J. 2006. 'Staying Power: Strong Brands.' *Canadian Business* 79, no. 22: 73–4.

– . 2005. 'Canadian Icons.' *Canadian Business* 78, no. 12: 32–3.

– . 2004. 'King of the Cruller.' *Canadian Business* 77, no. 12: 45–8.

Grayson, K. 2008. *Chasing Dragons: Security, Identity, and Illicit Drugs in Canada.* Toronto: University of Toronto Press.

Gruneau, R., and D. Whitson. 1993. *Hockey Night In Canada: Sport, Identities, and Cultural Politics.* Toronto: Garamond.

Gwyn, R. 1995. *Nationalism without Walls: The Unbearable Lightness of Being Canadian.* Toronto: McClelland and Stewart.

Habermas, J. 1989. *The Structural Transformation of the Public Sphere.* Cambridge, MA: MIT Press.

Hall, S. 1984. 'The State in Question.' In *The Idea of the Modern State*, ed. G. McLennan, D. Held, and S. Hall. Milton Keynes and Philadelphia: Open University Press. 1–28.

Harris, G. 2004. 'Canada's Military Planted Seeds for Flourishing Arts Scene.' In *News*, University of Calgary. http://www.ucalgary.ca/mp2003/news/nov04/wartime-shows/index.html.

Health and Health Services Research Workshop. 2002. 'Defining "Rural" and "Rurality." ' 23 October.

Heron, C. 2003. *Booze: A Distilled History.* Toronto: Between the Lines.

Hockey Canada. 2009. 'Mandate and Mission.' http://www.hockeycanada.ca/index.php/ci_id/6836/la_id/1.htm.

Hodgins, P. 2004. 'Our Haunted Present: Cultural Memory in Question. *Topia* 12 (Fall).

Hogarth, D. 2008. 'Reenacting Canada: The Nation-State as an Object of Desire in the Early Years of Canadian Broadcasting.' In *Programming Reality: Perspectives on English-Canadian Television*, ed. Z. Druick and A. Kotsopoulos. Waterloo: Wilfrid Laurier University Press.

Holman, A.C., ed. 2009. *Canada's Game: Hockey and Identity.* Montreal and Kingston: McGill–Queen's University Press.

Horkheimer, M., and Theodor W. Adorno. 1969. *The Dialectic of Enlightenment.* New York: Continuum.

Houpt, S. 2010. 'Tim Hortons: Where Commerce, Culture Intersect.' *Globe and Mail,* 5 March. http://www.theglobeandmail.com/report-on-business/industry-news/marketing/tim-hortons-where-commerce-culture-intersect/article1490187, accessed 10 May 2012.

Huizinga, J. 1955. *Homo Ludens: A Study of the Play Element in Culture.* Boston: Beacon.

Hurtig, M. 2002. *The Vanishing Country: Is It Too Late to Save Canada?* Toronto: McClelland and Stewart.

Hutcheon, L. 1990. *As Canadian as Possible under the Circumstances.* Toronto: ECW and York University.

Hutchison, B. 1985. *The Unfinished Country: To Canada with Love and Some Misgivings.* Vancouver: Douglas and McIntyre.

– . 1942. *The Unknown Country: Canada and Her People.* Toronto: McClelland and Stewart.

Innis, H. 1951. *The Bias of Communication.* Toronto: University of Toronto Press.

International Press Institute. 2002 Congress Report. http://www.freemedia.at/fileadmin/media/Documents/Boston_2000_Congress_Report_01.pdf accessed 12 March 2011.

Ipsos Reid. 2009. 'Defining Canada: A Nation CHOOSES The 101 Things That Best Define Their Country.' http://wwwdon.101things.ca/list.php, accessed 11 June 2009.

Jones, J. 2009. 'Share a Cup with a Brave Canuck! A Day as a Tim Horton's Clerk.' http://forums.army.ca/forums/index.php/topic,83803.0.html, accessed 24 March 2009.

Jones, R. 2009. 'Tim Hortons Contest Odds Give Ontarians Reason to Cry over Double-Double.' 11 March. http://www.cbc.ca/canada/new-brunswick/story/2009/03/11/nb-tim-hortons-rims-629.html#ixzz0qLx2wbkd, accessed 9 June 2010.

Joyrich, L. 2005. 'Good Reception? Television, Gender, and the Critical View.' In *Cultural Subjects: A Popular Culture Reader,* ed. A.J. Gedalof et al. Toronto: Nelson.

Kaufmann, E. 1998. 'Naturalizing the Nation: The Rise of Naturalism in the United States and Canada.' *Comparative Studies in Society and History* 40, no. 4: 666–95.

Keller, T. 2006. 'Forget Hockey Dad. Meet Anti-Hockey Grandpa.' http://www.macleans.ca/culture/media/article.jsp?content = 20060306_122383_122383URL, accessed 9 July 2006.

Kennedy, B. 2009. 'Confronting a Compelling Other: The Summit Series and the Nostalgic (Trans)formation of Canadian Identity.' In *Canada's Game: Hockey and Identity,* ed. Andrew C. Holman. Montreal and Kingston: McGill–Queen's University Press. 44–62.

Keohane, K. 1997. *Symptoms of Canada: An Essay on the Canadian Identity.* Toronto: University of Toronto Press.

Key, W.B. 1973. *Subliminal Seduction: Ad Media's Manipulation of a Not So Innocent America.* Englewood Cliffs: Prentice-Hall.

Kidd, B., and J. Macfarlane. 1972. *The Death of Hockey.* Toronto: New Press.

Kinahan, A.-M. 2006. 'From British Invasions to American Influences: Cultural Studies in Canada.' In *Mediascapes: New Patterns in Canadian Communication*, 2nd ed., ed. P. Attallah and L.R. Shade. Toronto: Nelson. 28–43.

Kinsman, G. 1996. *The Regulation of Desire: Homo and Hetero Sexualities*, 2nd ed. Montreal: Black Rose.

Kinsman, G., and P. Gentile. 2010. *Canadian War on Queers: National Security as Sexual Regulation*. Vancouver: UBC Press.

Kuffert, L.B. 2003. *A Great Duty: Canadian Responses to Modern Life and Mass Culture, 1939–1967*. Montreal and Kingston: McGill–Queen's University Press.

Laraque, G. 2011. 'The Worst: Pregame Stress about the Fight." *Globe and Mail*, 3 September, S2.

Laurier, E., and C. Philo. 2004. 'The Cappuccino Community: Cafés and Civic Life in the Contemporary City' (draft). Department of Geography and Topographic Science, University of Glasgow, http://web2.ges.gla.ac.uk/~elaurier/cafesite/texts/final_cappuccino.pdf, accessed 15 July 2005.

Leacock, S. 1916. *Essays and Literary Studies*. New York: John Lane; London: Allen Lane. http://gaslight.mtroyal.ca/amerhumr.htm.

Lipset, S.M. 1990. *Continental Divide: The Values and Institutions of the United States and Canada*. New York: Routledge.

Litt, P. 1992. *The Muses, the Masses, and the Massey Commission*. Toronto: University of Toronto Press.a

Livingstone, Charles, and R. Woolley. 2007. 'Risky Business: A Few Provocations on the Regulation of Electronic Gaming Machines.' *International Gambling Studies* 7, no. 3: 361–76.

MacGregor, R. 2011a. 'Sports Matter to the Nation, but Hockey Matters Most.' http://www.theglobeandmail.com/sports/hockey/sports-matter-to-the-nation-but-hockey-matters-the-most/article4250522, accessed 7 November 2011.

– . 2011b. 'Lords of Discipline Lacking.' *Globe and Mail*, 5 March, S1.

– . 2011c. 'March of the Penguins: Why It's Up to the Skilled and Dirty Team from Pittsburgh to Show the Way.' *Globe and Mail*, 14 February, A15.

– . 2007. *Canadians: A Portrait of Country and Its People*. Toronto: Penguin.

MacLean, Ron. 2009. *Hockey Day* telecast, February 21. CBC.

Magendanz, D. 2003. 'Governance in Morally Contested Industries.' Paper prepared for the Queensland Treasury Department, Brisbane, Australia.

Mahoney, J. 2005. 'Ice-Coffee Craving Gets Cool Reception.' *Globe and Mail*, 6 March, 2.

Maki, Allan. 2011. 'Bare-Knuckle Anguish.' *Globe and Mail*, 21 May, S4.

Manning, E. 2000. 'I Am Canadian: Identity, Territory, and the Canadian National Landscape.' *Theory and Event* 4, no. 4.

Marksbury, R.A. 2010. 'Ethnography in a Casino: Social Dynamics at Blackjack Tables.' In *Global Gambling: Cultural Perspectives on Gambling Organizations,* ed. S.F. Kingma. London: Routledge. 91–112.

Martel, M. 2006. *Not This Time: Canadians, Public Policy, and the Marijuana Question, 1961–1975.* Toronto: University of Toronto Press.

Martin, L. 2011. 'A Country of Dryden's Values Shifts to Cherry's.' *Globe and Mail,* 18 October. http://www.theglobeandmail.com/news/politics/lawrence-martin/a-country-of-drydens-values-shifts-to-cherrys/article2204000.

Marx. K. [1867]1967. *Capital,* vol. 1. New York: International Publishers.

McKenna, P. 2008. *Terminal Damage: The Politics of VLTs in Atlantic Canada.* Halifax: Fernwood.

McKinley, M. 2006. *Hockey: A People's History.* Toronto: CBC/McClelland and Stewart.

– . 2000. *Putting a Roof on Winter: Hockey's Rise from Sport to Spectacle.* Vancouver: Greystone.

McMullan, J.L., and D. Miller. 2009. 'Wins, Winning, and Winners: The Commercial Advertising of Lottery Gambling.' *Journal of Gambling Studies* 25, no. 3: 273–95.

Mercer, R. 2011. 'One Thing I'll Say for Bruce Carson,' *Maclean's,* 2 May, 24.

– . 2007. *The Rick Mercer Report.* Toronto: Anchor.

Meyrowitz, J. 1984. *No Sense of Place: The Impact of Electronic Media on Social Behaviour.* New York: Oxford University Press.

Morton, S. 2003. *At Odds: Gambling and Canadians 1919–1969.* Toronto: University of Toronto Press.

Mumford, L. 1934. *Technics and Civilization.* New York: Harcourt Brace.

Murphy, R. 2009. *Canada and Other Matters of Opinion.* Toronto: Doubleday Canada.

Nesbitt-Larking, P. 2007. *Politics, Society, and the Media: Canadian Perspectives.* Toronto: Broadview.

Nesrallah, J. 2009. 'CBC.ca/Radio2/Tempo.' On-air radio comments, 5 January.

New 7 Wonders 2008. http://www.new7wonders.com, accessed 25 February 2008.

Nietzsche, F. [1887]1989. *On the Genealogy of Morals* [and] *Ecce Homo,* trans. Walter Kaufmann. New York: Vintage.

Nimijean, R. 2006. 'Brand Canada: The Brand State and the Decline of the Liberal Party.' *Inroads* 19 (Summer).

Nora, P. 1996. 'Introduction.' In *Realm of Memory,* vol. 1, trans. Arthur Goldhammer, ed. Lawrence D. Kritzman. New York: Columbia University Press.

Novak, M. 1976. *The Joy of Sports: Endzones, Bases, Baskets, Balls, and the Consecration of the American Spirit.* New York: Basic.

Nova Scotia Gaming Corporation. 2006. Social Responsibility Charter.

OLG. 2010a. http://www.olg.ca/index.jsp, accessed 27 February 2011.

– . 2010b. 'About Economic Benefits.' http://www.olg.ca/about/economic_benefits/index.jsp, accessed 27 February 2011.

– . 2010c. 'Know Your Limit.' http://www.knowyourlimit.ca/setting-limits, accessed 27 February 2011.

– . 2010d. 'Superplayer Club.' http://superplayerclub.ca/winnersgallery.html, accessed 27 February 2010.

Osborne J. 1989. *The Legal Status of Lottery Schemes in Canada: Changing the Rules of the Game.* Unpublished LL.M. thesis, Faculty of Law, University of British Columbia, Vancouver.

Paletz, David L. 1990. 'Political Humor and Authority: From Support to Subversion.' *International Political Science Review* 11, no. 4: 483–93.

Pearce, T. 2011. 'As NHL Stars Suffer Potentially Life-Changing Injuries . . .' *Globe and Mail,* 19 February, A16.

Penfold, S. 2008. *The Donut: A Canadian History.* Toronto: University of Toronto Press.

– . 2002. ' "Eddie Shack Was No Tim Horton": Donuts and the Folklore of Mass Culture in Canada.' In *Food Nations: Selling Taste in Consumer Societies,* ed. W.J. Belasco. New York and London: Routledge. 48–66.

Pevere, G., and G. Dymond. 1996. *Mondo Canuck: A Canadian Pop Culture Odyssey.* Toronto: Prentice-Hall.

Postman, N. 1985. *Amusing Ourselves to Death: Public Discourse in the Age of Show Business.* New York: Penguin.

Priest, L. 2009. 'Special Investigation – Bad Bet: Government's Gambling Addiction.' *Globe and Mail,* 3 October, A1, A10, A11.

Rabinovitch, R. 2007. Opening remarks for CBC/Radio-Canada's appearance before the Standing Committee on Canadian Heritage. 27 November. http://www.cbc.radio-canada.ca/speeches/20071127.shtml, accessed 13 May 2010.

Rak, J. 2008. 'Canadian Idols? CBC's "The Greatest Canadian" as Celebrity History.' In *Programming Reality: Perspectives on English-Canadian Television,* ed. Z. Druick and A. Kotsopoulos. Waterloo: Wilfrid Laurier University Press.

Ramp, W., and K. Badgley. 2009. ' "Blood Money": Gambling and the Formation of Civic Morality.' In *Casino State: Legalized Gambling in Canada.* ed. J.F. Cosgrave and T.R. Klassen. Toronto: University of Toronto Press. 19–45.

Reith, G. 2007. 'Gambling and the Contradictions of Consumption.' *American Behavioural Scientist* 51, no. 1: 33–55.

Rider, D. 2010. 'Don Cherry Rips "Left-Wing Pinkos" at Council Inaugural.' http://www.thestar.com/news/torontocouncil/article/902903 – don-cherry-rips-left-wing-pinkos-at-council-inaugural, accessed 2 June 2012.

Robidoux, M.A. 2001. *Men at Play: A Working Understanding of Professional Hockey.* Montreal and Kingston: McGill–Queen's University Press.

Roseberry, W. 1996. 'The Rise of Yuppie Coffees and the Reimagination of Class in the United States.' *American Anthropologist* 98, no. 4: 762–75.

Rukszto, K. 2008. 'History as Edutainment: Heritage Minutes and the Uses of Educational Television.' In *Programming Reality: Perspectives on English-Canadian Television,* ed. Z. Druick and A. Kotsopoulos. Waterloo: Wilfrid Laurier University Press.

– . 2005. 'The Other Heritage Minutes: Satirical Reactions to Canadian Nationalism.' *Topia* 14 (Fall).

Rutherford, P. 1993. 'Made in America: The Problem of Mass Culture in Canada.' In *The Beaver Bites Back: American Popular Culture in Canada,* ed. D.H. Flaherty and F.E. Manning. Montreal and Kingston: McGill–Queen's University Press. 260–80.

– . 1990 *When Television Was Young: Primetime Canada, 1952–1967.* Toronto: University of Toronto Press, 1990.

Salming, B. 2007. *The Hockey News: Digital Issue.* 18 December.

Salutin, R. 2011. 'Wayne and Shuster's Comedy of Gratitude.' http://www.thestar.com/opinion/editorialopinion/article/1045153 – salutin-wayne-and-shuster-s-comedy-of-gratitude, accessed 25 August 2011.

Saul, J.R. 1998. *Reflections of a Siamese Twin: Canada at the End of the Twentieth Century.* Toronto: Penguin.

Scherer, J., and D. Whitson. 2009. 'Public Broadcasting, Sport, and Cultural Citizenship: The Future of Sport on the Canadian Broadcasting Corporation.' *International Review for the Sociology of Sport* 44, no. 2: 213–29.

Schor, N. 1994. 'Collecting Paris.' In *The Cultures of Collecting,* ed. J. Elsner and R. Cardinal. Cambridge, MA: Harvard University Press. 252–302.

Shilling, C. 1993. *The Body and Social Theory.* London: Sage.

Simmel, G. 1950. 'The Metropolis and Mental Life.' In *The Sociology of Georg Simmel,* ed. K.H. Wolff. New York: Free Press. 409–24.

Simpson, J. 2009. 'Fighting Hockey Violence Will Give You a Concussion.' *Globe and Mail,* 14 February. A.19.

Skinazi, K. 2009. 'The Mystery of a Canadian Father of Hockey Stories: Leslie McFarlane's Break Away from the Hardy Boys.' In *Canada's Game: Critical Perspectives on Ice Hockey and Identity,* ed. Andrew Holman. McGill–Queen's University Press. 166–210.

Slater, D. 2000. 'Looking Backwards.' In *The Consumer Society Reader,* ed. M.J. Lee. Oxford: Blackwell. 177–85.

Smith, G.J., D.P. Schopflocher, N. el-Guebaly, D.M. Casey, D.C. Hodgins, R.J. Williams, and R. Wood. 2011. 'Community Attitudes Toward Gambling in Alberta.' *International Gambling Studies* 11, no. 1: 57–79.

Smith, G.J., and C.S. Campbell. 2007. 'Tensions and Contentions: An Examination of Electronic Gaming Issues in Canada.' *American Behavioural Scientist* 51, no. 1: 86–101.

Smith, G.J., and H. Wynne. 2004. 'VLT Gambling in Alberta.' Edmonton: Alberta Gaming Research Institute.

Sontag, S. 1977. *On Photography*. New York: Picador.

Spencer, D. 2011. 'Science Looks to Learn from Boogaard's Death,' *Globe and Mail*, 16 May, S4.

Stempel, C. 2006. 'Televised Sports, Masculinist Moral Capital, and Support for the U.S. invasion of Iraq.' *Journal of Sport and Social Issues* 30: 79–106.

Stott, A. 2005. *Comedy*. New York and London: Routledge.

Stursberg, R. 2009. 'A Memo to Its Detractors: CBC TV's Never Been Better.' 3 May. http://www.thestar.com/article/627762, accessed 2 June 2009.

Taylor, C. 2004. *Modern Social Imaginaries*. Durham: Duke University Press.

Testa, B., and J. Shedden. 2002. 'In the Great Midwestern Hardware Store: The Seventies Triumph in English-Canadian Rock Music.' In *Slippery Pastimes: Reading the Popular in Canadian Culture*, ed. J. Nicks and J. Sloniowski. Waterloo: Wilfred Laurier University Press. 177–216.

TheStar.com. 2009. 'Donuts over Diplomacy.' 24 September.

– . 2008. 'Tim Hortons Fires Single Mom Over Free Timbit.' 8 May.

Thompson, C., and A. Zeynep. 2004. 'The Starbucks Brandscape and Consumers' (Anticorporate) Experiences of Glocalization.' *Journal of Consumer Research* 31, no. 3: 631–42.

Thompson, S., and G. Genosko. 2009. *Punched Drunk: Alcohol, Surveillance, and the LCBO*. Halifax and Winnipeg: Fernwood.

Tim Hortons, 2011a. 'Frequently Asked Questions.' http://www.timhortons. com/ca/en/about/faq.html, accessed 14 April 2011.

– . 2011b. 'Remembrance Day.' http://www.timhortons.com/ca/en/difference/ local-programs.html, accessed 12 April, 2011.

– . 2010. 'Tim Hortons CEO Spreads Holiday Cheer in Kandahar with Free Coffee and Tim Cards for Soldiers.' http://www.timhortons.com/ca/en/ about/4287.html, accessed 29 August 2011.

– . 2009. 'Medical Stories of Tim Hortons.' http://www.everycup.ca/story/ medical-stories-of-tim-hortons, accessed 26 June 2009.

– . 2008. 'Tim Hortons Launches Interactive Website for Customers and Fans.' 4 November. http://www.timhortons.com/ca/en/about/2359.html, accessed May 2010.

– . 2006. 'Joint Operation: Tim Hortons and Canadian Forces Announce Opening in Afghanistan.' 8 March. http://www.timhortons.com/ca/en/about/news_archive_2006b.html, accessed June 2007.

– . 2003. 'Tim Hortons and CBC Sports Team Up for CBC's Hockey Day in Canada.' http://www.timhortons.com/ca/en/about/news_archive_2003c.html, accessed June 2007.

Tim's Times. 2004. 17 May.

TV.com. www.tv.com/rick-mercer-report/show/22584/summary.html?q = Rick%20Mercer%20Report&tag = search_results;more;1, accessed 7 January 2009.

Tye, D. 2010. *Baking as Biography: A Life Story in Recipes.* Montreal and Kingston: McGill–Queen's University Press.

Vaillancourt, F., and A. Roy. 2000. 'Gambling and Governments in Canada, 1969–1998: How Much? Who Plays? What Payoff?' Canadian Tax Foundation (Special Studies in Taxation and Public Finance no. 2).

Valverde, M. 1991. *The Age of Light, Soap, and Water: Moral Reform in English Canada, 1885–1925.* Toronto: McClelland and Stewart.

Van Krieken, R. 1998. *Norbert Elias.* London: Routledge.

Vancouver Sun. 2011. 'They've Always Got Time for Tim Hortons.' 23 April. http://www.vancouversun.com/health/They+always+time+Hortons/4663833/story.html, Accessed April 24, 2011.

Veblen, T. 1953. *The Theory of the Leisure Class: An Economic Study of Institutions.* New York: New American Library.

Vipond, M. 1992. *The Mass Media in Canada,* 2nd ed. Toronto: James Lorimer.

Weber, M. [1905]1958. *The Protestant Ethic and the Spirit of Capitalism,* trans. T. Parsons. New York: Charles Scribner's Sons.

– . [1919]1946a. 'Politics as a Vocation.' In *From Max Weber: Essays in Sociology,* ed. H.H. Gerth and C.W. Mills. New York: Oxford University Press. 77–128.

– . [1918]1946b. 'Science as a Vocation.' In *From Max Weber: Essays in Sociology,* ed. H.H. Gerth and C.W. Mills. New York: Oxford University Press. 129–56.

Whitaker, R. 2001. 'Virtual Political Parties and the Decline of Democracy.' *Policy Options.* June.

Whittington, L. 2010. 'Jim Flaherty Blasted for $3,100 Flight.' *Toronto Star,* 9 March. http://www.thestar.com/news/canada/article/776967–jim-flaherty-blasted-for-3-100-flight, accessed 5 April 2010.

Willmott, G. 2001. 'Canadian Ressentiment.' *New Literary History* 32: 133–56.

Young, S. 1990. *The Boys of Saturday Night: Inside Hockey Night in Canada.* Toronto: Macmillan of Canada.

Index